HIGHLANDER

HIGHLANDER:
The History of the Legendary Highland Soldier

Tim Newark

A Herman Graf Book
Skyhorse Publishing

First Skyhorse Publishing edition 2009

Skyhorse Publishing books may be purchased in bulk at special discounts for sales promotion, corporate gifts, fund-raising, or educational purposes. Special editions can also be created to specifications. For details, contact the Special Sales Department, Skyhorse Publishing, 307 West 36th Street, 11th Floor, New York, NY 10018 or info@skyhorsepublishing.com

Skyhorse® and Skyhorse Publishing® are registered trademarks of Skyhorse Publishing, Inc.®, a Delaware corporation.

Visit our website at www.skyhorsepublishing.com.

10 9 8 7 6 5 4 3 2 1

Library of Congress Cataloging-in-Publication Data is available on file.

Cover design update by Rain Saukas

Print ISBN: 978-1-5107-0650-7

Printed in the United States of America

Contents

List of Illustrations

Jacobite Highlander of the clan MacLachlan in 1745. Coloured lithograph, by Robert Ronald McIan. © *Private Collection, Peter Newark's Military Pictures.*

James Stuart with his half-brother the Duke of Berwick. Oil on canvas, by Alexis Simon Belle. © *Private Collection, Peter Newark's Military Pictures.*

Wanted poster for Charles Edward Stuart issued during the Jacobite rebellion of 1745. Engraving. © *Private Collection, Peter Newark's Military Pictures.*

Officer and sergeant of the 42nd Highlanders, *c.*1750. Engraving published in 1786 by S Hooper. Based upon an earlier illustration by the brothers van der Gucht. © *Private Collection, Peter Newark's Military Pictures.*

Grenadiers of the 42nd (Black Watch) and 92nd (Gordon) Highlanders during the Napoleonic Wars. Coloured lithograph after painting by Charles Hamilton Smith for his *Costume of the Army of the British Empire* published in 1812. © *Private Collection, Peter Newark's Military Pictures.*

Black Watch at Bay. Oil on canvas, by WB Wollen. © *Private Collection, Peter Newark's Military Pictures.*

The Thin Red Line, the 93rd Highlanders stand firm before a Russian charge at the battle of Balaklava in 1854. Oil on canvas, by Robert Gibb. © *Private Collection, Peter Newark's Military Pictures.*

Sir Colin Campbell, commander of the Highlanders in the Crimean War and later during the Indian Mutiny. Engraving by DJ Pound from a photograph by Mayall. © *Private Collection, Peter Newark's Military Pictures.*

*Charge of the Black Watch, c.*1900. Coloured lithograph, by Stanley L Wood. © *Private Collection, Peter Newark's Military Pictures.*

Sergeant of the 2nd Gordon Highlanders, equipped as a mounted infantryman, 1896. © *Private Collection, Peter Newark's Military Pictures.*

The 1st Gordons and 1/2nd Gurkhas pose together, in mutual respect for each other's courage, after taking Dargai in October 1897. © *The Gurkha Museum.*

Statue commemorating Argyll and Sutherland Highlanders who died during the Boer War. © *Author's own collection.*

79th New York Highlanders, 1861. Painting by Michael Chappell.

Cape Town Highlander regimental mascot, 'Donald', with keeper Private MacDonald, 1887. © *Private Collection, Peter Newark's Military Pictures.*

Sir Harry Lauder, the popular music hall star. © *Private Collection, Peter Newark's Military Pictures.*

Exhausted 7th Argyll and Sutherland Highlanders during a break in the desperate fighting near Abbeville, France, June 1940. © *Private Collection, Peter Newark's Military Pictures.*

Cameron Highlander of the re-formed 51st Highland Division takes a prisoner after the battle of El Alamein, November 1942. © *Private Collection, Peter Newark's Military Pictures.*

Field Marshal Bernard Montgomery inspects the 5th/7th Gordon Highlanders prior to D-Day, 1944. © *Private Collection, Peter Newark's Military Pictures.*

American soldiers watch the arrival of the 1st Battalion Argyll and Sutherland Highlanders at Pusan in August 1950 during the Korean War. © *Private Collection, Peter Newark's Military Pictures.*

Cameron Highlanders on guard duty at Shaba Camp, Aden, 1957. © *Private Collection, Alfred Blake.*

Memorials to Black Watch soldiers who died in Iraq, in the grounds of Balhousie Castle. © *Author's own collection.*

Introduction

The Highlanders in my family had a tough time of it. My great-grandmother was a Ferguson from the southern Highlands. Born in Perthshire in 1857, Sarah Ferguson was the daughter of a shoemaker. The year before, her teenage brother Hugh had escaped their humble background by joining the Highland Light Infantry and served for twelve years. When Sarah was old enough, she left on the long journey to London.

Sarah Ferguson settled in the East End, probably working as a servant. In 1887 she married George Finch, my great-grandfather. She lied on her marriage certificate, saying she was twenty-six, when in fact she was five years older, but her husband hid the truth from her as well. He said he was twenty-eight, when he was thirty-one, and claimed to be a bachelor when he was in fact a widower with a child.

George worked on the railway at Stratford, but his money did not go far and they had to share a small workman's cottage with another family. They had the tiny ground-floor rooms, while the second family had to climb up to the first floor using a ladder. They shared the outside toilet with several other families. In this cramped slum space they brought up five children. One of them remembered their mother as being very intelligent and keen on books, but there was precious little opportunity for Sarah to make the most of her Scottish education. Eventually, her depressing circumstances wore her down and she took to drink. On one occasion she was arrested for drunkenness. But she was a robust old lady and lived to be eighty-one, dying in 1937.

Most of my family are Londoners, but that didn't stop them being

Highlanders too. Ernest Newark was working as a ledger clerk in the City of London when he was called up to fight in the First World War. Like many conscripts, he was used to fill a gap in a badly mauled regiment and ended up in the 1st Battalion Seaforth Highlanders. Surrounded by Scotsmen, he sailed to Mesopotamia to fight against the Ottoman Turks. It must have been doubly confusing for him – a London boy taking orders from Highlanders and fighting in a far-flung corner of the British Empire. Mesopotamia was a hard posting and many British soldiers died from disease.

Ernest Newark rose to the rank of lance-corporal and survived three years of campaigning before being demobilized in 1919. He wanted to return to his old job in the City but that was gone, so he applied to join the Metropolitan Police force. His years in the Middle East had left him chronically underweight, and he was turned down. He took a temporary job as a clerk, nursed himself back to fitness and was finally accepted into the police force, where he became a sergeant and then an inspector in 1936. The harsh life of a Highlander in Mesopotamia still dogged him, and he suffered terribly from gastric ulcers for the rest of his life.

In September 1940, a German bomb hit a civilian shelter in Tottenham, north London. Despite the blitz raging around him, Ernest Newark took control of the situation and helped organize the rescue of a hundred people trapped underground. For this act he was awarded the British Empire Medal by King George VI. It was a proud moment for a Seaforth Highland Londoner!

What is clear from this snapshot of my family – a Highlander coming to work in London, and a Londoner serving in a Highland regiment – is that the notion of the Highlander is fluid. My book tells the story of how a group of people from the edge of the British Isles came to be regarded as heroes of empire and how their warrior ideal was embraced by the rest of the world. It is a tale of a united nation in which Scots have served alongside English, Irish and Welsh in a British Army that has stood up to tyrants across the centuries. Tremendous strength and enterprise have come out of that union, and this book describes one brilliant aspect of it.

Tim Newark, 2009

Acknowledgements

Special thanks to all the Highland regimental museums who helped me most generously with my archival research for this book, especially Sarah Malone, Deborah Dunning and Major Malcolm Ross of the Gordon Highlanders Museum, Aberdeen; Tommy Smyth of the Black Watch Museum, Perth; Rod Mackenzie and Joyce Steele of the Argyll and Sutherland Highlanders Museum, Stirling Castle; and Lieutenant-Colonel George Latham of the Highlanders' Regimental Museum, Fort George, Inverness. Thanks for the kind permission of the trustees of these museums to quote from the unpublished material held in their invaluable archives.

Thanks also to Jonathan Ferguson and Stuart Allan of the National War Museum in Edinburgh Castle; Major Maurice Gibson, Regimental Secretary of the Highlanders; Captain Tam Henderson; Private Alfred Blake for his memories of Aden; Lieutenant-Colonel Andrew Brown, David Drinkwater, Derek Halley, Tony and Una Laycock for their memories of Korea; Chris Newark, George Newark and Michael J Newark for family history; Peter and Ollie Newark for their picture archive; the staff of the British Library, King's Cross and Colindale, and the National Archives, Kew; James Taylor of the Imperial War Museum; Gavin Edgerley-Harris of the Gurkha Museum; Freddy Berowski of the National Baseball Hall of Fame & Museum; Fergus Cannan, Eileen Stuart, James Opie; Stuart Reid for kindly reading through my draft chapters and giving me his expert advice; Victoria Newark, for being good company on my travels around the Highlands; my excellent agent Andrew Lownie and fine publisher Leo Hollis.

Tim Newark, 2009

Prologue: 'Run ye dogs!'

Captain John Maclean was the second son of a Highland clan chief. His father's estate was on the shores of Loch Linnhe, looking out across the sea to Mull, but he would not inherit that. He had to make his money from soldiering. Before he was thirty-six years old, Maclean had served King George II, first in the Black Watch, patrolling the Highlands for robbers and cattle thieves, and then abroad.

Overseas, the Black Watch had become a regular front-line regiment, and Maclean saw service in Flanders. But the service did not suit him. He had not joined the Black Watch to fight King George's foreign wars and he did not fit easily into a redcoat regiment. In 1744 he was dismissed from the ranks of the Black Watch for duelling with a fellow officer. Deprived of a regular income and with little hope of inheriting his father's estate, he had little left to lose.

Two years later, he stood at the head of a group of Maclean clansmen, impatient to fight the redcoats who had once been his comrades. For Maclean was now a Jacobite rebel, and rain and sleet lashed at him as he waited for action at Culloden, five miles east of Inverness. He was cold, wet and hungry. It was midday on 16 April 1746.

The land that Maclean stood on, Drummossie Moor, was typical of the Highlands – waterlogged and boggy. But it was the wrong sort of terrain for the Highland Charge – that traditional Celtic hell-for-leather attack unleashed at the climax of a battle. Previously successful charges depended on dry and firm ground, preferably on a slope, running down towards the enemy. You had to be confident of your foothold to run at full tilt across those deadly few yards inside the enemy's close musket range. You didn't want to be slipping and sliding and picking your way across clumps of muddy grass. But that was how it looked that afternoon.

Maclean tried to keep the locks of his pistols dry under his jacket. There was hope that the weather might be to the clans' advantage, as the British Army depended on firepower, and a whole host of dud shots would lessen the impact of their muskets. Nonetheless, there were other reasons for grumbling among Maclean and his Highlanders.

The night before had been the birthday of the enemy's commander – the twenty-five-year-old Duke of Cumberland – and he had given every man an extra ration of brandy and cheese. More than a few redcoats could have been expected to get drunk. But the Jacobites had squandered the advantage of a night attack by pointless marches through the dark that left Maclean and the Highland rebels tired and disappointed. They were hungry too; most of their supplies had been left behind at Inverness and a good number of them left the battlefield to scavenge for food. Those that did not, stretched out on the sodden ground to snatch any kind of rest. 'Many of them fell asleep in the parks of Culloden and other places near the road,' noted one witness, 'and never wakened till they found the enemy cutting their throats.'[1]

The early-morning exodus of hungry Highlanders to Inverness slashed the number of soldiers available to Prince Charles Edward Stuart – 'Bonnie Prince Charlie' – the twenty-six-year-old French-raised Jacobite leader. To counter any further desertions, the Prince issued a severe order threatening that 'if any man turn his back to run away, the next behind such man is to shoot him'.[2] This was perhaps why a unit of French troops, the Royal Ecossais, especially loyal to the Prince, was placed in the centre of the rear line behind the Highlanders.

But there was no fear of this with Captain John Maclean. He had no future with the British Army. His only chance of advancement was with Bonnie Prince Charlie and victory at Culloden. Nine months earlier, Maclean had rushed to pledge his support to the Prince, 'where I had the honour and satisfaction to get a kiss of his royal Highness his hand'.[3]

Back in '45, it had all seemed to be going so well. Early Jacobite victories led to an invasion of England, and the Highlanders marched as far south as Derbyshire. Maclean recalled with pleasure the friendly welcome they received. White sheets and napkins hung from windows alongside giant white cockades – the emblem of the Jacobites – nailed to the gables of houses. Crowds gathered and lit bonfires and cheered as the Highlanders swaggered past. One Englishman ran up to Maclean and wished him good luck. Such recollections raised rebel spirits on the mossy field of Culloden. If they had beaten the redcoats before, they could beat them again.

What Maclean did not fully understand, however, was that his senior commanders were split on what action to take that day; and his fate was in their hands. The main Jacobite commander was Lord George Murray, a fifty-two-year-old landowner with a professional military background. But Murray had fallen out of favour with the Prince, who now decided to take over direct command of his army for the battle. For military advice, the Prince deferred to his Irish friend, John William O'Sullivan, and Murray despaired of the decisions they made. He had wanted to attack the British Army at night while they were drunk as beggars. He also knew for sure that the moor was the wrong sort of ground for Highland warriors. The Prince and O'Sullivan ignored his criticism.

Murray was not the only senior Scot to disapprove of outside influences. David, Lord Elcho, a close associate of the Prince and Colonel of his Life Guards, voiced his dismay. 'Nothing displayed the Prince's want of insight better than to see him throwing himself into the arms of some Irishmen come from France to make their fortune by him,' wrote Lord Elcho, 'rather than consult the Scotch who formed his army and who were in their own land.'⁴

Captain James Johnstone was a twenty-seven-year-old aide-de-camp to both Murray and the Prince. The son of a well-to-do merchant in Edinburgh, he had left home to join up with the Jacobites as soon as the Prince landed in Scotland, but he was not blind to his leader's faults. He too thought the Irish gave poor counsel and overheard the Prince being told to withdraw his troops to higher ground and await the return of his missing hungry Highlanders. 'The Prince, however, would listen to no advice,' he noted, 'and resolved on giving battle, let the consequences be what they might.'⁵

Was John Maclean aware of this argument among his senior commanders? He had stopped writing entries in his journal a week before the battle. The small vellum-covered pocket book was tucked inside his jacket, and he hoped soon to write some lines about a great victory of the clans over King George. Elsewhere, the feeling was growing that the battle was lost before it had even begun. They had the wrong weather, the wrong ground and the wrong commander. To go into battle knowing this says a lot for the raw courage of the Highlanders. To top it off, the rebel force of around 5,000 was outnumbered by the British Army by at least two or three thousand men.

As midday came and went, Maclean and his Highlanders became more impatient. The cold wind was driving sleet into their faces and they had had enough of waiting on their Bonnie Prince. The Duke of Cumberland was satisfied with his redcoats organized in two broad lines, and both sides wanted to get on with it. At last, the combat opened with the boom of cannon. The British had more artillery than the rebels and their iron cannon balls skidded across the slick ground, bowling over Highlanders huddled in their clan groups. After about a quarter of an hour of this, the Highlanders snapped, just as Cumberland had anticipated. He wanted the clans to make the first move.

The Highlanders advanced from the left: 500 MacDonells of Glengarry, 400 MacDonalds of Keppoch, Clanranald and Glencoe, all under the command of the Duke of Perth. In the centre of the front line, from the left, came 100 Chisholms, nearly 200 MacLachlans and Macleans, 150 Deeside men and then 500 Mackintoshes, all led by Lord John Drummond. On the right, commanded by Lord George Murray, were 500 Frasers, 150 Appin men, 650 Camerons, and 500 Atholl men from Perthshire. Captain John Maclean led his men forward alongside the MacLachlans in the centre of the battleline.

All the Highlanders were instructed by the Prince to wear their traditional clothing of belted plaid to make the most of the Highland reputation for ferocity. Clan tartans were not invented until after the eighteenth century and so most tartan setts were red or brownish-red. As a Jacobite officer, John Maclean probably wore tartan trews, largely because they were more convenient than a kilt or plaid on horseback. All wore white cockades on their soft bonnets. Highland weaponry included the traditional basket-hilted steel broadsword and the round shield or targe, plus pistols and muskets – firelocks as they were called at the time. Many of the muskets carried at Culloden were made and supplied by the French.

In a Highland Charge, muskets and pistols were usually fired first and discarded, allowing the Highlanders to rush in with broadsword and shield for close combat. It was a savage onslaught but had many inherent defects. It allowed for only one undisciplined volley of fire and ignored the value of fighting with bayonet. As everyone knew, Highlander and enemy alike, the main impact of the Highland Charge was psychological, and so the purpose of the broadsword was mainly to hack down fleeing soldiers. But what if the enemy stood?

As a leader of his clansmen, John Maclean was in the front rank brandishing a pistol and broadsword. Yelling his battle cry, he rushed forward, pushing his tired legs over the boggy ground. He ran straight into the fire of the redcoats lined up before him. Musket balls buzzed past him, felling his clansmen following behind. One shot, maybe several, tore into his jacket and threw him down into the mud. Blood poured out and his life ended on Drummossie Moor.

Maclean's pocket book fell on the ground and was picked up by a fellow clansman, Donald Maclean. Donald later filled in the entry for the battle in John's journal and described the combat that killed its author.

> After a short stay and all the disadvantages any army could meet with as to their numbers they doubled or tripled ours and all the advantages of ground and wind and weather our cannon began to play upon them and they upon us. After we stayed about 10 minutes we were ordered to march hastily to the enemy which we did boldly. They began a smart fire of their small guns and grapes shots from their cannons till we were beat back ...[6]

As the Highland rebels emerged out of the clouds of artillery smoke, wielding their swords and pistols, they howled at the British infantrymen – 'Run ye dogs!' – hoping their Highland bloodlust would unnerve Cumberland's redcoats. They hoped too that the bad weather had dampened the rows of muskets aimed at them. But the redcoats had kept their powder dry within the lapels of their coats – shielding their muskets from the wet – and scarcely one gun in a battalion missed fire. At close range, Cumberland's artillery changed from round shot to grape, firing canisters loaded with dozens of small iron balls and creating the effect of massive shot guns blasting away in the faces of the Highlanders. The carnage was terrible. Iron balls ripped off heads, smashed arms and legs. The redcoats then unleashed volleys of disciplined musket fire, a hailstorm of lead tearing flesh and breaking bones. Because Jacobite officers led from the front, many of them were victims of the initial volleys, leaving their men leaderless.

The Highlanders could not reply with their guns – they had already fired them at some distance and dropped them, most of their ill-aimed shots going above the heads of the redcoats. Their only chance now was to rush through the gunfire and stumble into close combat, hoping that enough of them had survived to scare the redcoats into falling back. But the impetus of their Highland Charge had been slowed by the boggy, lumpy moor and, most importantly of all, the redcoats were not frightened and stood their ground. They fought back at close quarters with bayonets attached to the muzzles of their muskets. This gave them another advantage, as the reach of the bayonet was greater than that of the broadsword.

By sheer strength and courage some Highlanders broke though the front line to face units in the second line. In the heat of the fighting there were moments of individual combat evoking a more ancient age of Celtic duels. Lieutenant Loftus Cliffe of Monro's 37th Regiment was confronted by a Highland officer. 'In the midst of the action,' he recalled, 'the officer that led on the Camerons called to me to take quarter, which I refused and bid the Rebel scoundrel advance; he did, and fired at me, but providentially missed his mark; I then shot him dead and took his pistol and dirk, which are extremely neat.'[7]

The fighting lasted less than an hour. On the left, the marshy ground slowed the advance of the MacDonalds and they staggered forward to be easily mown down by the British before they had got anywhere near their lines. It was heartbreaking for the rebels. When they did get through on the right flank, they were met with redcoats wielding their bayonets with practised confidence. The traditional Highland broadsword that had done so much damage to redcoats in the past was now overtaken by the more deadly bayonet. 'They got a thorough dressing,' trumpeted one British officer, 'and it has convinced our soldiers that their broadsword and targe is only a bugbear, and nothing equal to a firelock and bayonet.'[8]

Not only had the Highland Charge failed in the face of superior firepower and across treacherously boggy ground, but the sword-swinging warriors had even come off worse in the close-quarter fighting. As redcoats closed in on the outnumbered and outfought rebels, firing point-blank volleys at them, some bitterly frustrated Highlanders were reduced to throwing stones at their enemies.

The collapse of the Jacobite army swiftly followed. Any High-landers able to get out of the killing ground made their way back across the moor. Captain Johnstone was at the heart of the action. He had given up a safe position near the Prince to join his friend, Donald MacDonald of Scothouse, a captain of the MacDonald clan. He was on the left of the army, at a distance of twenty paces from the enemy, when the rebels broke. He stood motionless, lost in astonishment. 'I then, in a rage, discharged my blunderbuss and pistols at the enemy,' he recalled, 'and immediately endeavoured to save myself like the rest; but having charged on foot and in boots, I was so overcome by the marshy ground, the water on which reached to the middle of the leg, that instead of running I could scarcely walk ...'[9]

When Johnstone came to write his account of the battle, he claimed it was lost 'rather from a series of mistakes on our part, than any skilful manoeuvre of the Duke of Cumberland'. The High-landers paid the price of these errors. 'No troops, however excel-lent, are possessed of qualities which will render them constantly invincible,' he concluded.

Bonnie Prince Charlie watched the rout, which was the result of his amateurish command. He tried to rally some of his troops but they streamed past him. Not even his most loyal soldiers were willing to fire on these beaten men, looking instead to their own survival and falling back. He soon joined them, along with the senior Jacobite commanders, including Lord George Murray.

It was then that the Duke of Cumberland unleashed his cavalry in pursuit of the rebels. It was a ruthless but standard military tactic to send in cavalry after a broken force and redcoat horsemen surged after the Highlanders, cutting them down as they fled. As British soldiers advanced across the battlefield, they finished off any wounded rebels. Quarter had not been expected from the High-landers and none was given.

Stuck on the moor with the redcoats fast approaching, Captain Johnstone searched desperately for a horse. He came across one being held by a man frozen with fear. He tried to take the horse from him, but it took the efforts of another Highlander to wrench the horse from the panicked man and help Johnstone, who barely had the strength to mount. As Johnstone rode away, he witnessed the fearless act of a Highlander caught in the open by the redcoats.

> One officer, wishing to take a Highlander prisoner, advanced a few paces to seize him, but the Highlander brought him down with his sword, and killed him on the spot; and, not satisfied with this, he stopped long enough to take possession of his watch, and then decamped with the booty.

Few Jacobite prisoners were taken on that day and they were mainly French soldiers serving with the Prince, accorded more civilized treatment than the native rebels. Cumberland wanted to end the threat of Jacobite Highlanders in Scotland once and for all, and through the next day the fleeing clansmen were slaughtered wherever they were found.

Months later, a British dragoon walked into a printer's workshop in Edinburgh and gave an eyewitness account of what happened after the battle. He remembered hearing the doleful sound of injured rebels huddling together, too weak to do anything but crawl across the ground. Then he saw small parties of the King's troops passing through the field and shooting the wounded men. 'Some of the rebels seemed pleased to be relieved of their pain by death,' said the dragoon, 'while others begged of the soldiers to spare them, which, however, was no ways regarded.'[10]

Between one and two thousand Jacobites died on the battlefield – there is no exact figure. In contrast, 310 Hanoverian soldiers were listed as killed or wounded (later rising to 364). Redcoat firepower had demolished the rebel army. While the relatives of Jacobite Highlanders mourned their losses, few other Scots were unhappy to see the back of Bonnie Prince Charlie. He had brought too much trouble to their land. When fourteen captured rebel standards were burned in public in Edinburgh, there were no great protests. The government then employed loyal Highlanders – the paramilitary Independent Companies – to hunt down the few rebels that remained defiant after Culloden. The defeated Prince fled back to his royal patron in France. The Jacobite cause was over.

*

Today, the battle of Culloden is viewed as the last tragic flourish of Highland culture in Scotland. It is also crudely characterized as a combat of Scots versus English – its brutality arousing nationalist anger north of the border. On the battlefield – preserved by the National Trust for Scotland – there is a memorial to the British dead. It is called, wrongly, the English Stone. A far larger memorial cairn, erected in 1881, commemorates the 'graves of the gallant Highlanders who fought for Scotland & Prince Charlie'. This is also far from the truth and yet is very much part of the later mythologizing of the battle.

The reality is that many Scots, including Highlanders, fought with the British Army against the Jacobite rebels at Culloden. In fact, Culloden was the climax of a fifty-eight-year-old civil war fought across Scotland. At the time, the rebels called the enemy not English or British but Hanoverians. It was a not a national war of Scots against English, but a dynastic and religious struggle – of Catholic Stuart-supporting Jacobites against Protestant Hanoverian loyalists.

At the battle of Culloden, the British Army, commanded by the Duke of Cumberland, included three regular Scots regiments numbering over 1,000 troops. In addition to these were a 500-strong unit of Highlanders, including Scots of the Argyle Militia, and tartan-wearing troops from the 64th Highlanders and 43rd Highlanders, the Black Watch. Some of them were used to guard the British baggage train but others fought valiantly in an action on the edge of the battle. Cumberland paid tribute to them in his report published shortly afterwards.

[The Rebels] came running on in their wild manner ... but the Royals [a Scots regiment] and Pulteney's hardly took their firelocks from their shoulders, so that after these faint attempts they made off; and the little squadrons on our right were sent to pursue them. Gen Hawley had, by the help of our Highlanders, beat down two little stone walls, and came in upon the right flank of their second line.[11]

Cumberland refers to 'our Highlanders' on three occasions in his report. He refers to the Jacobite Highlanders simply as the 'Rebels'. The British Highlanders at Culloden were clad in the traditional tartan belted plaid and distinguished themselves from the enemy by wearing red or yellow cloth crosses in their bonnets. Of course, the majority of recruits to the British regiments were English, but they all fought under the British Union flag. The only true Hanoverians on the field at Culloden were sixteen German Hussars, richly attired in their exotic Hungarian-influenced uniform, serving as Cumberland's personal bodyguard.

The outcome of the battle of Culloden was tragic for the Jacobite Highlanders. The lives of John Maclean and so many clansmen ended abruptly there. Their fighting talents were criminally betrayed by Bonnie Prince Charlie's foolish attempts at military leadership. They paid a heavy and bloody price for his mistakes. It was the end of the Jacobite cause, but it was not the end of the Highland soldier. Culloden was a key turning point in his advance. Liberated from the false hope of Jacobitism, Highlanders embraced the opportunities provided by a growing British Empire and would triumph in every corner of the globe.

Traditionally, young men from the Highlands of Scotland had escaped the poverty of their background by seeking military service abroad. Subsequent to their defeat at Culloden, several Jacobite rebels ended up as most distinguished servants of an emerging British Empire. Alexander Grant, for example, was a clansman from Glen Urquhart who stood in the ranks of Glengarry's Highlanders at Culloden, but after the battle, he sailed away to a new life in India. He joined the East India Company and ten years later found himself defending the British settlement at Calcutta against the Nawab of Bengal.

Unprepared and outnumbered, Grant and his colleagues fought a desperate house-to-house battle against the Indian warriors. In the end, he managed to escape but several of his comrades were imprisoned in the notorious Black Hole of Calcutta. Grant gained revenge when he urged Robert Clive to take on the Nawab at the battle of Plassey in the following year. It turned out to be a decisive victory in the expansion of British imperial influence in India. Alexander's cousin, Charles Grant, went on to become an important director of the East India Company.

Other former rebels sailed west to America. Simon Fraser was the son of Lord Lovat, a key figure in the Jacobite rebellion. On the morning of Culloden, Fraser was reported to be marching his troops towards the battlefield to join the other rebel Highlanders, but he lingered a little too long on the road until he met fleeing Jacobites. He then proceeded to turn round and surrendered his troops to the British. He spent the subsequent decade working hard to prove his loyalty to the Hanoverian monarchy. This culminated in his raising the 78th regiment of Highlanders for the British Army in 1757. The 78th included many former rebel soldiers and was dispatched to North America to fight the French during the Seven Years War.

On the morning of 13 September 1759, many of these ex-Jacobite soldiers found themselves standing on the Plains of Abraham outside the French-held city of Quebec. They wore red coats over their belted plaid and stood in line under the Union flag. Facing them across the battlefield, on the French side, there was at least one other Jacobite veteran of Culloden: James Johnstone, the aide-de-camp to Bonnie Prince Charlie who managed to escape from the battlefield by stealing a horse.

After Culloden, Johnstone went on the run, avoiding arrest by disguising himself as a beggar. Eventually he restyled himself the 'Chevalier de Johnstone' and sailed to Canada, ending up in command of a unit of French troops at the battle of Quebec opposite the 78th Highlanders. When his French commander was killed by British bullets, he feared for his life all over again. 'It was high time for me to extricate myself from this awkward situation in the best way I could,' he wrote, 'for I was now in as embarrassing and ticklish a position as that in which I was after the battle of Culloden.'[12]

Johnstone did so by throwing himself on the mercy of the British Army and in particular a redcoat who turned out to be a distant relative of his in Scotland whom he had last seen in 1745. The one-time rebel was sent back with a boatload of French prisoners and, on landing, walked straight into a French tavern where he found 'oysters and white wine in abundance'. A satisfactory ending to a tortuous military adventure.

Chapter 1
Making Hard Men

James Charles Stuart – James VI, king of Scots – was a spindly, neurotic monarch. In 1598, at the age of just thirty-two, he was convinced he was dying and wrote a book for his son, Henry, describing the state of Scotland, how it should be ruled and how he hoped the prince would follow his ambition to succeed to the English throne after the current Queen Elizabeth I. Originally written in Scots, it was called the *Basilicon Doron* – the Kingly Gift. It was meant to be a secret book, published in a very limited edition of seven copies, but news of its controversial contents leaked out.

Once the Scottish king became James I of England in 1603, a second, revised edition was widely published to great interest in England. In the original, uncensored copy of the book, James revealed his true Stuart arrogance and expressed especially his disdain for one group of his subjects – the Highlanders.

> As for the Highlands, I shortly comprehend them all in two sorts of people: the one, that dwelleth in our main land that are barbarous, and yet mixed with some show of civility: the other, that dwelleth in the Isles and are utterly barbarous, without any sort or show of civility.[1]

King James recommended they be treated as 'wolves and wild boars' and that his son establish 'colonies among them of answerable inland subjects, that within short time may root them out and plant civility in their rooms'. Yet, it was to these same Highland 'wolves' that the

Stuart dynasty would later turn to help them back into power after they were deposed at the end of the seventeenth century.

It was true, the Highlanders were not as sophisticated as the elegant Frenchified courtiers who thronged around James in Edinburgh, but this was hardly surprising. These were men and women surviving in a harsh environment, rain- and wind-swept, with the poorest soil in the British Isles. Once a family was fed, there was little left over for the fineries of 'civil' life. 'In dress, in the manner of their outward life, and in good morals,' wrote a sixteenth-century chronicler, 'these come behind the householding Scots – yet they are not less, but rather much more, prompt to fight ...'[2]

The Highlands of Scotland are hard in many ways. The rock that makes the landscape so dramatic is a barrier to drainage. When rain runs off the mountain tops it collects in valleys where there is no escape for it into subterranean chambers. Rain and snow are frequent, brought by Atlantic clouds, and moisture lingers on the surface to make the land marshy and sodden. If you make the mistake of stepping off the main road into this terrain, you quickly find yourself sinking into boggy ground that drenches your boots and makes walking tough work. A modern tarmac road is like a bridge across this water-soaked landscape.

For much of its early history, the north of Scotland was a virtual island, cut off from the rest of Britain by the Firth of Forth in the east and the Firth of Clyde in the west and the boggy land that spread out from around the heads of these inlets. The only place to pass though this 'moss' was at Stirling, which made the city crucial to controlling the north.[3] Only a few miles to the south, Robert Bruce made good use of the wetland, forcing invading English knights and archers to stagger and drown in the marsh around Bannockburn in 1314.

At this famous victory for the Scots, the Bruce numbered some 'Wild Scots' among his troops who rushed upon the enemy 'in their fury as wild boars will do'. They fought with daggers, spears and long-handled Lochaber axes, and when they came to close combat they did not hesitate to throw off their tartan clothes and 'offer their naked bellies to the point of the spear'.[4] It was an early demonstration of Highland battlefield rage.

For centuries, beyond this boggy barrier around Stirling, the north of Scotland evolved detached from the rest of Britain. It was a much more significant geographical frontier than the conventional Highland line, which follows a north-easterly geological fault line from the Clyde to just south of Aberdeen. It was only in the late eighteenth century that the marshy land around Stirling was drained, opening up the Highlands to modern roads and then railways. Until then, the more efficient method of transport was by sea. Highland merchants passed along the west coast and criss-crossed the Scottish islands of the Hebrides, Orkneys and Shetland, creating a trading network that stretched to Scandinavia.

The damp valleys and craggy mountains only allowed for the poorest kind of agriculture – the grazing of small herds of hardy cattle and sheep, with little profit to be made by the farmer. Large communities could not be sustained by this kind of living. Only the great estate owners – the clan chiefs – had any wealth, but this was paltry compared to southerners.

The food and drink available to the poor Highlander was meagre. Cattle were raised to be sold, so little meat was eaten, leaving only oats, barley, cabbage, potatoes, turnips and cows' milk to form the staple diet. Oat cakes and cheese might be a typical meal, with a winter breakfast, known as *tartan purrie*, being a porridge of oatmeal and the juice of boiled cabbage. Treats would be wild fruit or game, or fish and seafood if you lived near the coast.[5]

Alcohol featured significantly in the lives of the richer classes and hard drinking was expected. A Highland hierarchy of booze was described as claret and brandy for the lords and lairds, port or whisky punch for the tacksmen (tenant farmers) and estate managers, and strong beer for common husbandmen. In the *Memoirs of the Life of Duncan Forbes of Culloden*, Forbes's biographer made clear his disapproval of this excessive drinking.

> 'Tis a custom in the North of Scotland (highly indeed to be despised and abhorred) among the generality of gentlemen, to think that they do not entertain a visitor in a proper manner, unless they actually shall make him drunk: and indeed so far has the delusion spread that the visitor scarce judges himself well used, if he be left pass without the usual compliment ...[6]

Although Forbes was a Lowlander, his estate was in the Highlands and he was happy to join in the customs of his clan chief neighbours, so that he and his elder brother won the reputation of being 'the greatest *bouzers*, ie the most plentiful drinkers in the North'.

An Englishman travelling in Scotland in the 1720s heard of a drinking contest in which English officers unwisely challenged some Highland gentlemen. The Highlanders won, well practised in drinking quarts of whisky, while the Englishmen suffered badly. 'One of the officers was thrown into a fit of the gout without hopes,' it was recorded, 'another had a most dangerous fever, a third lost his skin and hair by the surfeit.'[7]

The geographical isolation of many Highland settlements meant they had to look after themselves. Young men were forced into the role of protectors, hunters or bandits, and it was customary to carry a weapon and maintain a fierce pride. Personal insults were settled by violence and injustices against a community by armed retaliation, raids and counter-raids. Highland songs and poetry demanded their young men be as fierce as wild cats.

O children of Conn of the Hundred Battles
Now is the time for you to win recognition
O raging whelps
O sturdy bears
O most sprightly lions
O battle-loving warriors
O brave heroic firebrands...
O children of Conn remember
Hardness in time of battle.

Conn was the mythical ancestor of the MacDonalds and his descendants were expected to act like ferocious animals in battle. Such expectations encouraged young men to push themselves forward as individual champions rather than working as part of a disciplined team. In battle, their natural instinct was to surge forward, running quickly to the combat, trusting on being 'chancy' (Scots for 'lucky') rather than 'canny'.[8]

Out of this landscape came the Highland warrior – physically tough, quick to attack, savage in close combat. Denied an income from his hard-pressed farming family, he would seek service with his feudal lord. Refused that, he would join the companies of strong-arm men paid by government to hunt down outlaws –

men like himself who had decided to go one step further to help themselves. Failing that, he would sail away across the sea to fight for a foreign army in Europe in French service or later in the Protestant forces of the Thirty Years War. Unemployed farmer, enforcer, mercenary, bandit, rebel – the first Highlanders were all these things.

The Highlander's reputation as a merciless warrior came from this desperation to win a place in the world, but it began to have a value of its own, gaining him employment as a professional fighter. This reputation grew as his settled southern neighbours became more prosperous. It is in the chronicles of John Major, a Scots Low-lander from Gleghornie near the border with England, that we see this clear distinction. In his *History of Greater Britain*, published in 1521, he gave full vent to the timeless prejudice of southerners against northerners. 'To the people of the North,' he wrote, 'God gave less intelligence than to those of the South, but greater strength of body, a more courageous spirit ...'

Major subdivided his people into 'Wild Scots' and 'householding Scots'. The Wild Scots spoke 'Irish' (Gaelic) and were more aggressive because 'born as they are in the mountains, and dwellers in forests, their very nature is more combative'. Some of these Highlanders were rich in cattle, sheep and horses and these were inclined to pay obedience to the laws of the land and their king, but other Highlanders were outlaws who liked to prey on their own people.

> The Scottish kings have with difficulty been able to withstand the inroads of these men. From the mid-leg to the foot they go uncovered; their dress is, for an over garment, a loose plaid and a shirt of saffron-dyed. [9]

In Major's early sixteenth-century Latin text, the character was already set of the Highlander as an untamed tartan-clad warrior who rushed upon his enemy like a wild animal. This was the image repeated by James VI, king of Scots in his *Basilicon Doron*.

If King James considered his own Highland subjects to be bar-barians then it was not surprising that this was a view held by many Lowlanders who failed to make any connection with them at all. It enhanced yet further their fearful reputation and turned it into a weapon that could be wielded by a Stuart ruler against disobedient Lowland Scots. Such an act of terrorism was unleashed in 1678.

*

Highland society was organized into clans. These began as extended family groups with a single surname which became associated with a particular region of the Highlands. The word comes from the Gaelic *clann* meaning 'children'. As a clan grew in size it became a political unit that could ally itself with other clans to protect its interests. The head of the clan was the chief and he formed the summit of the feudal pyramid. His duty was to maintain and secure the lands of his kinsmen – acting as both landlord and warlord – while those beneath him offered money or service in return for his protection and patronage.

Far away from central government authority, the clan chiefs also administered their own justice, having the power to imprison or execute lawbreakers. Lowly clansmen worked as farmers and often ended up borrowing money from their overlords or offering feudal dues in exchange for rent, giving themselves as servants or soldiers if their chief demanded it.

By the early seventeenth century, Highland society was caught up in the religious conflict that plagued the rest of Europe. Fighting had begun in Scotland with the Bishops' War of 1639. Two years earlier, the Scots had grown alarmed at the tyrannical rule of the Stuart king Charles I, son of the Highlander-hating James VI and I. When he tried to impose a new Book of Prayer on them, the Scottish Presbyterian opposition drew up a Covenant to oppose him. Because of their later support of Stuart kings, it is frequently assumed that all Highland clansmen were Catholics. This was not so.

The Campbells, Munros and Sutherlands were Presbyterian clans, and not all clan chiefs saw advantage in supporting the Stuart monarchy. The attitude of individual clan chiefs was based as much on personal relationships, rivalries and conspiracies as anything else, and these could often break into open fighting with each other. The most vicious of these clan conflicts was between the Presbyterian Campbells and the Catholic MacDonalds. The MacDonalds were the dominant clan of the western Highlands and islands and actively supported the Stuart monarchy, bringing over Irish warriors to assist them. The Campbells from the southern Highlands led the military opposition against them during the Civil Wars.

In 1660, following the Restoration of the Stuart dynasty, Charles II became king of England and Scotland. John Maitland, Duke of Lauderdale, became his Secretary of State and was allowed to rule Scotland as though he was its uncrowned king. Lauderdale constantly persecuted the more radical Protestants, and religion became even more of a polarizing factor in Scotland.

By 1678 Lauderdale was concerned about dissent among the defiantly Presbyterian population of south-west Scotland and chose to deal with this by physically intimidating them into submission. His weapon was the Highlander. The reputation of the Highlander was already poor among Lowlanders and it was about to get a lot worse. Lauderdale wanted to demonstrate that he could deploy their savagery against anyone he considered an enemy of the Stuart regime.

Lauderdale called on clan chiefs loyal to the Stuarts to send their vassals – the men on their estates who owed them service – to Stirling, where they would link up with soldiers from the king's army. The Catholic MacDonalds, along with the Macleans and Mac-Gregors, headed the list of clans that were particularly welcome. From there, the Highland horde of around 5,000 warriors marched into Presbyterian communities where they were given licence to behave as badly as they wished, abusing the inhabitants and stealing their property. The Highlanders were fully armed and backed up by government troops, and the terrified Presbyterians declined to face them in battle.

One inhabitant of Ayrshire recorded their behaviour, saying 'they pillaged, plundered, thieved, and robbed night and day; even the Lord's day they regarded as little as any other'. The marauding Highlanders came to his father's house and pointed at his shoes, saying they would take them off his feet. They grabbed the farmer.

> But he threw himself out of their grips, and turning to a pitch-fork which was used at the stalking of his corn, and they having their broadswords drawn, cried 'Claymore', and made at him; but he quickly drove them out of the kiln and chasing them all four a space from the house, knocked one of them to the ground.[10]

The next day, twenty Highlanders came back to the brave man's house, but, sensibly, he was not there. Instead, they plundered his home, taking pots, pans, clothes, bed linen, furniture, anything of value they could carry away. Another contemporary described their barbarity as 'more terrible than Turks or Tartars'. It was not the Highlanders' finest moment.

Few people were recorded as having died during this punishment raid, but it was estimated to have cost the Presbyterian communities in Ayrshire alone some £200,000 in damage and loss. It also confirmed the savagery and poverty of the northern clans in the eyes of Lowlanders. The Highlander was proved to be a frightening, hard man who could serve his government – if directed against a soft target – but what would happen if this same clansman fought against the government, against professional soldiers? What was his value then?

*

Within the next ten years, there was a political crisis in Britain. Charles II was succeeded in 1685 by his brother, James II, the first Catholic monarch in England since Mary I. It was too much for the Protestant establishment in England and they invited William of Orange, a Dutch Protestant, to rule jointly with his wife Mary, who was also James II's daughter. In 1688 William landed at Brixham in south-west England with an army of 20,000 Dutch, English, German and French Huguenot troops. James failed to oppose the landing and within weeks was forced to flee to Catholic France.

It was the beginning of almost sixty years of political intrigue during which James and his descendants would conspire with foreign support to win back their rule over Britain for the Stuart dynasty. Supporters of James II and his family were called Jacobites, a name derived from the Latin version of James, *Jacobus*. It was a name that would haunt the Highlands for decades to come.

The dramatic change in the fortunes of the Stuart monarchy suddenly placed in jeopardy those Highland clans who had risen to their support. Just ten years before, they had been happy to bully their fellow Scots whose religion put them at odds with the government; now, they faced a dose of their own medicine – unless they proved their strength. This opportunity came on 18 May 1689.

On that day, John Graham of Claverhouse, the forty-one-year-old Viscount Dundee, raised the Jacobite standard at a gathering of Highland clansmen at Dalcomera, near Spean Bridge. He was a passionate supporter of the Stuart cause and was known as 'Bluidy Clavers' after his brutal suppression of Scots Presbyterian Covenanters ten years before.

Today, the Jacobite Highland rebellions, stretching from 1689 to Culloden in 1746, are commonly viewed as a grand Scots-versus-English conflict, the last tragic gasp of Scots independence – but that is a false view of history. In reality, these were civil wars in which Scots fought on both sides. On the government side, Lieutenant General Hugh Mackay of Scourie was appointed the new commander of the army in Scotland. Mackay, who was around fifty years old, was a Highlander from Sutherland who had served abroad in the Dutch Army and was a key supporter of the Protestant William. Just seven months before William's accession, Mackay's nephew had been arrested and imprisoned in Edinburgh Castle because he was bringing a secret Williamite message.

In July 1689 Mackay took charge of a government army to hunt down Claverhouse. He was a good choice to take on the Highland Jacobite rebels: not only did he personally know the Highlanders' style of fighting, but he could counter this by deploying modern methods of warfare he had learned on foreign service. To underline the fact that this was a largely Scottish affair, of the six regiments Mackay took to face Claverhouse, five were Scottish, only one was English. He left Stirling on 25 July with his army and pursued Claverhouse to Blair Castle, which had declared its support for James. Sited at Blair Atholl in Perthshire, it guarded the main route through the mountains separating the Lowlands from the Highlands. Two days later, Mackay caught up with the Jacobites at the Pass of Killiecrankie, midway between Pitlochry and Blair Castle.

Mackay commanded 3,000 infantry and cavalry, trained in the latest Anglo-Dutch technique of firing well-ordered musket volleys. Claverhouse led a slightly smaller force, composed mostly of Highlanders ready to fight in their traditional way. It did not look promising for Claverhouse since the Highland way of war seemed out of date – suited to little more than raids and counterraids. They were irregular fighters expert in ambush but ill trained for an organized battle.

On the bright summer morning of 27 July, Claverhouse's Highlanders took a position on top of the steep wooded slopes overlooking the mouth of Killiecrankie Pass. General Mackay drew his troops up beneath them on a broad terrace, with their backs to a birch wood and a river that ran through the pass. Mackay deployed his units in the usual fighting formation he had practised in Europe, with his musketeers in three ranks to maximize their firepower. They looked the very essence of modern fighting men, wearing long red uniform coats with differently coloured cuffs signifying which unit they belonged to. They were regimented soldiers.

Due to the rough ground, there were gaps in the line between some of the government units. A bog a hundred yards across fell right in the middle of the redcoat battleline, separating Viscount Kenmore's recently raised Lowland regiment from the more experienced troops on the right flank, including the only English unit commanded by a Colonel Hastings. Mackay tried to cover this gap with three light artillery pieces and a few cavalrymen, but it was a definite weakness. He relied, perhaps too much, on his new methods of warfare and did not fully appreciate the fact that many of his soldiers were young, raw recruits.

Claverhouse's Highlanders were formed up in regiments but did not have the professional training of their opponents. He had asked one of his Highland commanders to instruct his followers in volley firing, but the Highlander refused, saying his men had neither the weapons nor the ammunition for such complex tactics. Most of the Highlanders on the battlefield that day were there because of feudal duty owed to their landowning masters. Some of the Highlanders were wealthy gentlemen who brought their own servants with them and could afford finely crafted firearms, broadswords and shields, but most were poor warriors who fought in clan gangs for booty and reputation. They carried simpler weapons such as spears or long-shafted axes – even bows and arrows. But, what they lacked in formal training, they more than made up in their experience of warfare and violence. They were tough men and knew how to present a fierce appearance.

Claverhouse's warriors wore the traditional Highland belted plaid. This was a long piece of tartan cloth wrapped over the shoulder and round the waist, secured with a belt and a brooch on the chest. It was a bulky piece of clothing that served well as a warm cloak or blanket. Although the lower part of the plaid hung loose over the knees, this was not a kilt.

If on a sunny day the belted plaid was too cumbersome to wear, a warrior would simply discard it and run into battle wearing only his voluminous shirt, with his shirt tails covering his groin. General Mackay later wrote his own report of the fighting at Killiecrankie and described the Highlanders in dismissive terms, mentioning their tendency to strip off for battle.

> To be sure of their escape, in case of repulse, they attack bare footed, without any cloathing but their shirts, and a little High- land doublet, whereby they are certain to outrun any foot, and will not readily engage where horse can follow the chase any distance.[11]

He said they came on slowly, fired their guns at a distance and threw them down. They then drew their long broadswords and ran towards the enemy, who 'if he stand firm, they never fail of running with much more speed back again to the hills'. Mackay's phrase 'if he stand firm' was to have particular resonance on that summer's day at Killiecrankie. He might well have understood the Highland way of fighting and considered them little better than half-naked savages, but many of his freshly recruited Lowland soldiers had grown up with tales of malicious Highlanders and were anxious to keep them a musket shot's length away. Mackay underestimated the value of the bogeyman factor presented by the Highlanders.

At Killiecrankie, neither side was keen to attack first. Mackay did not want his troops to tire themselves marching uphill to fight the Jacobites, while Claverhouse could see his poor Highlanders were seriously outgunned by the government troops in their regular ranks. As the hot day drew on, Mackay provoked the Highlanders into action by firing artillery rounds into their groups. In response, a party of Camerons ran down the slope to occupy two cottages in front of them. These Highlanders were driven off by musketeers from Mackay's own regiment on the right wing of his battleline. Mackay's men were Highlanders from Sutherland, but uniformed and trained, and their clash with the Camerons may well have infu- riated Claverhouse's warriors, who saw it as a challenge in the old clan style.

Having spent the long summer day anticipating battle, the Jacobite Highlanders were now impatient to fight or leave. Donald McBane was a twenty-five-year-old redcoat Scot fighting on the government side. Born near Inverness, he was himself a Highlander, but even he felt nervous as the rebels finally broke into a charge.

> The sun going down caused the Highlanders to advance on us like mad men, without shoe or stocking, covering themselves from our fire with their targes. At last they cast away their muskets, drew their broad swords and advanced furiously upon us, and were in the middle of us before we could fire three shots apiece, broke us and obliged us to retreat.[12]

In the face of this feral aggression, Mackay's recently raised soldiers in the centre of the battleline lost their nerve. Kenmore's Lowland troops dropped their guns and ran. Mackay's centre, bereft of any immediate support from the more experienced redcoats on the right flank – thanks to the extended gap caused by the boggy land – disintegrated. Donald McBane admitted they ran because many of them were new recruits.

They fled down the hillside towards the river. McBane grabbed a horse from the redcoat baggage train to ride through the water. A Highlander ran up behind him and started to fight him for the animal. McBane dodged around the horse, keeping it as a shield against the Highlander's blade. Eventually the clansman drew his pistol and fired after McBane as he bolted on foot for the edge of the river. He stood on a boulder and contemplated his escape route. 'It was about eighteen foot over betwixt two rocks,' he recalled. 'I resolved to jump it, so I laid down my gun and hat and jumped and lost one of my shoes in the jump.'

The location of McBane's legendary escape is now called the Soldier's Leap. Everyone wanted a quick exit. At least one redcoat officer died because one of his own men stole his horse to ride away. Mackay had hoped his personal presence among the troops in the centre would stiffen their resolve, but, as they flashed past him, he was in danger of being left alone, so he galloped over to his right wing.

But even there, the panic of Kenmore's troops had infected most of the two Scottish regiments, including government Highlanders, and they too fell back towards the river. Only one whole regiment remained standing and that was Hastings's Englishmen. They were experienced enough to know that flight offered no refuge from the fleet-footed Highlanders and that it was best to stick shoulder-to-shoulder and rely on their training. They shifted round to face the Highlanders running past them and poured volleys of fire into the flank of the clansmen as they sprinted after the fleeing redcoats.

Fortunately for Mackay, Claverhouse was killed at the moment of victory and the Jacobites lacked any further orders about what to do next. They ran down through the birch wood to the river. Not wanting to fight any more than they had to, the Highlanders turned their attention to looting the government baggage wagons and stripping the bodies of their victims. Having filled their pockets, the Jacobites drifted off into the night. It was a lucky escape for Mackay and those men that stood their ground. A more disciplined enemy would have returned to eliminate the fragments of government troops that remained.

As darkness fell, Mackay's right flank joined those redcoats on the left wing that had watched in dismay the collapse of their central battleline and withdrew safely from the battlefield. The bodies of both sides littered the ground. John Drummond wrote a detailed account of Killiecrankie, drawing on Jacobite eyewitness accounts to describe the battlefield on the day after the fighting.

'Many had their heads divided into two halves by one blow,' he reported, 'others had their skulls cut off above the ears by a back-stroke, like a night-cap. Their thick buff-belts were not sufficient to defend their shoulders from such deep gashes as almost disclosed their entrails … some that had skull-caps had them so beat into their brains that they died upon the spot'.[13]

It was the anticipation of such brutal hand-to-hand fighting that provoked panic in so many of the redcoats. It was their inadequate bladed weapons that had been shattered by the broadswords of the Highlanders. What characterized the battle was not training or skill, but fear. Most government soldiers were not killed in an initial clash with Highlanders – the redcoat units that broke crumbled before contact was even made. Most of them were killed in the pursuit, caught alone and cut down by the Jacobites chasing them.

As for the Highlanders rushing down the hill, most of them were not killed by volleys of fire to the front of them, because they, quite naturally, veered away from that and surged towards the gaps in the lines formed by those redcoats running away. The majority of their casualties came from the fire that tore into the side of their groups as they ran past Mackay's regiments that remained in the field – the figure has been estimated at over 700 clansmen. Neither side endured a frontal assault. Each had too much respect for the other's fighting skills for that.

Less than a month after the battle, Mackay wrote a report explaining the defeat to Lord Melville, Secretary for Scotland, in Whitehall, London. He admitted that several hundred of his men had 'fled without any firing'.[14] He later sought to explain this by saying 'all our officers and soldiers were strangers to the Highlanders way of fighting and embattailling, which mainly occasioned the consternation many of them were in'. This was not strictly true, as some of his troops were Highland veterans, but it did imply a high proportion of newly recruited Lowlanders in his army.

In addition to this, Mackay claimed that the speed of the Highland Charge at Killiecrankie was such that the redcoats did not have time to put plug bayonets into their muskets to meet the Jacobites with their swords and daggers. It was time to invent a new kind of bayonet, he argued, that could be used in this fast-moving fighting. It is not true that defeat at Killiecrankie was the reason for the introduction of the socket bayonet into the British Army – a weapon which could be fixed to the end of a musket without blocking up its barrel – but it must have encouraged interest in it. In 1693, a year after Mackay died fighting the French at the battle of Steenkirk, his *Rules of War for the Infantry* was published. It strongly advised that soldiers be provided with 'good Bayonets, fixt without the muzzels of their Pieces'.[15] Despite this practical advice, plug bayonets continued to be used in the British Army until 1703 when 1,200 socket bayonets were finally ordered by the Board of Ordnance.[16]

Killiecrankie was a terrible shock to those rulers that trusted in the potency of modern warfare. Until that point, Highlanders had been dismissed by Scots and English governments as barbarians. The true impact of Killiecrankie was not that Scots had defeated English – after all, it had been mainly Scots killing Scots – but that Highlanders using an ancient method of combat had beaten a modern regimented army equipped with muskets. That lesson shook the confidence of generals all the way from Edinburgh to London. But it also planted the seed of an idea.

If the triumph of the Jacobite Highland Charge at Killiecrankie had been more psychological than actual – the redcoats had broken before contact was made – then maybe the value of the Highlanders lay in their ferocious reputation rather than their actual fighting skills. It was the realization that appearance counted as much as regimental training that encouraged the English to think it would be a good idea to recruit these Gaelic wild men to their own ranks and put the fear of God in their enemies.

At Killiecrankie, it can be said that the legend of the Highlander was born, and their sprint pell-mell down the hill was a rehearsal for world-conquering charges in the following centuries. When the recruitment of Highlanders by the British Army began in earnest, the echoes of this battle would resonate on every battlefield where the British soldier stood.

Chapter 2
A Highland Mafia

For thirty-seven-year-old Donald Macleod, a tough, wiry ex-army sergeant, the appeal of joining the Highland Independent Companies was clear. He was 'fond of the highland dress and music, and of the society of his countrymen'. On top of that, the tasks demanded of him in this government police force were not too strenuous. Indeed, they were very much to his taste and included the following:

> Training up new soldiers ... hunting after incorrigible robbers, shooting, hawking, fishing, drinking, dancing, and toying ... with the young women.[1]

This was the life of Highland soldiers recruited by the British government in Scotland in the early eighteenth century and it was in stark contrast to the dangers they faced in battle. The *Memoirs of the Life and Gallant Exploits of the Old Highlander Serjeant Donald Macleod* tells the story of one such Highlander who experienced both kinds of duty. Like expert swordsman Donald McBane at Killiecrankie, Macleod would often stretch the truth to tell a good story, but dramatic memoirs like his established an audience for later Highland romances. Not everything Macleod says accords with the facts, but the account of his early career does have a ring of truth about it.

Born on Skye into a well-to-do landowning family, Macleod was abandoned by his father following the death of his mother in giving birth to a sibling when he was six years old. The father took to drink and then to a career at sea, leaving his son to be apprenticed to a stonemason in Inverness. It was an unhappy period for the little boy, who complained of always being hungry, and he was constantly running away. At the age of just twelve, he finally escaped by joining the Royal Scots in Perth.

Macleod's success in the British Army was down to natural intelligence, personal charm, and great ability with the broadsword. At the time, military commanders still liked to be surrounded by expert swordsmen who could take up any challenge delivered to them. During the Duke of Marlborough's campaigns on the Continent, Macleod was walking out with two ladies when a German soldier insulted him. The Highlander drew his sword and the German ran off, but a German officer stepped forward to accept the challenge. The officer had more courage than skill, and Macleod judged it would be easy to kill him, but he had no quarrel with the gentleman and proceeded to win the fight by wounding him on the calf and then the sword-arm. 'It is enough,' said the bloodied officer after a few more stinging blows and invited Macleod home to share a drink with him. 'They both cried,' noted Macleod's biographer, 'and kissed at parting.'

Macleod had learned sword fighting as a boy, filling in his spare time while an apprentice. His father was an expert swordsman too, though loathed by his neighbours for always challenging them to duels when drunk. A major headache for the British government, the easy availability of weapons in Scotland was considered to be a leading cause of lawlessness in the Highlands. Following the Jacobite Highland rebellion of 1715, the government passed an act prohibiting the carrying of weapons. From 1 November 1716, no Highlander was allowed to 'use, or bear Broad-Sword, or Target, Poynard, Whinger, or Durk, Side-Pistol, or Side-pistols, or Gun, or any other Warlike Weapons'.[2] If he were found carrying such a weapon, it would be confiscated and he would face a fine or imprisonment.

This was a significant assault on the very culture of the Highlands and a group of Scots gentlemen later published their response to the act. 'Our dispute is not whether we shall give up our arms or not,' they complained. 'But whether we shall deliver with them our poor people slaves to an unguarded clause in an act that may send us into captivity and ruin ...'[3] The act was too prone to error, they argued – a musket could be planted on an innocent, while the law-abiding individual was made vulnerable to criminals who ignored the act. Above all things, the Highlanders associated their weapons with freedom.

When the government employed Highlanders to police their communities, a key attraction of joining the Independent Companies was the right to bear traditional weapons. It appealed immensely to professional fighters like Donald Macleod, whose very character and personal progress depended on his talent with the broadsword.

*

Since the first Jacobite rebellion in 1689, the Stuart-supporting Highland clans had proved a surprisingly vigorous threat to the government of Scotland. In 1707, partly to help combat that menace, the separate parliaments of Scotland and England had come together in a Union that created the kingdom of Great Britain. This move was taken in anticipation of a succession crisis following the death of the childless Queen Anne, daughter of James II. The deposed king had died in exile in France in 1701, but his son James Edward Stuart took up the family claim to the throne he believed was rightfully his. The English parliament feared that the Scots might be tempted to back the Stuart pretender and plunge Britain into another damaging civil war.

Neither Scots nor English were especially keen on the Union, but it seemed the best way to preserve the Protestant regime in both countries. One side effect of the Union was that it pushed many disapproving Lowland Scots towards supporting their Jacobite Highland neighbours. A group of businessmen in Perth made their views clear in 1716:

> Before the Union we had no taxes but what were laid on by our own parliaments, and those very easy, and spent within our own country. Now we have not only the Cess or Land Tax, the Customs conform to the English book of Rates, near the triple of what we formerly paid ... But also the Malt-Tax, the Salt-Tax, the Leather-Tax, the Window-Tax, the Taxes upon candles, soap, starch ... and after all the Tax upon stamped paper and

parchments, by which alone vast sums of money are levied from the country.[4]

In 1715, the year after the death of Queen Anne, supporters of James Edward Stuart made their move. The standard of James VIII was raised by John Erskine, Earl of Mar, at Braemar in the heart of the Cairngorms. West Highlanders formed the majority of an army similar to that which followed Claverhouse in 1689, but Lowlanders angered by the Union also joined the cause. They clashed with a British government army led by the Duke of Argyll at the battle of Sheriffmuir, near Stirling.

Sergeant Donald Macleod was one of the redcoat Highlanders who fought with the Royal Scots at Sheriffmuir. His *Memoirs* mention a French officer fighting with the Jacobites who decided to take on his broadsword; within a few minutes, he had severed the Frenchman's head from his body. Seeing this, a Jacobite horseman sprang forward and with his longer cavalry blade managed to wound Macleod in the shoulder. In desperation, the redcoat Highlander thrust his sword into the horse's belly. 'The animal fell down,' recalls the *Memoirs*, 'and his rider was immediately hewn in pieces by the enraged Sergeant, who, in the act of stabbing the horse, had been cut in the head by the horseman's sabre, into the very brain. He bound his head fast with a handkerchief, otherwise, he says, he verily believes it would have fallen into pieces.'[5]

Sheriffmuir was a confused confrontation, and troops of both sides fled from the battlefield. The initial Jacobite Highland Charge created an impact which forced some redcoats to break, but this success was dissipated when the rebels followed them off the field. This left some resolute redcoats to stand their ground; they counter-attacked and forced the remaining Jacobites to withdraw.

The Stuart rebels had outnumbered the redcoats by two to one and their failure to win proved a decisive blow to their cause. By the time the 'Old Pretender', James Edward Stuart, landed at Peterhead, the campaign was already lost. Foreign support vanished and there was no heart left in the Highlanders to continue the struggle. At the same time, those Highland clans loyal to the government – Sutherlands, Frasers, Rosses, Munros and Forbeses – secured most of Scotland against insurrection. James Stuart was forced to flee back to France and the uprising of 1715 was over. Jacobite

Highlanders would have to wait thirty years before launching another full-scale rebellion.

*

Jacobite rebels were not the only problem faced by the British government in the Highlands. Banditry, cattle theft, protection rackets and blood feuds were rife. When Donald Macleod fled from his apprenticeship in Inverness, he was robbed by a highwayman who held a gun against the boy's head in return for a few coins. In many ways, the Highlands were like other remote mountain regions in Europe, such as the western half of Sicily, where clans were forced to police their own districts, protecting their people against rivals and outsiders.

Like the Mafia, the Highland clans developed tight, closed communities that depended on the favour of clan chiefs and the debts of service owed to them by people working on their land. A clan was only as secure as its toughest members and they enforced their rule by strong-arm methods. Violent acts of vengeance were essential for maintaining personal honour and reputation.

> If no immediate opportunity of obtaining complete satisfaction occurred, the hostile act was not forgotten, nor the resolution of avenging it abandoned. Every artifice by which cunning could compensate the want of strength was practised; alliances were courted, and favourable opportunities watched. Even an appearance of conciliation and friendship was assumed, to cover the darkest purposes of hatred … Revenge was accounted a duty, the destruction of a neighbour a meritorious exploit, and rapine an honourable occupation.[6]

In order to extend the rule of law over the Highlands, the government had raised Independent Companies as early as 1624. These were recruited from the Highlanders themselves to form armed bands that could intervene against outlaws, but they were notoriously corrupt, easily swayed by clan loyalties or the payment of bribes. They regularly defrauded the government by claiming expenses for more men on their payroll than were actually employed.

Having failed to play any useful part in halting the Jacobite rising in 1715, the Independent Companies were disbanded. The British government then introduced its Disarming Act, banning the carrying of weapons by Highlanders, but this was poorly enforced by redcoat soldiers who were isolated in garrisons and had little opportunity to penetrate clan communities.

The situation deteriorated until Simon Fraser, Lord Lovat, chief of the clan Fraser, put himself forward as a possible saviour. In 1715 Lovat had proved himself loyal to the British monarchy and nine years later he wrote a letter to King George I describing Highland lawlessness.

> One of the evils which furnish the most matter of complaint at present is the continual robberies and depredations in the Highlands, and the country adjacent. The great difficulty in this matter arises from the mountainous situation of those parts, the remoteness of towns ... the criminals cannot, by any methods now practised, be pursued, much less seized and brought to justice, being able to outrun those whom they cannot resist.[7]

Lovat insisted that the best measure against these outlaws had been the Independent Companies and that the Disarming Act had only made matters worse. It took weapons away from innocent Highlanders, so they could not protect themselves, but left them in the hands of bandits, many of whom had been heavily armed by the Jacobites. Lovat wanted to see the Independent Companies brought back and was happy to raise a unit of them for the king. His lengthy and detailed complaint struck a chord with the government in London, and later that year Major-General George Wade was sent to Scotland to check on the accuracy of Lovat's letter.

Wade was fifty-one years old and was leading a comfortable if unconventional life as MP for Bath. He never married but was a good father to his four children from various liaisons. A professional soldier and veteran of Marlborough's wars, Wade was also valued as an intelligence agent. He had uncovered two Jacobite conspiracies, one involving the sensational arrest of the Swedish ambassador in London. By the end of 1724, Wade had thoroughly investigated the threat posed by Highland renegades and sent his report to the king. He declared that the Highland clans most addicted to rapine and plunder were the Camerons to the west of Inverness, the Mackenzies in Ross-shire, the MacDonalds of Keppoch, and the MacGregors from the borders of Argyllshire.

> They go out in parties from ten to thirty men, traverse large tracks of mountains, till they arrive at the Low Lands, where they design to commit their depredations ... They drive the stolen cattle at night time ... and take the first occasion to sell them at the fairs or markets, that are annually held in many parts of the Country.[8]

Wade described the wide range of crimes committed by the Highland gangs, including a form of extortion, 'commonly called Black meal', which was levied by the Highland bandits on the Lowlanders bordering their territory. He agreed with Lovat that the Independent Companies had been an effective way of dealing with these outlaws, but suggested that their success had been marred by corruption and fraud.

Wade also noted the Highlanders' preferred method of fighting. 'When in sight of the enemy,' he wrote, 'they endeavour to possess themselves of the highest ground, believing they descend on them with a greater force; they generally give their fire at a distance, then lay down their arms on the ground, and make a vigorous attack with their broadswords; but if repulsed, seldom or never rally again.'[9]

King George was impressed by Wade's detailed report and on Christmas Eve 1724 promoted him to commander-in-chief of his forces in North Britain, as Scotland was then known. He was given a budget of £10,000 and with that was expected to start work on the construction of two new fortresses: one at Kilchuimen, that would become Fort Augustus, and one near Inverness, that would be Fort George. Most importantly, Wade was to improve the communication network between British garrisons and barracks in the Highlands. This included a Highland Galley, a small oar-powered vessel that would link forts along the shores of Loch Ness, but significantly, it also involved the improvement and construction of new roads throughout the Highlands.

The inaccessibility of their homeland had been the great natural defence for outlaw Highlanders. Now Wade was opening that

home up to his redcoats with modern roads spanning the moor
land. From 1725 to 1737 he oversaw the construction of 250 miles of
road and forty bridges. Captain Edmund Burt, a government engi-
neer sent to Scotland, wrote a detailed description of the boggy
landscape and the challenges it posed. He could not hide his pleasure when the terrain was finally conquered.

> The roads on these moors are now as smooth as Constitution
> Hill [in London], and I have galloped on some of them for miles
> together in great tranquillity; which was heightened by reflec-
> tion on my former fatigue, when, for a great part of the way, I
> had been obliged to quit my horse, it being too dangerous or
> impracticable to ride, and even hazardous to pass on foot.[10]

A new era was dawning and with it would come the end of the
Highland rebel.

Simon Fraser, Lord Lovat, had initiated this process in the hope
of gaining favour from King George, but as Wade compiled his
report he got some measure of the clan chief and did not find him
completely trustworthy. Lovat, Wade thought, was too involved
in Highland mafia politics. Nicknamed 'the Fox', he had a reputation for double-dealing. Although suspicious of the man, Wade
did approve his suggestion of reviving the Independent Companies, and six new militia units were raised from clans loyal to
the government.

Called Highland Watches, three units were recruited from the
Campbells, with one each from the Frasers, Grants and Munros.
Over several decades, the Presbyterian Campbells had used their
alliance with the government to strengthen their own hand in
their long-running war with the Catholic MacDonalds. This clan
rivalry had culminated in a bloody act of brutality in 1692 at
Glencoe, when troops commanded by a Campbell officer massacred thirty-eight Jacobite MacDonalds on government orders.
These ultra-loyal Highlanders were just the kind of paramilitary
policemen Wade could trust.

Despite his dubious past, Lord Lovat, chief of the Frasers, was
rewarded for his newly found support of the government by being
appointed captain of one of the new Independent Companies. His
police force, according to Wade's report of 1725, 'was posted to

guard all the passes in the mountains, from the Isle of Skye east-wards, as far as Inverness'. This took him deep into the territory of the Mackenzies and MacDonalds. It was just what Lovat wanted – a chance to raise troops to harass his clan rivals and impress the king, all funded by the British government. The five other com-panies were commanded by Sir Duncan Campbell of Lochnell, Colonel William Grant of Ballindalloch, John Campbell of Carrick, Colin Campbell of Skipness and George Munro of Culcairn.

The Highland Watches numbered around 500 troops each, and none of the soldiers was to be less than five feet six inches tall. Many of them were the sons of landed gentry and, unlike ordinary recruits, they were accompanied by their servants, who would carry their weapons for them while they rode. Although a red coat was listed as part of their parade uniform, it seems likely that in these first years they probably wore their own Highland clothes, ranging from elegant tartan jackets with gold lace embroidery, for the richer, more fashionably inclined members, to the traditional belted plaid. It was only later, from 1739, that a standard govern-ment tartan was worn, which may have derived from the Camp-bells' own pattern, and was a combination of blue, black and green threads. This dark pattern gave the companies the name they later became famous as – the Black Watch.[11] This was in contrast to the 'Red Soldiers' or *Seidaran Dearag*, the Gaelic name given to British redcoats.

*

The gentlemen members of the Highland Watches were balanced by more professional soldiers, including Sergeant Donald Macleod. Renowned as an excellent swordsman and recruiting sergeant in the British Army, he was garrisoned in Newcastle when he heard news that 'a certain number of independent companies were to be formed, under different commanders, for the purpose of prevent-ing robberies, enforcing the law, and keeping the peace of the country'.

Macleod was in his late thirties and looking for a more comfort-able life. His request to leave the army astonished his officers, who had thought that he might well join their ranks with a commission, but his mind was set. He paid fifteen guineas to release himself from the army and gave up his rank to enlist as a private in one of the new companies headed by Lord Lovat. He was soon raised to drill-sergeant and went on to spend twenty years in the Black Watch.

Macleod's duties were typical of those expected of the early Black Watch. From the start the regime was not all strictly above board and revealed a possibly too cosy relationship with many of the outlaws they were supposed to apprehend. James Roy Stewart was one of these gentleman cattle thieves, who haunted the countryside of Strathspey. Dubbed 'Red Roy', he had a reputation for conducting raids that drove away hundreds of cattle and horses, impoverishing the lives of the farmers he preyed upon. Part of his crime may well have been, like that of Mafia gangsters in Sicily, a kind of protection racket in which he would ransom the stolen livestock back to their owners.

Macleod was sent with thirty soldiers to arrest Red Roy at his home. The Independent Company men arrived early in the morning and caught the cattle thief in bed. Macleod left his comrades outside and entered the building by himself, armed with a sword, dirk and two loaded pistols. The thief's wife was greatly upset by his sudden appearance, and while Macleod tried to calm her, James Roy Stewart leapt out of bed in his clothes, grabbing his dagger and pistols. He tried to escape but Macleod blocked his way.

Knowing the building was probably surrounded by troops, the thief suddenly changed his attitude and tried to talk his way out of trouble. 'Very well,' he said to Macleod, 'but I hope you are not in a hurry; sit down, and let you and I talk together and take our breakfast.'

Macleod agreed and the two men shared a bottle of whisky, but the policeman had to bring the conversation back to why he was there. Red Roy tried to reason with him. 'Sergeant Macleod,' he begged, 'let me go for this time, and neither you nor the country will be troubled with me any more.'

'Jamie, I cannot let you go,' said Macleod, 'you have slashed many men, and stolen much horse and cattle. How many Straths are afraid of you? Jamie, you must go with me.'

Red Roy then offered Macleod a bribe of a hundred guineas to let him go. 'It was not for guineas that I came here this day,' said the proud Sergeant. 'Rather than be drawn off the duty of a soldier for a few guineas, I would go with you and steal cattle.'[12]

At this, Roy's wife threw herself on the floor and seized Macleod's knees, pleading with him to spare her husband for the sake of their four children. Never one to ignore the request of a woman, Macleod agreed to let Red Roy go on condition that he returned all his cattle to their rightful owners. The relieved thief insisted that Macleod take some money for his trouble, but all the Sergeant wanted was that he give breakfast to the thirty men waiting outside. A 'great part of the day was spent in conviviality', concluded Macleod's *Memoirs*, and the cattle were returned that evening.

This incident reveals how the Black Watch and the high-profile criminals they pursued regarded each other as equals. The task of arrest was more one of negotiation than heavy-handed punishment. Sadly, on many other occasions, the Watch was inclined to take the bribe and move on. Later, Red Roy bought his way out of trouble with another police officer, only to be betrayed by the same man, who pocketed the money and then ambushed him. This time there was no escape. Red Roy was taken to Perth and hanged. He made a full confession of his crimes on the scaffold and asked that his family be spared any punishment for his thievery.

*

In 1739, the approaching threat of conflict in Europe – the War of the Austrian Succession – put pressure on the British government to find more troops, and they looked to Scotland. Four more independent companies were raised and these were joined with the existing companies of the Black Watch to form a regiment of the line called the 43rd Regiment of Foot, the very first Highland regiment in the British Army. Highlanders had previously fought as redcoats for the English crown on many occasions, such as in the Royal Scots – Donald Macleod's old regiment – but the 43rd were the first regiment of Highlanders in the British Army to fight in their traditional tartan plaid with broadsword and dirk, in recognition of their particular fighting spirit and reputation. It was the beginning of the process by which Highlanders became a characteristic part of the British Army.

With the possibility of service abroad, Lord Lovat's loyalty was deemed suspect and he was removed from command of the Frasers.

He was furious and cursed the government, declaring that if an oriental Khan invaded the country, he would feel justified in joining him – words that would linger long in the memory of the government. Lieutenant-Colonel Sir Robert Munro of Foulis was considered a much safer pair of hands and became the regiment's new commander – the Presbyterian Munros having long proved their faith to the Protestant regime.

However, preparation for a foreign war was not exactly what many of the Highland gentlemen expected from their service with the Black Watch. It had been assumed that this was a cosy arrangement in which privileged Highlanders lived at home comfortably off government wages. They did not expect to face a high probability of death in the course of their work, but now their duty involved sailing abroad and serving in the front line of battle. On top of this, they were told to ditch their fashionable clothing and wear identical uniforms of scarlet jacket and dark belted plaid. For many, it was an order too far.

In 1743, the 43rd were instructed to march south for a review before King George II, but by the time they arrived the monarch had already sailed to Flanders to fight the French. Rumours of imminent embarkation stirred up concern among the ranks. Feeling betrayed and fearful of foreign service, over a hundred Highlanders deserted. The more professional soldiers among the 43rd were less appalled by the prospect. Sergeant Donald Macleod simply shrugged his shoulders and got on with it, but he was angered at what happened next to his comrades.

> The whole of the Guards, and all the troops stationed about London, were sent for to surround the Highlanders, quell what was now called a mutiny, and reduce them to obedience. The long swords of the horse-guards were opposed to the broadswords of the Highlanders in front, while one military corps after another was advancing on their flanks and rear.[13]

Macleod claimed that a portion of the Highlanders fought their way through the king's troops and made good their escape northwards. They got as far as Yorkshire, where a body of Horse Guards cornered them in a forest and forced them to surrender. Macleod's vivid recollection of the Black Watch mutiny is not supported by other versions, which state there was no confrontation with loyal troops, no bloodshed, and the deserters simply gathered one night on a common near Highgate before beginning their march north.

Nonetheless, punishment was swift. The Highland deserters were quickly court-martialled with many being transported to certain death in the disease-ridden West Indies. Three ringleaders were shot. Macleod was unhappy with this ill treatment of his comrades but he bottled his fury and joined the rest of the soldiers dispatched to Flanders. There, they would face their first test in battle. For their baptism of fire, the Black Watch would be up against the most powerful army in Europe – that of Louis XV of France – and the redcoat Highlanders had everything to prove.

Chapter 3
Loyal and Rebellious

Lieutenant-Colonel Sir Robert Munro of Foulis was enormously fat and when he inspected a military trench he sometimes had to be pulled out by his men, hauling and heaving on his arms and legs. Years of good living as an MP for the county of Ross had piled on the weight, but he knew his Highlanders well and he liked to lead from the front. He was not wanting in courage and, as a result, his soldiers were happy to follow him anywhere. He was chief of the clan Munro and the original commander of the 43rd Regiment of Foot – the Black Watch – the first Highland regiment in the British Army.

Munro presented two Black Watch soldiers, Gregor MacGregor and John Campbell of Duneaves, to King George II in London. The monarch had never seen a Highlander and was keen to view these exotic additions to his military forces. The Highlanders wore their belted plaids and exercised with broadswords and Lochaber axes before the king, the Duke of Cumberland, General George Wade and a number of senior officers in a gallery at St James's Palace. They were very impressed by the vigorous display of traditional weaponry and the king gave each of the Highlanders a gratuity of a guinea. Both considered themselves gentlemen and were insulted by the royal tip. As they left, they gave the coins to the porter at the gate of the palace.

Since then, others had taken over command of the Black Watch, with Lord John Murray, son of the Duke of Atholl, becoming its colonel in April 1745. A month later, the Highlanders were advancing into action against the French in Flanders and Munro, now sixty-one, was reappointed their battlefield commander. It was an excellent choice, for what happened next would set the Highlanders on the road to fame.

The Duke of Cumberland was the son of King George II and at twenty-four years old a very young commander-in-chief of the allied army in Flanders – a coalition of British, Hanoverian German and Dutch troops. Among them were the 43rd Highlanders who had already impressed their curious continental hosts with their courtesy and good behaviour. On 10 May 1745 they were set for some hard fighting. Their French opponents were led by Marshal Maurice de Saxe who had laid siege to Tournai. As in later centuries, the freedom of Flemish towns was of prime strategic and economic concern to the British.

The two armies met at Fontenoy. The French were dug in behind a line of trenches and redoubts. Saxe was so ill that he had to be carried to the battlefield on a stretcher but he refused to give up command to anyone, especially King Louis XV who accompanied the army. It was not unusual at this time for monarchs to appear in combat; just two years before, King George II had led his soldiers into battle at Dettingen.

Cumberland decided to take on the French defensive line and smash his way through it. Three lines of redcoats, some 15,000 men, advanced. Just before they came to blows, Cumberland halted his men to ensure their ranks were precisely in order. Famously, Lieutenant-Colonel Lord Charles Hay stepped forward in front of his Grenadier Guards and pulled out a flask. The enemy paused as Hay raised his flask in a toast. He led his troops in three hearty cheers and then bolted back to his ranks. As the surprised French returned the salute, the redcoats unleashed an almighty volley of musket fire.

The shattered French fell back as the British and Hanoverian troops surged forward. It looked as though victory was theirs. At least two eyewitnesses claimed that the Highlanders were part of this initial assault.

> The Highland Regiment of Foot and some light armed Corps which formed the Forlorn of the Allied Army, began the attack between six and seven with great bravery, but were most of

them cut off by the prodigious fire of the batteries, as well by the close and vigorous fire from their small arms.[1]

The Forlorn [Hope] was usually a group of soldiers flung into battle at the beginning to test the resolve of the enemy. This view of the battle was matched by a private letter from an anonymous officer in the allied army.

> About seven the Horse coming up we began to charge, the Battalions of Guards and the Highlanders beginning the engagement on the right wing, which they did with so much bravery, that they forced the enemy from their first entrenchment which they had flung up only knee deep, and drove them to another, which they had flung up as high as their noses. Here we suffered greatly ...[2]

As his troops fled past him, Louis XV was advised to remove himself too, but he refused. Saxe got off his sickbed and mounted a horse to rally his soldiers. They re-formed a line and well-timed volleys halted the allied advance. Crucial to this French counter-attack was the Irish Brigade, made up of Irish and Scottish Jacobites, fervent supporters of the exiled Stuart king. The recently raised Royal Ecossais, a 500-strong group of Jacobite Scots commanded by Lord John Drummond, may well have been among their number. The stubborn ferocity of the Irish Brigade saved the French from defeat and persuaded Cumberland to command an orderly withdrawal.

With Jacobite Irish and Scots running across the battlefield towards them, Cumberland ordered Sir Robert Munro's Highlanders to cover the retreat. Munro had petitioned his commander to allow his troops to fight in their traditional style and this included, sensibly, ducking out the way of enemy musketry. Given permission, Sir Robert ordered the whole regiment to drop to the ground on receiving French fire. The only problem was that when Munro told his men to lie down, he was too fat to join them. So he stood alone with the Union colours fluttering behind him – striking an unintentionally heroic pose as he faced the whole of a French volley by himself. 'His preservation that day was the surprise and astonishment,' wrote a contemporary biographer, 'not only of the whole army, but of all that heard the particulars of the action.'[3]

Inspired by their fearless leader, the Highlanders sprang back to their feet, unsheathed their broadswords and fought tenaciously, driving the French back through their own lines. It was during this bitter close-quarter fighting that Sergeant James Campbell achieved fame by killing nine Frenchmen with his sword. A cannon ball severed his left arm just as he was about to finish off a tenth. Elsewhere, Munro ordered a Highland chaplain to move back to the rear or face losing his commission. Brandishing his broadsword, the chaplain bellowed 'Damn my commission!' and threw himself at the enemy.

Expert swordsman Sergeant Donald Macleod was in the ranks of the Black Watch and gave a good account of himself. His adversaries included Jacobites of the Irish Brigade.

> Serjeant Macleod, with his own hand, killed a French Colonel, of the name Montard; and, in the midst of dangers and death, very deliberately served himself heir to 175 ducats which he had in his pockets, and his gold watch. He had not well gone through this ceremony, when he was attacked by Captain James Ramievie, from Kilkenny, an officer in the French service, whom he killed after an obstinate and skilful contest.[4]

Macleod was then set upon by several French soldiers who might well have cut him to pieces had not a fellow Scot intervened. A Cameron clansman, he was one of the Scots in the Irish Brigade. He helped Macleod fight off the French. Although a Jacobite and serving Louis XV, the Cameron could not bear to see a Scot slaughtered by the French. It was a moment when shared Highland blood proved more important than politics or religion. It also reflected the fluid nature of loyalties in this war, with several Highlanders from the 43rd having earlier deserted to the Irish Brigade, but others, as on this occasion, refusing to see a fellow Highlander killed by foreigners.

The ferocity of the Black Watch at Fontenoy was enough to help stop the British retreat turn into a rout. It was a victory for the French but a narrow one, since both sides had lost heavily. Despite the defeat, Cumberland was impressed by the 43rd Highlanders and asked them to let him grant them a favour. The Highlanders requested only that the Duke release one of their men who had been court-martialled for allowing a prisoner to escape. Cumberland happily gave them their wish and made a mental note of their relentless aggression. It would come in useful later when he led an army into Scotland.

The Highlanders were celebrated far and wide for their perform-ance at Fontenoy. A French report of the battle praised them for the moment 'when the Highland furies rushed in upon us with more violence than ever did a sea driven by a tempest'. Colonel David Stewart in his 1822 history of the Highland regiments cites this as their first real battle honour. Sir Robert Munro was rewarded for his leadership in the battle by being made colonel of the 37th Regi-ment of Foot. Laurence Macpherson, a chaplain in the 43rd High-landers, was moved to write *A New Form of Prayer as used (since the battle of Fontenoy) by the British Troops in the Allied Army of Flanders*. His fellow Protestant officers were so impressed by its sentiments they urged him to have it published. In it, Macpherson expressed thanks to God for a new pride in Britishness. He defined what it meant to him and his redcoats – those values to be defended by both Scots and English:

> The Britons were ever thy favourite People! Thou hast distin-guished them above all the Nations of Europe: They were renowned for their bravery, their courage, their magnanimity, and generos-ity; their ardent zeal for liberty and freedom, their eager thirst after military glory, (when only honour and justice drew them into the field) and their constant success in the day of battle; their kings were heroes, their ministers were patriots, and their parliaments uninfluenced by anything but the interest and glory of the people, whose laws and liberties were committed to their charge.[5]

Macpherson may well have been the chaplain who refused to with-draw to the rear of his unit, preferring to take up a broadsword and charge the enemy, but his pride in military success was matched by his quieter appreciation of parliament and its rule in favour of the people. The final paragraph of his prayer was dedicated to the Highland regiment: 'May the courage and intrepidity of the brave Highlanders be a continual terror to the enemy, and a distinguished example to their fellow soldiers ... Amen.'

*

Just three months after Fontenoy, Bonnie Prince Charlie – the Young Pretender – landed in Scotland and raised a Highland army to put a Stuart king back on the English throne. This campaign was part of the wider war in Europe between Catholic France and Protestant Britain. At Fontenoy, Hanoverians and Jacobites had fought ferociously. This dynastic clash simply continued on to Scottish soil with many of the same soldiers and personalities involved. The Duke of Cumberland brought his troops back from Flanders to fight in Scotland. It also helps to explain how what seems in retrospect a relatively minor threat to the British nation was seen at the time as part of a greater European menace, which deserved a strong and ruthless response.

To head the British Army against the Jacobite rebellion of 1745, King George II turned to that old trooper Field Marshal George Wade, whose campaign of road building had proved so effective in opening up the Highlands to government control. But Wade was seventy-two years old, had proved inadequate in Flanders and had resigned his command. King George put him back in charge of soldiers rapidly brought back from Flanders to confront the Young Pretender, but Wade was outmanoeuvred by the Jacobite Army – ironically – making swift use of his military roads.

In the meantime, the Duke of Cumberland had his hands full with a confident Marshal Saxe and his French Army, who followed up their victory at Fontenoy by methodically capturing major towns in Flanders. By September the French had captured ports on the Flemish coast and were planning an assault on the Netherlands. In that same month, more bad news came from Scotland. Bonnie Prince Charlie had occupied Edinburgh and was rapidly descending on Sir John Cope's outnumbered British force at Prestonpans.

It was Killiecrankie all over again. An early-morning autumn mist screened the Jacobite advance, but barking dogs alerted the British who formed into lines. The rebels had seized an upland position, perfect for delivering a Highland Charge downhill, but then discovered at the last moment that they would be running into bogland. They manoeuvred round it, and the redcoats had the disconcerting experience of hearing the Highlanders rustling through newly harvested corn, their voices carrying spookily across the misty fields.

As the sun rose, both sides began to catch sight of each other. The redcoats were terrified by the vision of sword- and axe-wielding Jacobite Highlanders coming at them. The last-minute move of the Highlanders meant they avoided a direct attack on the lines of redcoats in the centre. Instead, they appeared before the weaker flanks, which collapsed almost immediately. As a result, they were spared volleys of musket fire, which allowed many more Jacobite officers to survive; they could thus rally Highlanders who might otherwise have chased the fleeing redcoats off the field.

The rebels turned on the remaining redcoats and butchered the panicking troops; no mercy was shown by the Highlanders, who happily cut down the defeated enemy. It was the blood-curdling savagery of Prestonpans that encouraged the equal ferocity of redcoats in later battles. As at Killiecrankie, the majority of the redcoats were newly recruited from Lowland Scots who knew only too well the reputation of the Highlanders. This sense of fear had yet again done its job and won the battle before substantial contact was made.

Jacobite victory at Prestonpans encouraged many more Highlanders wavering in their support to join the march southwards. Not least of these was that old fox Simon Fraser, Lord Lovat. On 11 October 1745 he wrote a letter to another influential Highland figure, Duncan Forbes, Lord President of the Court of Session in Scotland. He explained the reality of the situation he was caught in:

I had a vast deal of trouble in keeping my men from rising at the beginning of this affair; but now the contagion is so universal, by the late success of the Highlanders, that they laugh at any man that would dissuade them from going; so that I really know not how to behave. I wish I had been in any part out of Britain these twelve months past, both for my health and other considerations.[6]

A few days later, he elaborated on the support swinging the way of the Young Pretender. 'It is certain, that almost all the Highlanders in Scotland love the Pretender,' he insisted, 'more than they do the interest of the present government; and if he be assisted by the English friends of the Pretender, & by a foreign force, he believes he will succeed with his enterprise.'[7]

The implication was clear. The Highlanders loved a winner and you would have to be a fool not to join in. Lovat thought he was being clever by covering himself with these letters of doubt written to the top lawyer in Scotland, so that if the campaign turned against the Jacobites he could use them as evidence of his reluctance to get involved. He protested that his son was raising soldiers for Bonnie Prince Charlie against his will. In reality, he was encouraging the young man.

Duncan Forbes was not fooled by the old fox and wrote back to him from Inverness on 28 October 1745:

> I can no longer remain a spectator of your Lordship's conduct and see the double game you have played for some time past … Your Lordship's actions now discover evidently your inclinations and leave us no further in the dark about what side you are to choose in the present unhappy insurrection: you have now so far pulled off the mask, that we can see the mark you aim at though on former occasion you have had the skill and address to disguise your intentions in matters of far less importance.[8]

Forbes went on to berate him for betraying a benign government that had entrusted him with the command of one of the Independent Companies: 'So that both Duty and Gratitude ought to have influenced your Lordship's conduct, at this critical juncture …' With this letter published widely in London, Lovat and his family faced severe punishment if he was caught – but for a few months, it looked as though he had chosen the right side.

The question of how far to trust loyalist Highlanders was exemplified by the Black Watch. Heroes of Fontenoy, their mutiny a few years earlier was not far from the minds of British commanders and this overrode their performance against Jacobites on the Continent. The sense of community shared by Sergeant Macleod and the Jacobite who saved him at Fontenoy suggests that the generals may well have been right not to take a chance. When the Black Watch returned to Britain, they were kept south of the border, eventually ending up in Ireland. Only one company of Black Watch would be at Culloden but that distinguished itself as part of a loyal Highlander attack on the right flank of the rebel army.

Prestonpans unleashed a flood of new recruits for Bonnie Prince Charlie. These included a great number of Lowlanders who now thought it wise to fight alongside the rebel Highlanders rather than against them. Interestingly, the Lowlanders were instructed to wear Highland clothing and use Highland weapons in order to make the most of the northerners' terrifying reputation. Their mere appearance was a battle-winning weapon as far as Bonnie Prince Charlie was concerned.

With an army almost doubled in size, the Jacobites felt confident enough to cross the border and invade England. They advanced as far south as Derby in the hope of encouraging a French invasion and stirring up English Jacobite rebellion. Neither of these happened. Faced with launching an assault on London with inadequate forces and supplies, Bonnie Prince Charlie had to accept there was no place to go but back to Scotland.

Scottish Jacobites consolidated their grip on their own country by besieging the strategically important city of Stirling. On 17 January 1746 a British Army was advancing towards them and the Jacobites decided to confront them at Falkirk Moor in the midst of a storm. Both sides raced to get the advantage by taking the higher ground. The redcoats won and their commander, Lieutenant-General Henry Hawley, unleashed his cavalry on the Highlanders, knowing from past experience that they were ill-equipped to deal with them. But by now the Jacobite Highlanders had armed themselves with many more muskets than was usual and as the British dragoons came close they fired a volley that thinned the cavalry's ranks. The Highlanders then took on the horsemen in brutal hand-to-hand combat, stabbing at the bellies of the animals to bring them down.

Having dispatched the threat of cavalry, the Highlanders charged the redcoats, with the storm of wind and rain behind them beating into the faces of the British. Many redcoats lost their nerve and fled, but two regiments held their ground. Their disciplined fire shook the Highlanders and it was now their turn to fall back.

Sir Robert Munro, hero of Fontenoy and much beloved by the Black Watch, was at Falkirk in command of the 37th Regiment of Foot. He was accompanied by his brother. The 37th were one of the redcoat units to panic in the face of the Highlanders, leaving their officers to face the rebel warriors alone. Munro's son, Sir Harry, heard from the survivors of the battle what happened to his sixty-two-year-old father.

> My father, after being deserted, was attacked by six of Lochiel's regiment, and for some time defended himself with his half pike. Two of the six, I am informed, he killed, a seventh coming up fired a pistol into my father's groin, upon which, falling, the Highlander with his sword gave him two strokes in the face, one over the eyes and another on the mouth, which instantly ended a brave man.[9]

On hearing of the lonely death of their chief, a Munro clansman cursed the soldiers who had abandoned him and declared it would never have happened 'had his own folk been there'. His son raised an elaborate sarcophagus for him and part of the inscription bore the proud boast, 'He commanded the Highland Regiment which will be remembered as long as the battle of Fontenoy.'

*

The British licked their wounds after Falkirk and Field Marshal Wade was retired from commanding forces in Scotland. He was old and ill and had not performed well. Two years later, he would die in Bath at the age of seventy-five, and in his will he paid for an elaborate monument to be built in Westminster Abbey. The most striking memorial to him was a verse in *God Save the King*, composed by Thomas Arne and first sung in 1745. The triumphal lines were later removed when it became the British national anthem.

> Lord, grant that Marshal Wade,
> May by thy mighty aid,
> Victory bring.
> May he sedition hush and like a torrent rush,
> Rebellious Scots to crush,
> God save the King.

The Duke of Cumberland took over command and brought with him battle-hardened troops from the Continent. Many Highlanders knew this did not bode well and they were reluctant to face this strengthened army. Poor weather forced the redcoats into winter quarters at Aberdeen, but they used the time to practise their skills with the bayonet – the weapon that would challenge the supremacy of the broadsword.

In April 1746 the weather was still poor but good enough for the Duke of Cumberland to emerge from his winter camp and advance rapidly on the Highland rebels based around Inverness. Bonnie Prince Charlie's army was scattered throughout the Highlands and could not concentrate fast enough to deal with the threat.

Failing to surprise the redcoats during the night, the Young Pretender led his outnumbered and exhausted men on to a rain-lashed battlefield at Culloden on 16 April. His defeat that day brought a decisive end to the Jacobite cause and allowed the British to thoroughly crush the rebellious Highland clans. From warrior to chieftain, very few rebels escaped. Lord Lovat hoped his letter writing might save him and he was not too proud to address a begging note to the Duke of Cumberland at Fort William. 'If I have the honour to kiss your Royal Highness's Hand,' he pleaded, 'I would easily demonstrate to you, that I can do more service to the King and government than destroying a hundred such old men like me, passed 70 (without the least use of my hands, legs or knees) …'[10]

It was not enough. The next month, the old man was taken to Stirling under armed guard and by August was sitting in prison in the Tower of London, where he confessed, 'What a turbulent life has mine been.' After a five-day trial, on 9 April 1747, he was executed by having his head cut off with a sword – a privilege reserved for peers.

Lord Lovat's eldest son, also called Simon Fraser and nineteen years old in 1745, was studying law at St Andrews University. When his father finally chose to support the Jacobites, he was dispatched to raise a unit of Frasers to join Bonnie Prince Charlie in January 1746. He fought in the front line at the battle of Falkirk and would have been at Culloden, but for his lateness in bringing recruits to the battlefield. Fortunately, this allowed him to turn round and surrender to the British at Inverness.

Young Fraser was imprisoned for ten months in Edinburgh Castle but survived the investigation and execution of his father, eventually being granted a pardon in 1750. Two years later, he was practising as an advocate and had even managed to shake off the

Machiavellian reputation of his father. In 1757 he was commissioned as a Lieutenant-Colonel in the British Army. With that rank came the responsibility of raising a new Highland regiment. Within a few weeks he had recruited 800 men, many of them veterans or relations of veterans of the Jacobite rebellion. Captain Simon Fraser of Inverallochy was one of the officers and he was the brother of the man who commanded the rebel Frasers at Culloden. Colonel Fraser's unit was numbered the 78th Regiment of Foot.

Following the violent suppression of Jacobites in Scotland after Culloden, the only military route out of the Highlands for many young men was to take service with the British Army. New companies of the Black Watch were deployed to ravage the lands of rebel Highlanders and burn their houses. It was a dirty business but it helped extinguish the flame of Jacobitism once and for all. The 43rd Regiment of Highlanders remained based in Ireland with occasional expeditions to fight the French. In 1748, they were renumbered as the 42nd Regiment. In the same year, Loudoun's Highlanders – the 64th – were disbanded.

Perversely, with the threat of Jacobite invasion safely past, the lost cause of Bonnie Prince Charlie suddenly became fashionable in southern England. Visiting the resort town of Bath in the spring of 1748, a Scottish tourist was shocked to see public displays of support for the Jacobites. He wrote to his friend in Leith telling him all about it:

> I believe I forgot to tell you that the gay world at Bath and other parts of southern England seem very fond of white rosed buttons, plaid or tartan. Some of the very horses furniture is so [decorated] ...

At the Theatre Royal in Bath, he attended a musical play in which '20 lads and lasses dress'd after the Highland fashion' danced before scenery representing the mountains of Scotland. They sang songs dedicated to the Stuarts and Bonnie Prince Charlie to the accompaniment of bagpipes. 'In short it is so ravishing seemingly to the whole audience' reported the surprised visitor, 'that the people express their joy and clap their hands in a most extraordinary manner indeed.'[11]

There was a darker history to this entertainment. Jacobite sympathies had been strong in Bath in 1715 and this was why General

George Wade was originally sent to the city to guard against it with his militia. But by the late 1740s sedition had been replaced by an anti-establishment Highland fashion.

*

If Fontenoy had opened the eyes of the British Army to the tremendous fighting abilities of the Highlanders, then the '45 had clouded this view. It would take another major confrontation with the French to change their perception yet again – and this time the fighting would take place far away from Scotland.

In 1756, the Seven Years War began – a European conflict, with France, Russia and Austria lining up against Prussia. But as Britain took the side of Prussia it spread globally, with the British and French battling to expand their colonial empires. In North America, fighting had already been going on since 1754 and this part of the conflict became known as the French and Indian War. It centred on the British blocking French expansion southwards from their possessions in Canada and then developed into a struggle for the control of French Canada itself.

As the fighting in America became part of the Seven Years War, the British government grew hungry for more and more troops to protect its interests around the world, and a pacified Scotland proved a good recruiting ground. In addition to the 42nd Highlanders, two more Highland regiments were raised in 1757, numbered the 77th and 78th Highlanders. The 78th was Simon Fraser's, while the 77th was raised by a Lowlander from Ayrshire, Major Archibald Montgomerie. He recruited clansmen from all across the Highlands, including the traditionally rebellious western Highlands and islands. Within just a few months, the 42nd, 77th and 78th Highlanders took ship across the Atlantic to the New World, disembarking at Halifax in Nova Scotia in June 1757.

It was the adventure of a lifetime for all the soldiers involved. For some, it would mean an early death and for some of those it would be a painful and lingering end at the hands of an equally ferocious warrior race – the American Indians.

Chapter 4
American Adventures

At the age of just thirty-two, Brigadier-General James Wolfe had already demonstrated his great talent as a military commander fighting the French in North America. In September 1759 he was leading a British force towards French-held Quebec in the hope of delivering a knockout blow. In his army was a Highland regiment – the 78th. Wolfe knew well their way of combat; as a nineteen-year-old captain, he had faced charging clansmen at Culloden, but the bayonets of his redcoats had proved more deadly than the broadswords of the rebels. His Highlanders were now armed with both bayonets and broadswords.

In America, Wolfe faced new challenges. As his army marched through dense forest, he recorded his experience of the tough terrain:

> The obstacles we have met with in the operations of the campaign are much greater than we had reason to expect or could foresee. Not so much from the number of enemy (tho' superior to us) as from the natural strength of the country, which the Marquis de Montcalm seems wisely to depend on. [1]

The French commander could also call upon 'several Nations of Savages', which waited to pounce on the advancing redcoats. These Native Americans were superb irregular fighters, especially skilled at ambush. 'The French did not attempt to interrupt our march,' reported Wolfe, 'some of their Savages came down to murder such wounded as could not be brought off, and to scalp the Dead, as their Custom is.'

Several Highlanders in America had already experienced this brutality at first hand. Allan Macpherson was a soldier in the 77th Highland Regiment when he was captured, along with several of his comrades, in an ambush. He was then forced to watch while his fellow Highlanders were slowly tortured to death by the Indians. Macpherson decided he could not face such a drawn-out fate and beckoned to one of the tribesmen. He explained that he could give them the secrets of a miraculous medicine that would toughen the skin of anyone covered with it, so it could stand up to the strongest blows of a tomahawk.

The tribesmen were intrigued and allowed Macpherson to go into the woods, under guard, to gather the plants he needed to make the ointment. He had the herbs boiled up in a pot and then smeared the medicine over his own neck. To test its effectiveness, he lay down with his neck on a log and told one of the Indians to raise his axe and demonstrate the power of the medicine. The Indian obliged and brought down his blade with a tremendous blow, severing Macpherson's head with one sickening thump. The tribesmen were stunned. The Highlander had cleverly avoided being tortured to death. Such was their admiration for this ruse, that the tribesmen spared their remaining prisoners any cruelties.[2]

*

In the early hours of 13 September 1759, Wolfe and his British Army closed in on their target – the city of Quebec, capital of French Canada. In the rain, they arrived by river and landed on a beach at the foot of a short slope at Anse au Foulon, about a mile and a half from the city. Through the darkness, French Canadian militia spotted the activity, but Captain Donald MacDonald of the 78th Highlanders boldly stepped forward. He spoke to the Canadian sentries in French and managed to convince them that he was a French officer bringing reinforcements. He told the sentry to remove all his men from the top of the slope and, if the British came, he promised he would 'take care to give a good account of the B-Anglois [sic], if they should persist'.[3]

The thirty-five-year-old MacDonald had learned French while

serving as a lieutenant in the *Royal Ecossais*, a regiment of Scots in the service of the French king. Like Wolfe, he had been at the battle of Culloden, but on the other side. The *Royal Ecossais* were part of the French task force sent to support the Jacobite rebellion of Bonnie Prince Charlie. Now, he was helping the British against the French. He was reputedly a tough officer and was nicknamed Donald Goran – 'Donald the Sinister'. His bluff gave the British just enough time to scramble ashore.

Much has been made of the ascent of the slope above the beach. It has been portrayed as a precipitous cliff calling for mountaineering skills from the redcoats. In fact, it is a steep but short slope with slippery shale under foot but plenty of roots and tree trunks to grab on to. Not easy for soldiers in the dark carrying weapons, with rain running down their faces, but little more than a rigorous ten-minute climb.[4]

Once up the escarpment, British light infantry fanned out across the Plains of Abraham in front of the city of Quebec. The ground was used mainly for grazing but there were patches of crops and lots of brushwood to hide in. The Marquis de Montcalm, the French commander at Quebec, was confident that just a hundred troops posted along this ridge above the river and in the scrubland could delay any British advance and give him time to assemble his men. But in the dim light of dawn, British light infantry went to work and captured or silenced most of the French guards.

By 6.00 a.m., Wolfe had assembled his troops on the Plains of Abraham with Quebec just a mile away. Montcalm was panicked by the sudden appearance of the British outside the town – his guards had failed him – but he had beaten the redcoats the year before at the battle of Ticonderoga and was confident that he could repeat the experience. To buy time to organize his regular forces, he sent out his own light infantry to harass the British with skirmishing fire. These soldiers were mainly local Canadians and Indians who knew the territory and chose their hiding places well.

Malcolm Fraser was a twenty-six-year-old lieutenant in the 78th Highlanders and as he assembled in the gloomy dawn with his comrades, it was the pot shots of the Indians and Canadians that bothered them most:

We had several skirmishes with the Canadians and the Savages, till about ten o'clock, when the army was formed in line of battle, having the great river, St Lawrence on the right ... Their advanced parties continued to annoy us and wounded a great many men.[5]

The fire of the French skirmishers proved so damaging at one point that Wolfe had to tell his soldiers to lie down to avoid the bullets. He could not take the same advice and had to expose himself to this deadly sniping throughout the morning in order to walk around the battlefield, inspecting his position and giving orders. The largest British unit on the battlefield was the 78th Highlanders with over 500 men;[6] they stood to the left centre of the main battleline.

Many English officers wondered at the loyalty of this Scottish unit as it was generally regarded as a 'turned' Jacobite regiment. Raised by Simon Fraser, son of the executed Lord Lovat, many of the troops recruited to the 78th were also descended from or related to former rebel soldiers, while several of its senior officers were Fraser clansmen once sympathetic to the Jacobite cause. Only John Campbell of Ballimore was notable among the officers of the 78th for being the son of a Hanoverian loyalist. His father had been killed while serving in one of the Scots units that fought for King George at Culloden.

The shadow of Culloden hung over Quebec, but it may also have been a positive influence. Many of the former rebels in the 78th Highlanders were said to hold Wolfe in high affection because of his restraint after Culloden when the young captain was, reputedly, asked to execute a Jacobite leader. He refused the Duke of Cumberland's direct command and a private soldier stepped forward to shoot the rebel. The dead man was Charles Fraser, older brother of Simon Fraser of Inverallochy of the 78th. If this were true, then Wolfe's clemency would no doubt have impressed Captain Simon Fraser and his fellow officers and explained their willingness to serve him so well at Quebec.[7]

By 10.00 a.m., both armies were assembled on the Plains of Abraham, the French lined up with their backs against the city of Quebec. Montcalm had managed to put 2,000 French soldiers into his main battleline, in addition to the 1,500 Canadians and Indians already sniping from the undergrowth. Wolfe had little more than 1,700 troops to call on and only two cannon to support them. But the French were not well served with artillery either, and this would be a combat settled by foot soldiers. Lieutenant Malcolm Fraser of the 78th Highlanders recalled the advance into battle:

> The Army was ordered to march on slowly in line of battle, and halt several times, till about half an hour after ten, when the French began to appear in great numbers on the rising ground between us and the Town, and having advanced several parties to skirmish with us; we did the like. They then got two Iron field pieces to play against our line ...[8]

The Highlanders and the rest of the advancing British regiments continued to suffer from the fire of the Canadians and Indians – bullets buzzing among their ranks and felling many redcoats.

Captain John Knox, standing in the centre of the British line, also wrote an account of the combat. He described how the French came on briskly in three columns with loud shouts. They were led personally by Montcalm, who bravely advanced at their head waving his sword in the air, until they were 130 yards from the redcoats. They then tried to form into a line to bring the highest number of muskets to bear on the British, but in doing this they fell into some confusion, partly thanks to well-aimed shots from a British cannon. The distance of 130 yards was a long one for effective musketry and when the French fired their guns, the resulting volleys did little damage to the lines of redcoats. Observing the discipline expected of them by Wolfe, the British did not return fire.

The French reloaded and advanced rapidly to within forty yards. They had entered the maximum killing zone and wanted to get their muskets off one more time before the British. But, according to the Highlander Fraser, braced beside his kilt-wearing comrades, this volley 'did little execution'. Many of them must have fired high, being nervous and not having the eye for a target that the more patient Canadians and Indians had as experienced hunters.

Having withstood this assault, it was the turn of the British to respond. Fraser and his Highlanders and all the rest of the redcoats levelled their muskets and let rip with one great volley. That morning, Wolfe had ordered them to load their weapons with two balls rather than one, so their fire would have more impact at a short range. '[It was] as remarkable a close and heavy discharge as ever I saw performed at a private field of exercise ...' said Knox, 'well might the French officers say that they never opposed such a shock as they received from the centre of our line …'[9]

Montcalm and two of his brigadiers went down immediately before the storm of fire. Within minutes, with so many comrades slumped and moaning around them, the French formations crumbled. One great volley had broken the French lines, and their courage deserted them. It was the turning point of the battle but the fighting was far from over.

That this one shattering blast of musket fire had won the battle was taken up by Sir John Fortescue in his grand history of the British Army. He called it the 'most perfect volley ever fired on battlefield'.[10] Since then, conventional histories of Quebec have tended to follow the same line, crediting victory to a perfect display of English-trained musketry. 'Quebec was therefore to be that rare thing in the gunpowder age, a firefight pure and simple between two lines of opposed infantry …' wrote military historian Sir John Keegan. 'At one moment the French line engaged the British in equal combat; at the next it was flying to the rear as a broken force.'[11]

Lieutenant Malcolm Fraser of the 78th Highlanders saw it differently. There was not one great volley.

> We returned it and continued firing very hot for about six, or (as some say) eight minutes, when the firing slackening, and the smoke of the powder vanishing, we observed the main body of the enemy retreating in great confusion towards the town, and the rest towards the river St Charles.
>
> Our regiment were then ordered by Brigadier-General Murray to draw their swords and pursue them; which I dare say increased their panic but saved many of their lives, whereas if the artillery had been allowed to play, and the army advanced regularly there would have been many more of the enemy killed and wounded …[12]

Tragically, at this moment of his greatest victory, Wolfe was mortally wounded. One of the Canadian or Indian snipers who had bothered the British all morning finally struck down their commander as he observed the action from the right flank. Effective command of the British Army was taken over by Brigadier-General James Murray, a thirty-eight-year-old Scot.

With the French falling back before him, Murray led the charge at the head of over 500 screaming, broadsword-waving High-landers. They hurtled across the scrubland towards the broken French formations. It was a Highland Charge, the sight of which was enough to unnerve any remaining French soldiers. Fraser claimed that it saved many lives. While English musketry had halted the French columns, it was the charge of the 78th High-landers that ended any further thought of resistance.

Fraser and his Highlanders pursued the French as far as the gates of Quebec. They were then ordered to stop and form up on the ground previously held by the enemy. The rest of the British Army caught up with them, but it was at the head of the 78th Highlanders that General Murray placed himself as they marched off, in recog-nition of their special contribution to the battle. The combat was not over and more Highlanders lost their lives in the fight with the enemy skirmishers who remained in the scrubland around the city than during the actual battle. Among the casualties was Captain Simon Fraser of Inverallochy.

Despite the British victory, the struggle for Quebec continued. French forces remained in the region throughout the following bitter winter and besieged General Murray and his garrison, includ-ing the 78th Highlanders, in Quebec in the spring. Murray aggres-sively marched his troops out into the melting snow and attacked the larger French force. It looked as though his Highlanders might repeat their earlier success but the French counter-attacked, and Culloden veteran Captain Donald MacDonald of the 78th was among 300 redcoats killed. Murray quickly withdrew into Quebec and resolved to stick it out. It was now a race between French and British ships to see who would be the first to break through the ice to bring reinforcements and supplies. Three British warships got through first and the French had no choice but to withdraw from their Canadian realm.

Lieutenant Malcolm Fraser, who had played his own small part in the British triumph at Quebec, fully recognized the significance of the battle:

> Thus ended the battle of Quebec ... which has made the king of Great Britain master of the capital of Canada, and it is hoped ere long will be the means of subjecting the whole country to

the British Dominion; and if so, this has been a greater acquisition to the British Empire than all that England had acquired by Conquest since it was a nation ...[13]

The importance of this victory was even greater than Fraser appreciated, because by removing French imperial presence from North America the British had ensured that, despite their American colonies becoming independent just a few decades later, the entire continent remained part of the Anglo-Saxon world.

This victory built on the success of Fontenoy and helped dispel the shadow of Culloden. It presented the Highlander as a key warrior in the development of the British Empire. For a century before Quebec, the Highlander had been reviled as a bandit and rebel, but with this decisive battle won under the Union flag, his character was, in part, transformed and assumed a global significance.

Just a few years later, the new role of the Highlander in helping to create a British Empire was best expressed in a speech of 1766 by the English statesman William Pitt the Elder, the strategic mastermind behind the triumphs of the Seven Years War:

I sought for merit wherever it was to be found; it is my boast that I was the first minister who looked for it and found it in the mountains of the north. I called it forth and drew into your service a hardy and intrepid race of men, who when left by your jealousy became a prey to the artifice of your enemies, and had gone nigh to have overturned the State in the war before last [the '45]. These men in the last war [Seven Years War] were brought to combat on your side; they served with fidelity as they fought with valour and conquered for you in every part of the world![14]

Pitt's enthusiasm for Highland warriors was reflected in the raising of three more Highland regiments in 1759, numbered the 87th, 88th and 89th. The latter was commanded by Staates Long Morris, an American married to the Duchess Dowager of Gordon. Assembled at Gordon Castle and given officers in Aberdeen, this regiment was the precursor of the famous 92nd Gordon Highlanders. All these regiments, along with the later 100th, 101st and 105th, served all round the world before they were disbanded at the end of the Seven Years War.

The claim that the Highlander was partly responsible for the triumph of the English language in North America may well seem hyperbole to many Britons living south of the border, but the combat on that sodden day was a devastating display of a method of warfare that would prove remarkably effective. Combining disciplined English gunfire with a shattering Celtic charge did produce a breathtaking ability to win battles that was quickly exported around the world. It was the violent engine that forged British world dominion over the next 150 years.

*

Back in Scotland, the new appeal of the Highland regiments was immense and young men were keen to join up. The Black Watch was especially popular and recruiting parties from other regiments sometimes clad themselves in the dark sett to attract them. On one occasion, a party of Scots were tricked into joining the 38th but when they arrived in Dublin they refused to serve with anyone else but the 42nd. Some were gaoled while a court of enquiry investigated the skulduggery. It was found that the recruiting party had falsely posed as Highlanders and although the form the recruits signed mentioned the 38th, most of them only spoke Gaelic and did not read English. Once this deception was revealed, the young men were released and allowed to re-enlist in the 42nd.

Less than twenty years after the triumph of Quebec, Britain's North American possessions were dealt a severe blow. Following an armed clash at Lexington in 1775, the thirteen colonies rose in revolt against the British government. American militia set siege to Boston and Colonel George Washington of Virginia was put in command of a Continental Army to fight the British regulars. Several years of major battles and campaigning followed and the British turned to the Highlanders to help them enforce their rule. Simon Fraser raised a new Highland regiment, numbered the 71st, and in 1776 these sailed with the 42nd to America.

Before leaving Scotland, some Highlanders were issued with the traditional broadswords they had brandished in their charge at Quebec. But arriving in America, these same swords were said to hamper the soldiers marching through dense undergrowth and were withdrawn from service, along with the traditional brace of

Highland pistols. It was a symbolic moment for Highlanders as they now fought with bayonets rather than swords, like every other redcoat regiment. Colonel David Stewart in his 1822 history of Highland regiments could not see the sense of it:

> I have been told by several old officers and soldiers ... that an enemy who stood for many hours the fire of musketry, invariably gave way when an advance was made sword in hand. It is to be regretted that a weapon which the Highlanders could use so well, should ... have been taken from the soldiers, and, after the expense of purchase had been incurred, sent to rust and spoil in a store.[15]

Although the broadsword ceased to be an official weapon for the Highlander in the British Army, it did not mean that he could not purchase it privately, and Highland officers continued to use the blade in combat for years afterwards.

Many of those who had originally served with Fraser's 78th at Quebec chose to settle in America after their military service ended, each being given a grant of land to farm and raise their families on. This was also true of the 77th Highlanders, who had many ferocious clashes with Indians during the same war. When rebellion came in 1775, several hundred of these veteran Highland soldiers chose to stand by the British government and formed a loyalist Highland Emigrants corps as part of the 84th regiment.

Even as late as 1781, Highland settlers were offering their services to the British. Following a minor British victory at the battle of Guilford in the southern states, a Highland community at Cross Creek offered to bring 1,500 men into the field. The British commanders declined the offer, but one former Highland officer from the Seven Years War called MacNeil led his own guerrilla raid against the rebels. A tall, imposing figure, MacNeill was said to have all the authority of an old clan chieftain. With a combination of old country Highlanders and those born in America to Highland families, he captured an American governor, his council and garrison. Intending to march them to a British base at Wilmington on Cape Fear, his 300-strong force outwitted pursuing rebels by advancing through swampland. When they were finally confronted by a hostile force, MacNeil drew his broadsword and led the Highlanders in a charge. The rebels fled, but MacNeil was killed in the pursuit. Sorely missing their leader, the Highlanders pressed on to deliver their high-ranking prisoners to Wilmington.[16]

King George's Highlanders performed well in America but they could not win the war for him and the thirteen colonies became the independent United States of America with the ending of hostilities in 1783. It has been suggested that their Declaration of Independence in 1776 was modelled on the Arbroath Declaration of 1320, the document drawn up by supporters of King Robert the Bruce which maintained the right of a people to choose who would govern them:

> So long as but a hundred of us remain alive, never will we on any conditions be brought under English rule. It is in truth not for glory, no riches, nor honours that we are fighting, but for freedom – for that alone, which no good man gives up but with his life.[17]

Thomas Jefferson, principal author of the Declaration of Independence, could well have been introduced to this document by his influential Scottish professor, William Small, at William and Mary College in Virginia.

*

While many Highlanders were benefiting from the new global opportunities provided by the expanding British Empire, as traders and colonists, other Scots embarked on more personal enterprises outside the British Army. The most extraordinary of these Highland adventurers in America was Gregor MacGregor. Although born in Edinburgh in 1786, he claimed descent from an illustrious family of Highlanders. His grandfather was the Black Watch MacGregor who came to London to display his fighting skills before King George II. The adventurer also insisted he was related to Robert MacGregor, more famously known as Rob Roy, the Highland outlaw. He certainly inherited his buccaneering attitude. He joined the Royal Navy in 1803, then gained valuable combat experience fighting in Spain during the Peninsular War.

With a good knowledge of Spanish, MacGregor sailed to South America in 1811, arriving at Caracas in Venezuela. Boasting the rank of colonel, he lent his military service to the colonial wars of independence from Spanish rule and came to the attention of the Latin American liberator Simon Bolivar, who promoted him to general. Making the most of his military heritage, MacGregor wore full Highland regalia, reputedly dressed some of his native warriors in tartan and led them into battle to the sound of bagpipes.[18] The Scots–Indian combination worked brilliantly and his army captured several towns, their campaign culminating in the independence of Venezuela in 1817.

Having achieved so much, including marrying the daughter of Bolivar, MacGregor was hungry for more conquests and, no doubt, a fortune of his own. In the same year, he struck a deal with wheeler-dealers in the United States of America, who sent him a challenging commission. 'It is highly important to the interest of the people whom we have the honour to represent,' they said, 'that possession should be taken, without loss of time, of East and West Florida, and the blessings of free institutions and the security of their natural rights imparted to their inhabitants ...'[19]

Florida was then part of the Spanish Empire and these Americans wanted MacGregor to take it from Spain. In June 1817 he led a small army of marauders to capture Amelia Island, off the coast of Florida. From there, he proposed to invade the rest of the country, but his backers failed to provide reinforcements and he was forced to abandon the island in the face of the Spanish. For the next few years MacGregor embarked on a freelance life, undertaking several precarious missions to help Latin Americans win independence from Spanish rule.

In 1819 MacGregor took 250 desperadoes in an eighteen-gun ship called the *Hero* to attack Port Bello in present-day Panama. He employed professional officers to knock them into shape, but these men, some of them military veterans, ended up duelling on the decks. A companion described the crew as 'scraped together anyhow, from anywhere, for a voyage to the Torrid Zone, in a ship scarcely sea-worthy'.

The mercenary army captured Porto Bello, but then faced the inevitable Spanish counter-attack. This time it came while MacGregor and his officers were sleeping. One of MacGregor's aides-de-camp, Cornet Colclough, fought the Spanish with sword and pistol as they ran up the steps into their house.

> MacGregor in the mean time leaped (in his shirt only) out a window of his bedroom, that looked towards the harbour, and was soon followed by Colclough. They both jumped into the sea, and swam on board the Hero in safety.[20]

It was a narrow escape, and MacGregor next sought a safer way to make his fortune. In London, in 1821, he set up a legation in the City to represent the Kingdom of Poyais, a piece of land along the Mosquito Coast in Central America he said he had obtained from the Indian chief of the region. He claimed it was a fully functioning state with schools, banks and farms just waiting for bold settlers to sail out there. Off the back of this promise he raised a £200,000 loan and sold land rights in the kingdom, allowing him to live like a prince in Essex.

In reality, when over two hundred Scots emigrants set off for the Caribbean and landed at Poyais, all they found was untamed jungle. One committed suicide, many others succumbed to disease and starvation. It was a terrible confidence trick, and in the end Mac-Gregor was forced to flee to Paris. Shamelessly, he repeated the entire Poyais trick on French investors, which earned him a short spell in prison. He then returned to his homeland, settling in Edinburgh for a few years, but he found no more British takers for his dream investments and he lived a meagre life. Finally he was granted a military pension by the Venezuelan government in thanks for his past services and he died in Caracas in 1845.

America had offered Scots an escape route from Hanoverian Britain, especially valued after Culloden and the end of the Jacobite cause. It also enabled many poor Highlanders to start afresh and build a fortune for themselves and their families, while making a useful contribution to a new nation. Their numbers grew steadily over the next century until they formed an important and respected part of communities in both the USA and Canada. Other Highlanders chose to go east and many of them faced a completely different kind of challenge in India.

Chapter 5
Vengeance at Seringapatam

Alexander Grant had watched the redcoats run at Prestonpans. A clansman from Glen Urquhart, he had led rebel Highlanders to Derby and back again and stood by them as the Duke of Cumberland's artillery laid them low on that rain-sodden moor in April 1746. As a fervent Jacobite, he could expect little mercy or employment from the British. So, rather than sign up with a Highland regiment for America, he chose to take ship to the Far East.

As a trained officer, Grant enlisted with the military forces of the East India Company. A private business venture, the Company did not care about the political background of their soldiers and did not require them to swear an oath to King George. The irony is that Alexander Grant's subsequent service would contribute enormously to the wealth and power of the government he had fought so hard against.

Ten years after Culloden, Captain Grant found himself in a desperate situation in Calcutta. The Nawab of Bengal, Siraj ud-Daulah, was angered by British traders defying his laws and taxes and, encouraged by the French, he raised an army to take the capital of Bengal. Grant was tasked with the job of defending this valuable prize, but as he checked through the garrison's arsenal, he found a chronic shortage of ammunition. 'When the Nawab's intention of marching on Calcutta was known,' wrote Grant in his report, 'it was felt time to enquire into the state of defence of a garrison neglected for so many years, and the managers of it lulled in so infatuate a security, that every rupee expended in military services were esteemed so much loss to the Company.' Grant discovered that most of the gunpowder was damp and the few primed shells exploded dangerously short of their targets. On top of that, he was the only officer to have seen active service.

In June 1756 the Nawab ordered his mighty army towards Calcutta. A probing attack on an outlying bastion was met by just twenty-five Company men and the guns of a ship moored in the nearby river. A lucky shot detonated some gunpowder barrels of the Nawab's artillery, and the assault faltered. It was an encouraging start for the Company, but Grant knew the rest of the city was woefully vulnerable and this proved to be the case when the Nawab's warriors overran the native and European quarters. They plundered the rich houses, forcing terrified traders and their families to seek the protection of the main garrison inside Fort William. It was up to Grant to organize a hasty defence, but panic and indecision surrounded him. The most obvious measures of defence were avoided for financial reasons.

> It may be justly asked, why we did not propose the only method, that as I thought then, and do now, could give us the least chance of defending the place in case of a vigorous attack – the demolition of all the houses adjacent to the Fort, and surrounding it with a ditch and glace [earthwork]?[1]

But even up to the very day of the attack, European merchants preferred to ignore the threat posed by the Nawab rather than see their houses destroyed – and so the path was laid for disaster and great slaughter. When it was clear the Company garrison could no longer mount an adequate defence against the Nawab's assault, the British Governor, Roger Drake, tried to organize an orderly evacuation of women and children from the Fort into boats on the river Hugli. As they assembled on the shore, the Nawab's troops opened fire and the frightened refugees stampeded the boats, overturning several of them.

By now, the men defending the Fort wanted to escape too and Grant was outraged to see the Governor join the fleeing crowds on the riverside. 'I first thought he only wanted to speak to his servant to secure the boat,' he observed, 'but seeing him step in it in somewhat of a hurry I followed, and before I came into the boat desired to know what he was about.' The Governor snapped at Grant, saying there was no time to inform the garrison of his withdrawal. They could see he was going and should join him if they could find any boats.

> Looking behind ... I considered the retreat to be general, and that everyone who could lay hold of a conveyance would choose to escape falling into the hands of a merciless enemy, and so [I] thought it justifiable to follow the Governor in a state of such apparent confusion and disorder, though greatly grieved to see how many of my friends and countrymen were likely to fall a sacrifice for want of boats.[2]

They rowed in their little craft towards a ship moored in the river. Once on deck, Grant was embarrassed to see mostly women and children. He argued with the Governor and the captain of the ship that they should take her back to rescue more of the refugees, but Grant was told it would be too dangerous and they sailed away. It was an appalling moment for all concerned and condemned those left behind to a cruel fate at the hands of the Nawab's soldiers.

That night, between fifty and a hundred Europeans captured in Fort William were crammed into a prison cell eighteen feet square that became known as the Black Hole of Calcutta. In searing summer heat, with little fresh air and no water to relieve them, only twenty-three of them survived to emerge from the cell twelve hours later.[3] A survivor of the atrocity later wrote a sensational account that turned it into one of the darkest crimes inflicted on defenders of the British Empire.[4] But few of the senior commanders involved in the scandalous defeat were punished. The Governor kept his job and so did Grant. The debacle did little to dampen the ambition of the East India Company and the following year they returned to Calcutta with an army led by Robert Clive. In the face of this, the Nawab's troops withdrew.

Having easily recaptured the important trading city, Clive was reluctant to fight the far larger force of the Nawab in a pitched battle outside Calcutta; but key figures among the Company men spoke up for an attack – among them Captain Alexander Grant. Their blood was up and they wanted revenge. Thus persuaded, Clive took his small force to attack the Nawab near the village of Plassey in June 1757. As part of Clive's army, Grant commanded a company of Europeans recruited from Bengal during the earlier clash.

A sudden torrential downpour soaked the gunpowder of the Nawab's soldiers as they tried to surround the Company army, but Clive stood his ground and his artillerymen, who had wisely covered their powder, blasted away. Eventually, the Indian army disintegrated and Grant charged after them in a pursuit that more than made up for his humiliating retreat from Fort William. A few days later, the Nawab was assassinated and Bengal fell under Company control. It was a major addition to what would become British Imperial India – and Grant, the former Jacobite, had played his full part in the historic victory.

*

Alexander Grant received £11,000 for his role in the battle, just part of the fortune extracted from the new Nawab by the Company. With this prize he returned to London and set up a trading business dealing with the East India Company's ships. A few years later, a young man came to work for him – a cousin called Charles Grant. He was recommended to the Captain for his 'good genius for writing, ciphering and keeping of accounts',[5] but it may well have been his family history that appealed to Alexander.

Charles Grant was born at Aldourie on the eastern shore of Loch Ness in the month before Culloden. His father, also named Alexander, was known as 'the Swordsman'. He had rallied to Bonnie Prince Charlie and named his newborn son after the Young Pretender. At the baptism, as a sign of his dedication to the Jacobite cause, his father got the baby to clasp the hilts of swords crossed over him by his comrades.

At Culloden Alexander the Swordsman was badly wounded and he went on the run, hiding out in caves and woods. After a year he returned home to find his property destroyed by redcoats. He struggled for the next few years to earn a living and eventually signed up, like so many other former Jacobites, to the British Army, joining either the Black Watch or Montgomerie's Highlanders. He was shipped off to the West Indies, where he took part in the conquest of Havana in 1762. Shortly afterwards, he died of fever.

The Swordsman's wife had already passed away, just two years after he left her. Their five children were looked after by members of their family. At the age of thirteen, Charles Grant was apprenticed to a merchant in Cromarty, where he learned the skills of a clerk and the rudiments of business. After five years of this, he travelled south to London to work for his successful cousin, Alexander. The tragic story of the boy's Jacobite father must have struck a deep chord with Captain Grant and he was keen to help. When Alexander returned to India, Charles was left in charge of his business, but dealing with the accounts of trade in India filled the young man with a desire to visit the country. In 1767 he enlisted as a cadet in the East India Company's army and set sail. A year later, Captain Grant died in Calcutta.[6] Charles was now on his own, but his ambition knew no bounds.

Having left Inverness with only half a guinea in his pocket, it took Charles a little over twenty years to make a fortune manufacturing silk in Bengal. As a successful businessman, he was appointed to the Board of Trade of the East India Company, possibly the richest commercial organization in the world at that time. He returned to London to become MP for Inverness-shire and continued to exert his influence on the East India Company, eventually becoming its Chairman in 1805. Not bad for the orphaned son of a renegade Jacobite Highlander.

Although Captain Grant, perhaps unwittingly, had played his full part in extending British rule over India, Charles Grant was not so sure about this imperial role. He was a businessman and saw the defence of trade as the purpose of the East India Company, not grabbing land. He believed it was a false dream that every conqueror of the subcontinent had, that they could unify it into one dazzling realm. To empire-makers he quoted the India Act of 1784, which forbade any further conquests as 'repugnant to the wish, the honour, and the policy of the British nation'.[7]

Grant's criticism of empire brought him into conflict with Richard Wellesley, Governor-General of India since 1798. Richard was the elder brother of Arthur Wellesley, later to become the Duke of Wellington. When Richard took up his post, he employed his young brother, who was then a colonel, as an unofficial military adviser. Richard Wellesley had a far more aggressive approach to British rule in India and, shortly after arriving there, he targeted Tipu Sultan, ruler of the kingdom of Mysore in southern India. Wellesley feared that the French, who had just landed in Egypt, were planning to move on to India and use Tipu to push the British out. But in the case of Tipu, there was also some unfinished business.

Tipu's father, Haidar Ali, had sided with the French to fight the British in the Second Mysore War of 1780–3. In the first year of the conflict, he had cut to pieces a small British force and held some of them prisoner in terrible conditions. By 1783 Haidar Ali was dead, but his son, Tipu, took over his rule and he harboured a special loathing for the redcoats in his country. He famously commissioned for his amusement a mechanical model of a tiger mauling a Company soldier.[8]

A Third Mysore War followed in which the British put Tipu under siege in his fortified palace at Seringapatam. This time, Tipu was forced to hand over half his lands to the Company, but he was still not tamed and continued to conspire with the French against the British. In 1799 Wellesley decided to extinguish this threat once and for all. Normally, Charles Grant would have opposed such military adventuring, but he made an exception of Tipu and was happy to see a British Army move against him. Perhaps, it was because Grant knew that some of those British soldiers who had been so badly treated by Tipu's father were fellow Highlanders.

*

David Baird was forty-two years old when he stood before Seringapatam in 1799. A tall man with a powerful voice, a natural leader of men, he shivered at the sight of the city walls. As a young man, almost twenty years before, he had been brought to Seringapatam as a prisoner of war. At that time, Baird was captain of a company of the 73rd Highlanders, raised by the former Jacobite Lord Macleod for service in India (they later became the 71st Glasgow Highland Light Infantry). Baird was himself from East Lothian and a good quarter of the thousand-strong 1st Battalion were Lowlanders too, plus a few English and Irish. They arrived in Madras in January 1780. By September, under the command of Colonel Baillie, they were part of a small force advancing on the army of Haidar Ali. They were split from the main British force in the area of Perambaukum and the Mysore army seized this opportunity. Haidar Ali and his son Tipu led their mail-clad warriors in a devastating charge on the isolated group.

The outnumbered redcoats put up a good fight but then two of their wagons containing gunpowder exploded, depriving them of much of their ammunition. The 73rd Highlanders and their comrades fought on for over an hour, repelling thirteen separate assaults, but the armoured cavalry and Indian war-elephants overwhelmed them. Amid the slaughter, with his ranks thinning around him, Colonel Baillie raised his handkerchief on a sword as a sign of truce. The redcoats laid down their weapons, but Tipu rushed in with his horsemen and hacked away at them. Captain Baird received two sabre wounds to his head, a musket ball in his thigh and a spear wound in his arm, collapsing soon afterwards from loss of blood. It was only when disgusted French officers intervened that the massacre stopped.

The British survivors were taken as prisoners before Haidar Ali where they were horrified to witness the heads of their comrades being exchanged for a reward of five rupees each. Baird and some other officers were then marched to Seringapatam. On the journey, Baird's open wounds were crawling with maggots. Having reached the palace, the redcoats were chained to the walls of a cell. A French surgeon tended Baird's suppurating wounds and allowed him to go without irons, but as soon as he recovered he was placed in chains like the rest of the British prisoners. So poor were the conditions and so meagre the food that several officers died from illness, including Colonel Baillie. One went mad. Baird kept himself sane by making his own shirts.

Later, Baird told his biographer that he never yielded to despondency and 'never doubted that he should somehow and at some time get out of the hands of his enemies'. But there were many dark times inside the prison at Seringapatam. During one bleak period, he was suffering terribly from dysentery. As he slowly recovered, he craved food to rebuild his strength but there were few extra rations available. At this point, he looked around his cell at his companions and the desire 'to snatch a portion of the food from others was almost unconquerable, and that if the least morsel was left by any of them, he swallowed it with the greatest eagerness and delight'.[9]

So as not to upset the more genteel of his readers, Baird's biographer failed to mention the full extent of the torture endured by the Highland prisoners of war. Cromwell Massy was a lieutenant in the 73rd regiment and one of 200 prisoners held in the Muslim Sultan's palace. Along with many of his fellow Highlanders, he was forcibly circumcised and recorded the brutal event in his prison diary.

> They immediately informed us that we should be, that night, circumcised ... you Sir who have tender and delicate feelings, sure will conceive what our situation was, drag'd to what every Christian in the universe utterly abhors, surrounded by enemies whose very soul is many times darker than their visage ... A little after [sun] set the Surgeon came and with 30 or 40 Coffries who seized us and held us fast till ye operation was performed ...[10]

As far as we can tell, Captain Baird was spared this assault, but none of the lower ranks was so lucky. There is at least one other written account of these forced circumcisions at the hands of Muslim captors in Seringapatam. Henry George Jennings Clarke was asked if he wished to join the Sultan's army and embrace Islam. He refused and on the second night of his captivity 'lost with the foreskin of my yard all those benefits of being a Christian and Englishman, which were and ever shall be my greatest glory'.[11]

After three years of confinement in Seringapatam, Captain Baird was finally released in 1783 with a handful of survivors. Weakened by disease and despair, they would not quickly forget the experience. Sixteen years later, however, Baird had risen to the rank of Major-General and had become commander of the 73rd, renumbered as 71st Highlanders, and had led them in several more campaigns in India. When in 1798 they finally returned to Scotland, after an absence of nearly two decades, Baird decided to stay in India and in May 1799 was put in charge of Governor-General Richard Wellesley's final assault on Tipu Sultan.

The task should have gone to the young Colonel Arthur Wellesley but he had fumbled a night attack on Seringapatam a few days before. A sense of revenge might also have swayed the choice of leadership. Among the British and native troops that Baird commanded were the 74th Highlanders. A mixture of Highland and Lowland recruits, their kilted garb was deemed too warm for the heat of India and they fought in red jacket and lightweight white trousers.

Baird's attack focused on a breach in the city wall defences, but to reach it his men would have to cross a shallow river under the heavy fire of the defenders. On the morning of 4 May, Baird's soldiers assembled in their siege trenches, concealing themselves from the gaze of the garrison. British artillery pounded away at the breach. The sun was relentless and the Highlanders were impatient to get on with their work. Around 1.30 p.m., Major-General Baird judged the time was right. He drew his broadsword and clambered on to the edge of the trench. 'Come, my brave fellows,' he boomed to the men behind him, 'follow me, and prove yourselves worthy the name of British soldiers!'

Only a Forlorn Hope of seventy young men beat the middle-aged Major-General to the river, otherwise Baird led his troops across the wet rocks up the debris of the breach into the city. They came under a storm of musket fire and rockets, but it took just a few minutes for the Highlanders and their comrades to sweep the defenders from the wall. They then advanced along the battlements of Seringapatam to the Mysore Gate. Traditionally, a city taken by assault became the prize of the victorious soldiers and the vengeful Highlanders were in no mood to take prisoners, but Baird understood that most of the inhabitants of Seringapatam had little to do with Tipu Sultan and would become innocent victims. He sent messengers ahead to Tipu Sultan's palace to demand surrender. It was not to be.

An account of the war against Tipu Sultan, published just a year after Baird's attack, described the scene later that day when the body of the Sultan was discovered.

> About dusk, Major-General Baird, in consequence of information he had received at the palace, came with lights to this gate ... and after much labour it was found and brought from under a heap of others to the inside of the gate. The countenance was no way distorted, but had an expression of stern composure ... He who had left the palace in the morning a powerful Imperious Sultaun [sic], full of vast ambitious projects, was brought back a lump of clay.[12]

Major-General Baird gazed down at the dust-covered corpse at a place barely 300 yards from where he had been held prisoner in

chains for three years. This exquisite moment of imperial vengeance captured the imagination of the British public who liked to see
an exotic villain brought down by a tough Briton – and a Scotsman
at that.

The image was captured in a painting by Sir David Wilkie, portraying Baird standing in the gateway with a Highlander to the side
of him looking down at the dead Sultan. The Storming of Seringapatam was also depicted in a 120-foot-long panoramic canvas by
Robert Ker Porter, which went on display at the Lyceum in the
Strand in April 1800. It attracted thousands of visitors and afterwards went on a national tour, ending up in a purpose-built gallery
in Belfast.[13] On his return to Britain, Baird was treated as a hero and
received a knighthood.

*

Although East India Company Chairman Charles Grant joined in
the national acclaim at the death of Tipu Sultan, he did not applaud
Governor-General Richard Wellesley's 'perpetual warfare' against
Indian princes. He saw it as a recipe for being drawn into expensive wars of no great commercial benefit. But he was in a minority,
as Wellesley spread British rule across India in a series of campaigns and treaties. His younger brother Arthur Wellesley was
also caught up in the fever of imperial expansion and when, as the
Duke of Wellington forty years later, he was asked what his greatest military success was, he did not mention any of his victories
against the forces of Napoleon, but one combat in India – Assaye.[14]
It was there that he won one of the bloodiest contests of his career
and it was there that his Highland regiments proved their courage
beyond doubt.

Four years after Seringapatam, Arthur Wellesley had risen to the
rank of Major-General. He now commanded his own army as he
marched into the land of the Marathas in central India in September
1803, where he faced a formidable foe. The Maratha clans had
recruited European military advisers and transformed their native
warriors into musket-firing soldiers, supported by strong artillery.
They had already defeated a redcoat army in 1779 at the battle of
Wadgaon and their continued independence threatened British
dominion. Hoping to split the clans, Wellesley advanced with the

aim of helping one tribal chief against another. What he found at the junction of the Juah and Kaitna rivers was an enormous Maratha army that far outnumbered his own – 300,000 native cavalry with 10,000 French-trained infantry and 200 pieces of artillery. Wellesley's army was only 4,500 strong and composed mostly of local sepoy soldiers, but marching alongside them were two Highland Regiments, the 74th and the 78th Ross-shire Highlanders.

Colin Campbell was a young lieutenant in the 78th when he came to the attention of Wellesley earlier in the campaign. On that occasion, just after dawn, the Highlanders had been ordered to take the Maratha town of Ahmednuggur, surrounded by a mud-brick wall and towers. Campbell was the first man to reach the assault ladders, drew his broadsword and clambered up the wooden rungs, but the battlements were filled with warriors who threw stones and spears down at him. Knocked off the ladder, he brandished his sword and went back up. Again, he was wounded and thrown down. This time he let his sword hang from his wrist, allowing him to use both hands to climb up. Under a covering fire of muskets, Campbell told his men to follow him quickly. With both hands free, he sprinted up the ladder and was quickly over the wall where he grabbed his sword and hacked at the defenders. The 78th followed and they took the bastion, killing everyone inside. With the job done, Campbell collapsed from his wounds.

Wellesley watched the whole incident. He made Campbell his aide-de-camp and the young Highlander accompanied him through all his future campaigns from India to Spain and Waterloo. With Ahmednuggur swiftly taken, the redcoats went back to camp for their first food of the day. A Maratha chieftain who had decided to join Wellesley took note. 'These English are a strange people,' he said, 'they came here in the morning, looked at the wall, walked over it, killed all the garrison and returned to breakfast! What can withstand them?'[15]

On 23 September, as Wellesley approached the Maratha village of Assaye, he personally rode out to inspect the enemy's position. He did not trust the information coming from local scouts and liked to get to know the terrain of a forthcoming battle. He discovered a ford across the Kaitna river and used this to surprise the enemy. Splashing through the water, his troops rapidly advanced on the enemy who thought this river would protect them. Their artillery opened up, but the fire was half-hearted as concern spread through their ranks.

The advantage was with Wellesley and he pressed it home. His Madras sepoys advanced between the two Highland regiments on either flank. He rode with the 78th, anticipating they would be the first to attack. The Highlanders' morale was high because of their previous success against the Marathas, but what they did not know was that the army facing them had been trained by a senior German military adviser, a Colonel Pohlmann. The valiant Scots faced a ferocious storm of fire as they moved forward.

At sixty yards from the enemy, the 78th Highlanders halted in unison, levelled their muskets and fired a mighty volley at the Maratha artillery, then attached their bayonets and plunged forward. They took the guns, regrouped in line and fired a second disciplined volley which broke the Maratha infantry, already unnerved by the sight of the tall Highlanders crashing through their artillery. Several European mercenary officers took to their horses and fled. Emboldened by the triumph of the 78th, the Madras sepoys followed on and shattered the centre of the Maratha line. In the midst of the fighting, Wellesley had his horse shot from beneath him. On the other flank, the 74th Highlanders advanced across rough ground studded with cacti that ripped their legs and feet. When they confronted the enemy they came under intense fire and had to form a square with ramparts built of dead Marathas. They stood their ground long enough for the 19th Dragoons to gallop past them and sweep away the enemy before the village of Assaye.

The entire British line swung round and pushed the Maratha army back towards the river Juah. Wellesley had a second horse fatally wounded, his courage inspiring his men further, in stark contrast to the Maratha leaders who were more concerned with their personal survival and were nowhere to be seen. Colin Campbell of the 78th recognized a fellow brave man in his leader. 'The General was in the thick of the action the whole time,' he wrote in his despatches. 'No one could have shown a better example. I never saw a man so cool and collected ...'[16] Faced by a renewed attack by the Highlanders and Madras sepoys, the Marathas finally decided they had had enough and withdrew across the river, leaving behind piles of weapons and equipment.

Wellesley's Highlanders and sepoys had won a decisive victory, but the cost had been heavy, with some 1,500 of his troops dead and wounded – a casualty rate of more than 27 per cent. Not until Waterloo would Wellesley again experience such heavy losses, which is why he regarded the combat so highly. The 74th had been particularly badly mauled, with 124 killed and 277 wounded out of a regimental strength of around 750. The Marathas lost at least 1,200 dead and abandoned ninety-eight cannons on the field.

Wellesley's brother, the Governor-General, was delighted by the victory at Assaye and took on board the key role of the Highlanders in winning it. In his General Orders of 30 October 1803 he made the following recommendations:

> The names of the brave officers and men who fell at the battle of Assaye will be commemorated together with the circumstances of the action, upon the public monument to be erected at Fort William [in Calcutta], to the memory of those who have fallen in the public service during the campaign. The honorary colours granted by these orders to his Majesty's 19th regiment of dragoons, and to the 74th and 78th regiments of foot, are to be used by those corps while they shall continue in India ...[17]

The battle honour won at Assaye lived a lot longer than that. A version of the colour presented to the 74th by the East India Company was carried on parade until very recently by the Royal Highland Fusiliers, the late-twentieth-century British Army regiment incorporating the old 74th.

In the eyes of the British public at the beginning of the nineteenth century, Highlanders were at the heart of many of their greatest overseas victories – from Quebec to Seringapatam to Assaye. From being untrustworthy Jacobites they had become warriors of empire. With that grew a public affection and a sense of romance. This could only be enhanced when Britain faced a direct threat from Europe in the shape of revolutionary France. The role of the Highlander in defending his islands against Napoleon Bonaparte raised his reputation to yet another level.

Chapter 6
Scotland For Ever

Private Dixon Vallance of the 79th Cameron Highlanders was twenty-two years old when he arrived in Belgium in May 1815 – the year of Waterloo. The 79th was quartered in Brussels along with other Highland regiments. Vallance and three Highlanders were billeted in a pub – perhaps the best result you could hope for as a soldier. Vallance had been brought up on a humble moorland farm in Lanarkshire, and was embarrassed by his lack of formal education. 'In my youth I learned the exercise of the cart, plough and harrow,' he recalled, 'but I soon abandoned this peaceful employment for the exercise of the gun and bayonet.' He had joined the 79th two years earlier. On the evening of 15 June 1815, Vallance and his regiment were told that Napoleon and the French army were marching on Brussels and it was up to them to halt the advance.

In the previous year Napoleon Bonaparte had been defeated by an alliance of European armies and been dispatched to the island of Elba. Less than twelve months later, he returned to France, resuming power in Paris before he struck north to defeat the separate forces led by the British Duke of Wellington and the Prussian Marshal Blücher. It was the Emperor's last roll of the dice.

As news of the French advance swept through Brussels, terrifying the civilian population, Private Vallance rushed to retrieve his spare shirts from a washerwoman. They were soaking wet and he just had time to have them wrung out before packing them damp into his knapsack. Wearing his full uniform and equipment in anticipation of an early start the next day, the Highlander tried to get some sleep, but it was near impossible. Just after dawn, Vallance and three comrades were called to action by the sounds of bagpipes, bugles and drums. While the 79th's piper played *The Gathering of the Camerons* and the *War Note of Lochiel*, their excited landlord gave them each a bumper of gin and a loaf of bread. He shook their hands and kissed his guests farewell.

Vallance and the rest of the 79th mustered in the Grand Place in the centre of Brussels where they received another allowance of gin. The crowds cheered them loudly and girls rushed forward to embrace the kilted soldiers. By midday they were in high spirits and left the city to the sound of their band playing *Loudon's Bonny Woods and Braes*.

It was a bright sunny day and as the Highlanders marched along the road from Brussels to Waterloo they began to feel the heat. Alongside his knapsack, Vallance was carrying a blanket and camp-kettle plus a ten-pound India Pattern flintlock musket and sixty rounds of ball cartridge. By midday it was feeling very heavy. They stopped for a moment in a wood to drink some water and Vallance laid out his damp shirts to dry. As he placed the clothing on the ground, he noticed his bible at the bottom of his pack. 'I took up my best, but much-neglected, companion,' he recalled, 'and retired a little into the wood, in order to avoid the taunts and scoffs of some of my profligate comrades.'[1] Alone, he read the psalms he felt most suited a soldier going into battle.

With his shirts dry, Vallance fell into place in the ranks once more. As they marched, villagers came out and gave them wooden cups of water to slake their thirst, but ahead they began to see the signs of combat. Dutch and Belgian troops were falling back past them, some sitting on the side of the road tending their wounds. Vallance saw some faint from loss of blood. In the distance, he could hear the sounds of cannon fire and they marched on until they came to a place called Quatre Bras – a crossroads about twenty miles south of Brussels. It was 2.00 p.m.

The 79th were part of General Sir Thomas Picton's 5th Division, which was divided into two brigades, one commanded by Sir Denis Pack, and the other by Sir James Kempt, which included the 79th. An allied Hanoverian Brigade stood to their rear. In total, there were three Highland battalions present at Quatre Bras, the others being the 42nd Black Watch or Royal Highlanders and the 92nd

Gordon Highlanders, both in Pack's brigade. There were no British cavalry present, meaning the British foot had to stand up to both infantry and cavalry assaults.

Vallance and his battalion took up their position in a field full of tall rye and thick clover. As they formed their battlelines on the left flank of the British force, they came under immediate and intense artillery and musket fire. An older soldier next to Vallance had his feather bonnet knocked off by a musket ball. The veteran laughed and said, 'I have had many a one of that sort.' Then a musket ball shattered Vallance's canteen at his side and wounded a man behind him.

The 79th were burning to get to grips with the enemy but they could only just see their heads above the tall rye. Their commanding officer gave them orders to load, fire and charge. From feeling tired and stiff, the young Highlander was suddenly energized. As he forced his way through hedges, he recalled, 'I never felt my feet touch the ground, my gun and bayonet seemed as light in my hands as a feather.'

> If the French had made a stand against us at the hedge we would have thrown them over the hedges from the points of our bayonets like corn sheaves. Our passion of rage and fury had risen to such a height, that we were like madmen all the time we were engaged.[2]

At one stage in the battle, Vallance and his comrades were ordered to lie down in a field of rye to lessen the impact of the French fire. A musket ball struck his camp-kettle with a clang and embedded itself in his knapsack. Another bullet cut his belt. A man next to him was hit on the crown of the head and was killed instantly.

When the French counter-attacked, the 79th rose to their feet to pour more fire into the enemy ranks. Their Captain told them to 'take a good aim and bring down the ruffians'. French bullets whizzed past their ears. 'My face, hands, clothes and belts were bespattered with the blood of my killed and wounded companions,' remembered Vallance. 'We were ordered to charge the French – we gave them three hurras and again drove them through the hedges.'

The battle went back and forth all afternoon. French cavalry charged in, but not even the breastplates of the cuirassiers could protect them from the Highlanders' musket balls and they rode away. At one point the 79th were cut off from the main force and the French soldiers surged forward to surround them. The French taunted them, telling them to make themselves prisoners, but Vallance and his comrades were not too proud to 'run like devils' through a hedge, re-form their lines then attack again.

Elsewhere on the battlefield, the 42nd and 92nd Highlanders were having a stiff fight against the French cavalry and infantry. Captain Thomas Hobbs was with the 92nd Gordon Highlanders and recalled seeing the Duke of Wellington, their supreme commander, just to the rear of their regiment, fearlessly observing the enemy with his spyglass: 'Several shells and round shot fell close to him.' At about 5.00 p.m., a French column marched up the road towards the British line and Wellington told the Gordons to attack them. Their Colonel, John Cameron of Fassiefern, led the charge but was mortally wounded.

'The French opposed us most obstinately,' noted Hobbs, 'but the brave conduct of the men could not be sustained, we completely routed them, and pursued them some distance when we charged in turn. Thus we were warmly engaged until the Brigade of Guards came to our assistance.'[3] At 7.30 p.m., Hobbs was shot in the thigh and was forced to quit the field. He was helped to the rear of the battle where his wound was dressed by a Prussian doctor, but he was out of any further fighting and was returned to Brussels in a wagon. The losses suffered by the 79th were recorded by Lieutenant Alex Forbes as one staff officer and twenty-eight rank and file dead, with three field officers, six captains, seven subalterns, ten sergeants and 248 rank and file listed as wounded.[4]

Only sunset brought an end to the fighting at Quatre Bras. All the Highland regiments, alongside their redcoat comrades, had fought well. By standing against the French, the British had won a temporary victory; but Napoleon had defeated the Prussians at Ligny on the same day and this meant Wellington had to order the withdrawal of his troops back towards Brussels. For the moment, however, the British enjoyed their triumph.

Private Vallance spent the night on the battlefield with the sound of the wounded and dying around him. It was a horrific scene. 'Many of the slain were shockingly mangled,' remembered

Vallance. 'Some with their innards torn out and scattered all over the ground.' The weather had turned stormy and the wind howled around him as he stood guard. A few of his companions took the opportunity to loot the knapsacks of the dead Frenchmen.

The next morning, the victorious Highlanders were given a ration of beef for their breakfast. With a morbid sense of humour, some of the 79th removed the breastplates from dead French cuirassiers and used them as pans to fry their steaks. 'They suited our purpose well,' said Vallance, 'only we lost a little of the gravy by the holes which our bullets had made.' Some Belgian soldiers were upset by the sight of this breakfast, believing that the Highlanders were living to up their fierce reputation by cooking portions of the dead Frenchmen.

> We invited the [Belgians] to partake with us; the men looked horrified and ran after their companions and told them the Scotch Highlanders were cannibals and, not content with killing the French, they were frying them in their iron jackets ...[5]

Mindful of the psychological impact this could have on their enemy, Vallance and his comrades left the unusual cooking utensils near their fires 'to let the enemy see that we had used the iron jackets of their slain companions for frying pans'.

Vallance had survived Quatre Bras; but this was just the opening round of what was to come – the battle of Waterloo.

*

Highland regiments had fought magnificently in the earlier wars against Napoleon. Several of these were new regiments raised specifically for campaigns against revolutionary France. Private Vallance's regiment, the 79th, had been established by Alan Cameron of Erracht in 1793. He claimed to have originally recruited mainly from around Inverness, although later recruits, like Vallance, were Lowlanders.

The 79th made a name for themselves during the Peninsular War in Spain, especially in the bitter street fighting at Fuentes de Onoro in 1811. 'The town presented a shocking sight,' wrote Sir Charles Oman, the leading historian of the campaign, 'our Highlanders lay dead in heaps.'[6] Colonel Cameron's eldest son died in the house-to-house combat. Cameron lost his second son from illness while on service, but the old man himself never missed a day of duty, leading his troops on campaigns in Flanders, the West Indies, Egypt, Portugal and Spain. It was an exhausted 79th that returned to Scotland from Spain with many losses. Vallance joined them in 1813 during a new recruitment drive.

Another famous Highland regiment born out of the Napoleonic Wars was the Gordon Highlanders. Raised by the 4th Duke of Gordon and his wife, the Duchess of Gordon, in 1794, they took men from their estates of Badenoch, Lochaber and Strathspey, but a good quarter were from around Aberdeen. The 92nd distinguished themselves in Spain, with one particularly heroic moment at Col de Maya in the Pyrenees in 1813. There, two lines of fewer than 400 Gordons held off a whole French division for twenty minutes. 'They stood there like a stone wall,' said an eyewitness, 'overmatched by twenty to one, until half their blue bonnets lay beside those brave highland soldiers. When they retired, their dead bodies lay as a barrier to the advancing foe.'[7]

Four other Highland regiments were raised during the French wars, including the 78th Ross-shire, the 97th Strathspey, the 98th then 91st Argyllshire, and the 93rd Sutherland Highlanders. The pressure to raise large numbers of fighting men meant many of these units were obliged to recruit from far beyond the traditional Highlands. As a result, while early recruiting of Highland regiments had depended on feudal obligations to Highland landlords, a bounty was now paid to anyone serving in Highland ranks, including Lowlanders, English, Irish and Welsh. Arthur Wellesley – the future Duke of Wellington – was born in Ireland but started his illustrious military career in the 73rd (Perthshire) Regiment of Foot – the renumbered 2nd battalion of the 42nd Black Watch.

Colonel Cameron of the 79th Highlanders was not happy with this dramatic change in the regiments' character and expressed his views strongly in a letter of 27 October 1804.

I have to observe progressively, that in course of the late war several gentlemen proposed to raise Highland Regiments – some for general service, but chiefly for home defence; but most of these corps were called upon from all quarters, and thereby adulterated by every description of men that rendered them anything but real Highlanders, or even, Scotchmen (which is not strictly synonymous): and the colonels themselves being generally unacquainted with the language and habits of High-landers ...[8]

Above all, he was furious at the suggestion that his Highlanders should stop wearing the kilt in favour of breeches. He declared that the kilt was perfectly suited for campaigning and kept his soldiers healthy and clean as they could more easily wash themselves in a brook on a forced march than soldiers dressed in tight-fitting pantaloons. But moves were ahead to remove the kilt from most Highland soldiers. In 1809 the Adjutant-General issued an order to all Britons, in which he claimed that as the population of the Highlands of Scotland was insufficient to supply recruits, troops from elsewhere should be attracted to the regiments by laying aside the kilt 'which is objectionable to the natives of Southern Britain'.

As a result of this official policy, six Highland regiments exchanged their kilts for trousers. By 1814, only the 42nd wore kilts. Yet, strangely, the soldiers were allowed to keep their Highland title. It indicated a major shift in the character of British Highland regiments. In this context, a Highlander was no longer a clansman from the Highlands, but an elite soldier belonging to a unit known for its aggression and relentless attack in battle. The Highlander was, in the description of the day, 'a stormer', and any Scotsman, Englishman, Irishman or Welshman could be a Highlander if he was tough enough.

*

Following Quatre Bras, Wellington and his British and allied troops fell back towards Brussels to take up a position near the village of Waterloo on 17 June 1815. It was sorely disappointing for those who had fought so hard to win the crossroads to be forced to retreat. As they marched, the weather changed dramatically and a thunderstorm cracked above them, soaking them with heavy downpours. That night, Private Vallance and the 79th Highlanders bedded down in a sodden rye field. Some of them took to dancing and jumping to keep themselves warm. 'The ground was so flooded, soft and miry,' said Vallance, 'that when we tried to leap and dance we stuck in the mud and mire, and had to pull one another out.'

The next morning the rain ceased and Vallance began cleaning his gun and looking for dry ammunition. To raise their spirits, the soldiers were issued with a ration of gin. Wellington positioned his troops along the slope of a ridge running beside the road to the village of Ohain. It was a good choice of ground as Wellington's troops could be hidden on the reverse side of the slope, while the French would have to march uphill towards it when they attacked. Vallance had scarcely finished his breakfast when he was told to stand to arms as the French columns were advancing. He could hear them shouting 'Vive l'Empereur!'

The battle of Waterloo began just before noon with Napoleon's 72,000 men attacking Wellington's 68,000-strong allied army of British, Dutch and Belgians positioned along the ridge. Vallance and his 79th Highlanders stood alongside the 42nd and 92nd Highlanders and other British regiments in the centre of the position near the farmhouse of La Haye Sainte. As at Quatre Bras, they were part of Kempt's brigade, under the divisional command of Sir Thomas Picton. Having first tested the allied right flank, after 1.00 p.m. Napoleon turned his attention to Wellington's centre, sending forward four divisions, preceded by a ferocious artillery bombardment.

Vallance and his men were told to lie down during the massive barrage, although the wet soil mercifully meant that the cannon balls tended to sink in harmlessly rather than bounce around. 'A cannon ball struck the ground a short distance from my head, and covered me with earth,' said Vallance. When a second ball struck the soil a few inches from his feet, an older comrade advised him to move as a French gunner had his cannon aimed straight at him. 'I shifted a little off the line and another ball sunk deep in the spot where I lay only a few minutes before.'

A soldier nearby stood up to take a view of the action and had his cheek torn off by a cannon ball, leaving him screaming in agony. When the French artillery ceased, Vallance and the 79th scrambled to their feet to face the chilling spectacle of 16,000 Frenchmen advancing towards them. Vallance and his men were ordered to hold their fire until the French got closer. The French let loose their muskets at a greater distance, sending a hail of balls among the

Highlanders, but their tall feather bonnets helped protect them – at long range, the French aimed at the hats rather than their heads. Several bullets went though Vallance's feather bonnet.

The 79th had some difficulty holding their ground against the weight of the French divisions pressing on them. Sir Thomas Picton was at the front of the action, cheering on his men. 'The noise was dreadful,' remembered Vallance – a combination of booming cannon and the roar of musket volleys. Picton – 'our gallant leader' – was killed in the close fighting, struck in the head by a musket ball. It was a severe blow to the morale of his troops. As fearless as always, the Duke of Wellington personally intervened, later recalling the critical moment.

> I saw about two hundred men of the 79th, who seemed to have had more than they liked of it. I formed them myself about twenty yards from the flash of the French column, and ordered them to fire; and, in a few minutes, the French column turned about.[9]

Perhaps as a result of this brief success, Vallance found himself advancing past wounded French soldiers who opened their knapsacks to him, hoping the British would take their belongings rather than kill them. They spared them, not having time to take their property. The French fire was relentless and the redcoat line wavered, with some of the Highlanders falling back.

Around 3.00 p.m., sensing that the British infantry were having a hard time of it, the Earl of Uxbridge, commander of the allied cavalry, unleashed the three horse regiments that stood behind the Highlanders. The charge included Sir William Ponsonby's Union Brigade, so named because it included English, Scots and Irish troopers – 1st Royal Dragoons, 2nd Royal North British (Scots Greys) and 6th Inniskilling Dragoons. The British cavalry surged between the Highlanders in front of them, who had to quickly step aside to let them through. Vallance watched their impact on the French column.

> Our three regiments of cavalry rushed upon this powerful column, the Scots Greys taking the lead – they seeing their countrymen on both right and left of them, cheering and shout-

ing 'Scotland for Ever'. While the other Scotch regiments returned the ever memorable salute, 'Hurrah, Scotland for Ever'.

The 92nd and 42nd were the other Highlanders present, and Major Robert Winchester of the Gordons remembered the scene. 'The Scots Greys came up at this moment, and doubling round our flanks, and through our centre where openings were made for them, both Regiments charged together calling "Vive Scotland for ever".'[10] In less than three minutes, the French column was totally destroyed – some 2,000 Frenchmen killed and wounded with two of their prized eagle standards captured. The ground was so thick with their discarded knapsacks and equipment that the redcoats could hardly walk across without stepping on them.

The charge of the Scots Greys was the stuff of legend and at least one eyewitness described the Highland infantry grabbing hold of their stirrups and dashing into the combat with them. As the horses appear not to have been charging at full tilt – indeed, Winchester says they 'walked' over the French – it is possible that some Highlanders may have increased the momentum of their run by grabbing hold of cavalry stirrups on horses briskly trotting towards the action. The ground was wet and heavy too, hindering any fast movement by horses.

Lieutenant Charles Wyndham of the Scots Greys remembered the 92nd mingling with the British cavalry. 'The 92nd Highlanders passed though the intervals of the Greys,' he said, 'and several went down the hill from the hedge with the Regiment, and it was at this moment when the 92nd cheered the Greys, and cried "Scotland for ever!"' Wyndham could not be certain, but presumed the 42nd Highlanders were in the same brigade with the 92nd and 79th regiments.[11]

Cornet W Crawford of the Scots Greys also recalled that the 92nd Highlanders 'turned and ran into the charge with us'. The exuberance of this moment was later turned into an iconic Victorian military painting by Lady Elizabeth Butler in 1881, called *Scotland for Ever*, but her hurtling horses seem far from the truth of the scene.

Having had his main infantry thrust blunted, Napoleon sent in his cavalry regiments under the command of Marshal Ney to break the British resistance. Thousands of magnificently attired French cuirassiers, hussars and lancers launched forward. Private Vallance and the 79th were told to form squares to resist the mounted onslaught. The front row of Highlanders knelt on one knee, holding their bayonet-tipped muskets to present a rampart of pointed steel directed at the breasts of the advancing French horses.

Riding up the slope, across the muddy ground, the French cavalry lost much of their impetus and were vulnerable to well-timed volleys of musket fire. Sometimes they could do little more than slash at the forest of bayonets with their sabres and fire pistols at the redcoats inside the squares. A few Highlanders laughed at their frustration. 'We continued for a considerable time in square,' said Vallance, 'as large bodies of the French cavalry were hovering near us. They made several furious attacks on us, but were often repulsed by our impregnable barrier of British steel.'

Eventually, tired horses just refused to close on the British formations and the French cavalry withdrew. This failure to break the British squares was a major blow to Napoleon, but the fighting continued long into the evening. The wind blew the clouds of gunpowder smoke back into the faces of the Highlander, so at times they could barely see the French. They just aimed their muskets at where the smoke was thickest, presuming that this marked an eruption of enemy fire.

In went more waves of French attacks, including Napoleon's most loyal infantry troops, the elite Old Guard. Even they were unable to shift the exhausted but stubborn allied soldiers. The defeat of the Old Guard was the last straw for most of the French. By then, the Prussians were closing in and threatening Napoleon's right flank. It was a welcome relief for Vallance and his comrades who had been fighting for over seven hours.

As the sun dipped towards the horizon, Vallance, so lucky through so much of the fighting, was hit. A musket ball smashed his cheekbone and tore out his right eye. The wound was so severe that he just lay down on the ground with his wounded companions. By 8.30 p.m., the fighting was mostly over. Wellington and the allied army had won a tremendous victory and Napoleon was soundly defeated, but there was little mood of celebration. 'It had been too much to see such brave men,' said Wellington to a mortally wounded friend, 'so equally matched, cutting each other to pieces as they did.'

Private Vallance was left on the battlefield along with the rest of the dead and dying, allies and enemies all mixed together. The victors were too exhausted by their own efforts to provide much help for the wounded and Vallance had to endure the horrors of the long night. Next to him lay a soldier he knew well. He was severely wounded in the stomach by a musket ball and cried out to Vallance to shoot him and end his pain. Within a few hours he was dead.

> About midnight a party of plundering Prussians came to me. One of them looked in my face – it was clear moonlight – and he saw my face all covered with blood and went off cursing the French. They plundered and stabbed a wounded Frenchman that lay a short distance from me.[12]

The next morning, half-blind, Vallance rose to his feet and got some water for himself and those wounded around him that had survived the night. As he helped them, field parties from different regiments came to bury the dead.

Nearly 2,000 British soldiers died at Waterloo and over 7,000 were wounded. The wounded of both sides, some tens of thousands of men, were treated by British and Belgian doctors at a field hospital at Mont St Jean farm and then taken to hospitals in Brussels.[13] Vallance's wound took a long time to heal, but eventually he was returned to Dundee. In early 1816, he was discharged from the army with a pension of ninepence a day.

*

The battle of Waterloo brought an end to the Napoleonic Wars. Over the next few weeks, Napoleon was made a prisoner and the allied armies occupied northern France. They headed for Paris and the city surrendered without resistance. The 71st Glasgow Highland Light Infantry was one of the victorious regiments to march into the capital. Originally the 73rd or Macleod's Highlanders, the 71st recruited so many men from Glasgow that it was renamed in their honour. One of these soldiers was surprised to hear female Scots voices among the French crowd. 'There is a music in our native tongue,' he recalled, 'in a foreign land where it is not to be looked for, that often melts the heart when we hear it unexpect-edly.'[14] The two girls had made their way from Paisley to Paris, where they were working as embroiderers, and they were as delighted to see their fellow Scots as were the soldiers.

Private James Gunn of the Black Watch was proud to tell his grandson of the day he saw the allied armies on parade in Paris.

> The Prussians were smart active looking like soldiers. I never did see any men marching with such precision. Indeed compared with [us] they might well be called Giants but I hope that it might and still be said of the British soldier what was said of Rob Rorison's bonnet that it was not the bonnet but the head that was in it – that it was not the size of his body but the soul that was within it.[15]

Then came the greatest praise of all for this Highlander. 'We was in company with some of the Cossacks,' said Gunn, 'who hon-oured us by saying that we were the English Cossacks as they were the Russian.' The Highland Regiments of the British Army had won an international reputation for hard fighting that had now spread as far as the steppes of Russia. They would spend the rest of the nineteenth century living up to it.

Chapter 7
Fashionably Violent

Major David Stewart knew how to choose a spectacular wedding present. In a letter to Lord James Murray in 1810, he sent his congratulations on the peer's recent marriage and delighted in telling him that he had dispatched a case full of the most beautiful tropical birds he had collected while stationed on Trinidad in the West Indies. Later, he would charm the new bride by sending her a live flamingo. He mischievously compared the ravishing pink of the bird to the sunburnt skins of the white ladies on the island – 'the vermilion of the ladies not being of that showy brightness which makes my Flamingo look so gorgeous as he stalks with his awkward gait among the fowls'.[1]

There was little to indicate in this letter that the forty-two-year-old Major Stewart was soon to become the man most responsible for the cult of the Highlander in nineteenth-century Britain, or that he would entertain a king of England in Scotland, assist him to dress in a tartan kilt, and help spread the popularity of the Highlander around the world in a best-selling book. The purpose of Stewart's exotic gift to Lord James Murray was to gain his influence in securing a job for himself as a colonial governor in the Caribbean, where he could pursue his studies of its exquisite flora and fauna. He wanted to thrive in the tropical sun, not in the rain and snow of Scotland.

Stewart was born to a landowning family in Perth and Kinross. At the age of fifteen, his father bought him a commission in the British Army in the Black Watch – the 42nd Highlanders – yet his military future did not look especially bright as he was small of stature and very short-sighted and always wore thick-rimmed spectacles. His courage in battle, however, more than made up for any physical failings. In 1795 he accompanied the Black Watch to the Caribbean where they were deployed to suppress the revolts of slave workers in some of Britain's richest colonies. Stewart was annoyed to see the Highlanders' traditional clothing replaced by a felt hat and linen trousers, arguing that the kilt and feather bonnet were more effective against the heat and sudden downpours of the tropical islands.

> When the kilt and hose got wet, if they were taken off (a very easy operation) and wrung in the same manner, they might be immediately worn with perfect safety. The mosquitoes were the most troublesome annoyance to be guarded against by those wearing the kilt; but as these insects seldom attacked people in day-light, and only in particular places at night, this objection might be overcome.[2]

After success in the Caribbean, Stewart was sent with the 42nd to Egypt to face a French army at the battle of Alexandria in 1801, where the Highlanders distinguished themselves in hard fighting and Stewart was wounded in the arm. He was promoted to major in 1804 and was in the front line in the bitter combat of Maida in Italy – the first defeat suffered by Napoleon's forces in Europe and widely celebrated in Britain. Stewart was wounded for the second time in the arm, but this did not prevent him from seeing further service in the Caribbean in 1810.

By this time, Stewart was aware that his fighting days were coming to an end and he had to seek another source of income. Ideally, he wanted to spend his middle age in the tropics pursuing his interests in natural history, but this was not to be. In 1812 he returned to Scotland where he received a military pension that allowed him to become absorbed in another pursuit – recording the history of the Black Watch and other Highland regiments. He travelled all around his native land visiting archives and libraries and speaking to veteran Highland soldiers. His passion for the subject soon brought him to the notice of other Scottish enthusiasts and in 1815 Stewart was appointed the vice-president of the Highland Society of London. The year before, despite being retired from the army, he was promoted to the rank of colonel.

The Highland Society of London was originally formed by twenty-five Highland gentlemen at the Spring Garden coffee house in London in 1778. Lieutenant-General Simon Fraser of Lovat, founder of the 78th and 71st Highland Regiments, was its first President. Its mission was to preserve traditional Highland culture, endangered ever since the British government's Disarming Act of 1746. This not only continued the earlier anti-Jacobite ban on Highlanders carrying traditional weapons, but extended it to the wearing of seditious tartan clothing, including the belted plaid and kilt. A notable exception to this ban was, of course, the wearing of tartan kilts in the British Army. Contrary to popular myth, the playing of Highland bagpipes was not prohibited after Culloden[3] but its popularity had declined to the point where the Highland Society of London considered the instrument needed patronage, and they introduced prizes for exemplary playing.

After intense lobbying by members of the society, the Disarming Act was repealed in 1782 and, with the death of Bonnie Prince Charlie in exile in 1788, the British establishment could allow itself to become more relaxed about the Highlands in general. A newspaper report of 1787 mentioned with delight the appearance of Highlanders at a London theatre:

> Last night, at Sadler's Wells, no less than five Highlanders appeared in different parts of the house, all dressed in the true national style of their country. The bonny Chiefs from Scotland now take a particular pride in exhibiting their Tartans at public places, especially where they are complimented with any thing in their own way.[4]

This public affection derived to a large extent from the brave performance of Highland regiments in wars for the British Empire in North America and India. The Highland Society of London, including a large number of military men among its members, was very aware of this and part of their early commitment was to celebrating military success. In 1801, after the battle of Alexandria in which Major Stewart had been wounded, the society presented a silver plate and medallions to the Black Watch Officers' Mess. Seven years later, after the battle of Vimiero, the role of the 71st was commemorated when their piper George Clark was awarded a gold medal and a set of silver-mounted bagpipes. He was among several pipers to win celebrity for playing his pipes after being severely wounded. 'Deil ha' my soul, lads,' he shouted, 'if ye sall want music!' Corporal John Mackay of the 71st received a gold medal for capturing the French General Brenier during the battle and – most amazingly of all, it seems – not stealing his watch and purse.

The Highland Society of London also pledged itself to preserve the traditional life of the Highlands in the face of land clearances and agricultural change. In 1786 they raised the sum of £40,000 to purchase land and establish free towns, villages and fishing stations in order to slow down the rate of emigration. A similar Highland Society of Scotland was established in 1784 in Edinburgh and it too concentrated on improving the everyday life of Highlanders, especially in encouraging effective farming.

Improvement was a subject close to Colonel David Stewart's heart. He strongly criticized the greed of landowners who discouraged the enterprise of Highland farmers with short leases and frequent rent rises. 'If men live in the dread of being ejected at every term,' he protested, 'or contemplate the probability of being obliged to emigrate to a distant country, the best education, unless supported by a strong sense of religion and morality, will hardly be sufficient to produce content, respect for the laws and a love of the country and its government.'[5] Stewart applauded the work of both societies in trying to moderate the impact of modernization on Highland farming.

Stewart's love of the Highlands also led to his taking an interest in preserving its tartan culture. He could find no Stewart tartan, except for that worn by Bonnie Prince Charlie in a portrait hanging in the family house on their estate at Garth. Further research exposed a poverty of general knowledge about tartans: were they related to particular areas or families? Without proof, Stewart proposed the idea that certain clans could be identified by different tartan patterns or setts, but believed that much of the original information about these had long been lost. In 1815, the Highland Society of London wrote to all the clan chieftains, asking them to 'furnish as much of the tartan of their clans as will serve to show the patterns'.[6] These were then gathered into a forty-five-page book with the sett of each clan certified by the chieftain's seal. It was part of the process that led to the invention of clan tartans.

However, the book that eventually made Stewart famous came about because of a shipwreck. The historical records of the Black Watch were being transferred by sea with much of their baggage when the regiment moved their base from Dublin to Donaghadee in northern Ireland in 1771. The ship was driven ashore by a gale and much of the regimental baggage lost. This loss was compounded when what remained of the regimental archives was captured by the French in Holland in 1794. Faced with a virtually blank canvas when it came to the history of his regiment, Stewart was asked by the commanding officer of the 42nd in 1817 to fill in the considerable gaps.

Colonel Stewart set about the task with great thoroughness and decided that, while conducting this research, he might as well tell the story of the other Highland regiments too. What emerged was a two-volume history of the Highlander as warrior both before and after 1745, with one of these volumes devoted completely to the history of the Highland regiments in the British Army. Rich in anecdote and dramatic accounts of battle, it drew attention to the tremendous contribution of the Highland soldier to Britain's rise to world power in the late eighteenth, and early nineteenth, centuries. As a veteran himself, he celebrated the achievements of the humble private soldier as well as the wealthy and influential men who established the regiments. It was a highly readable work that helped advertise the reputation of the Highland regiments throughout Britain and abroad.

Published in Edinburgh in 1822, Stewart's *Sketches of the Character, Manners and Present State of the Highlanders of Scotland; with details of the Military Service of the Highland Regiment* sold well. In London, five hundred copies were bought in just six days. The author received royalties of £159 2s 1d for the first edition and an advance of £300 for the second edition. It was good money but not nearly enough to settle the debt of £40,000 he had acquired since taking over the family estate in 1820 and spending large sums on its improvement. Money problems would continue to dog Stewart for the rest of his life.

The quality of research in the *Sketches* was quite rightly recognized at the time but one anonymous reviewer found the book a little too exciting for his taste. 'Some of his notes and digressions are very entertaining,' wrote a Scottish critic, 'but from the quantity of old tradition of doubtful authenticity which has crept into them, some readers may be disposed to think ... he has no objection to blend truth and fiction together, and to avail himself of the taste of the day for raids and romances to please all descriptions of readers.'[7]

It was an interesting observation and a temptation to which any historian of the Highlander is vulnerable, since so many good stories of the early period come from soldiers with a tale to tell and every incentive to make it larger than life. But the critic also reveals that by this time there was a considerable audience for fictional romances set in the Highlands, and Stewart's vision of the Highlander played well to this readership. One of Colonel Stewart's most enthusiastic literary friends was Sir Walter Scott. While Stewart was in the early stages of researching *Sketches*, Scott was writing *Rob Roy*, and it was no surprise that Stewart should have provided an extensive appendix in his book on the true story of the Highland bandit, information he may well have shared with Scott.

If Stewart provided the factual backdrop for a celebration of the Highlander, it was Scott who created the imaginative landscape for Highland adventures. Born in Edinburgh in 1771, the son of a solicitor, Scott studied law but had early literary ambitions. At the age of fifteen, he met Robert Burns, the Ayrshire poet who had begun the process of turning the tales of the Highlands into a literature worthy of international attention. As a lawyer's clerk, Scott witnessed the bleak side of Highland life when he had to direct an eviction. In his mid-twenties he published a three-volume collection of Scottish ballads. With the profits from his legal work, he set up a printing press and published more of his poetry. When the press got into financial difficulties, he decided to write a novel and in 1814 produced *Waverley*, an adventure story set during the Jacobite rebellion of 1745. It was a huge success and he followed it with several more novels in historical Scottish settings, including *Rob Roy* in 1817.

A leading figure in Edinburgh society, it was Scott who organized a Waterloo public dinner to welcome back the officers of the Black Watch from their overseas service in March 1816. Scott and Stewart got on very well, sharing an interest in Scottish military history, and there is evidence to suggest that the original idea may well have been for Stewart to carry out the research for a factual Highlander book which Scott would actually write.

An early fan of Scott's novels was the Prince Regent, later King George IV, and he arranged a private meeting with the author. Scott successfully filled the Prince's mind with all sorts of Highland fantasy, convincing him that he was the true heir to Bonnie Prince Charlie and should embrace the wearing of tartan. Throughout the late eighteenth century, the fashion for tartan had been somewhat daring and no doubt appealed to the dandy prince. Contemporary portraits of Bonnie Prince Charlie depicted him in a tartan patch outfit more akin to that worn by Harlequin – a pantomime character that delighted audiences with his cunning and subversion.[8]

In 1815 the Prince Regent accepted the post of President of the Highland Society of London. With Jacobitism safely in the past, it was an appointment symbolic of how far the former outlaws and rebels had come. They were now set to become part of the establishment.

*

When the Prince Regent became king in 1820, it was suggested that he visited Scotland. By then, Scott had been knighted by the king and was invited to organize the reception for him in Edinburgh. The royal visit was arranged for August 1822 and Scott turned to Colonel Stewart, whose Highlander *Sketches* had just been published, to help him present a Highland pageant.

In order to look the part, the king ordered an extravagant Highland outfit from George Hunter & Co of Princes Street, Edinburgh, at a cost of £1,354 18s. The invoice survives and lists every rich detail of the Highland fantasy costume, including a goatskin sporran lined with silk, decorated with Scottish gems and tassels of gold thread, and a sword-belt with a buckle sporting the figure of Saint Andrew in gold against a saltire of garnets. His dirk – once an item banned by the Hanoverians – had an emerald mounted on the hilt, and the blade of his broadsword of polished steel was inlaid with gold. Over all he wore a belted plaid of flaming Royal Stewart Tartan.[9] The king was not in great health, however, and in order to keep himself warm, he was provided with a pair of flesh-coloured tights to wear beneath his kilt.

The strong Highland element to the 'King's Jaunt', as Scott called it, was thanks to the influence of the Royal Celtic Society set up in Edinburgh by Colonel Stewart with Sir Walter Scott as its president. With a membership of about a hundred Edinburgh professionals and a few true Highlanders, it was dedicated to 'reviving the national costume of the mountains' and was given a key role in the events of 1822.

In preparation for the royal visit, Sir Walter Scott and Colonel David Stewart led a civic ceremony in which they presented colours to members of the Celtic Society. Dressed in Highland garb, the members were to act as an escort for the royal regalia of Scotland, consisting of a crown, sceptre and sword of state. 'The duty of guarding the ancient emblems of the independence of this kingdom has devolved upon you,' said Scott, with great solemnity, 'and should the hour of real danger arrive, I have no doubt that you will do credit to the lineage from which you are sprung, and stand forward in the foremost ranks of danger for the rights and liberties of your country.'

The Times ran verses of poetry by Sir Walter in celebration of the visit, but not even Scott could resist slipping in a carping reference to the Disarming Act.

> But yonder come my canty Celts,
> With dirk and pistol at their belts,
> Thank God, we've still some plaids and kilts –
> Carle, now the King's come![10]

Two days before the visit, an English journalist in Edinburgh was charmed by the festivities held on the king's birthday, but could not completely ignore past enmities.

> The appearance of the principal streets this day is extremely picturesque from the bodies of Highlanders who promenade the town, playing national airs, with their favourite instrument the bagpipes. The shrill and discordant notes of this instrument seem to give the utmost animation to their movements, and the various hues of the Tartan dresses, while they distinguish the different

clans, give a pleasing variety to the appearance of this martial costume ... It is a peace-giving occasion, and these Highland warriors are generous in forgetting the past.[11]

The fortnight-long royal visit was partly in aid of making the Scots feel good about themselves. It included the laying of the foundation stone of the National Monument, which was originally intended as a memorial to those Scots who died in the Napoleonic Wars and took the form of a Greek temple. That the visit was also very much about fostering a Highland fantasy that would fuel Scotland's tourist industry for centuries to come was proved when, at his last formal appearance, the king attended a showing of *Rob Roy* at the Theatre Royal. The boxes were filled with the rich and famous, including the war hero and defeater of Tipu Sultan, Sir David Baird. In this one evening, reality and myth were blended in a way that would serve the Highlander very well in the future.

King George IV's visit was a triumph for the Union. The previously unpopular monarch was cheered by thousands of Scots, establishing a link that would endure for two centuries. It was also the moment when Highlanders could stand tall, no longer regarded with suspicion by the British establishment but welcomed as a vital part of its machinery. All the accoutrements of the Highlander were worn with pride – even by the king in his pink tights – and it marked the beginning of a strong personal affection between the British monarchy and the Highlands. That Sir Walter Scott and Colonel David Stewart were at the heart of this successful public relations event cemented their roles as the leading publicists for the Highlander and his way of life.[12]

With the king's visit and the publication of his book, 1822 was the year of national acclaim for Colonel Stewart; but it did not put money into his bank account and he continued to struggle to maintain his family estate. In 1825 he was promoted to the rank of Major-General and, finally, three years later, he got the appointment he had been awaiting for so many years. He was given the governorship of St Lucia in his beloved Caribbean and sailed away from Scotland to study tropical birds. He would never return. In December 1829, having hosted a St Andrew's Night party in full Highland regalia, he caught a fever and died. Just under a century later, a Black Watch honour guard attended the unveiling of a statue to

Stewart carved in black granite at Keltneyburn, but, of course, his true monument is the *Sketches*, the first book to fully recognize the Highlander as a military phenomenon.

Sir Walter Scott's career had also reached its pinnacle with the king's visit and just three years later his publishing company ran out of money. Rather than declaring himself bankrupt, his put his house and future income into a trust for his creditors and kept on writing until he died in 1832. His best-selling books continued to pay off his debts after his death. An enormous rocket-like monument finished in 1846 commemorates Scott in Princes Street in the heart of Edinburgh.

*

The British royal love affair with the Highlands grew in intensity with the accession of Queen Victoria in 1837. She visited Scotland in 1842 and a few years later work began on her Scottish residence at Balmoral in Aberdeenshire. In 1845 Robert Ronald McIan dedicated his two-volume *Costumes of the Clans* to her Majesty; Queen Victoria and Prince Albert headed the list of the original subscribers to the book. Curiously, it was published to coincide with the anniversary of the 1745 rebellion and some of its most dynamic illustrations depict Jacobite rebels, but clearly this was all thought to be long in the past and of no offence to the Queen.

The text of *Costumes of the Clans* was written by James Logan, a one-time secretary of the Highland Society of London. In 1831 he had written *Scottish Gael*, a study of Highland lore, and presented the book to Victoria's royal predecessor, William IV, while wearing full Highland dress. The Scottish artist McIan began his life as an actor in Bristol and Bath, performing in stage versions of *Rob Roy*. In his early thirties he turned to painting and had one of his dramatic works accepted by the Royal Academy. Following in the wake of Sir Walter Scott's literary achievements, many artists of this period turned to painting scenes from Scotland's past, especially those depicting Jacobites. So successful was McIan in meeting this demand for romantic images of the Highlands that he gave up acting to concentrate on art.

Both McIan and Logan were known as hard drinkers, but the writer let it get out of hand and was expelled from his charitable residence at Charterhouse in the City of London. McIan was more moderate, being mainly criticized for an excessive enthusiasm for singing Scottish songs. In preparation for his famous book, McIan visited many Highland locations, making sketches and collecting reference material. The book was a hit and helped fuel the popular craze for tartans and their association with particular clans. This process of identification – and invention – had already begun with the research carried out by Colonel Stewart and the Highland Society of London, but the beautiful paintings of clansmen in McIan's book added tremendously to the popularity of tartan as both a costume and a decoration for Victorian interiors.

Another Highlander, John Ban Mackenzie, caught the eye of Queen Victoria thanks to his expert bagpipe playing, but refused her invitation to take royal service. She then asked him to find another piper of similar good looks and talent. Cheekily, he replied this would be impossible, but he could recommend another Highlander of some musical skill – Angus MacKay. Born in Raasay, MacKay was just thirteen years old when he won a prize for writing bagpipe music. In 1835 he won a gold medal in a piping competition in Edinburgh and three years later he published *A Collection of Highland Pipe Music*, which he dedicated to the Highland Society of London. It included his own composition of music dedicated to the memory of the battle of Waterloo. Recent research suggests that it was during this period that the form of Scottish bagpipe used today was invented, being a more sophisticated version of earlier pipes.[13] It is certainly thanks to music scholars such as MacKay that it became a much loved instrument in Victorian Britain.

MacKay became the first personal Piper to the Sovereign in 1843. He played for her regularly after breakfast and at balls and on special occasions. In 1852 he played to celebrate the building of a cairn to commemorate Victoria's purchase of her Balmoral estate. He continued in royal service until 1854, when his role was taken over by William Ross from the Black Watch. The position still exists today and is awarded to a serving soldier and Pipe Major. Sadly, MacKay lost his job because he suffered from mental problems and was confined to Crichton Royal Asylum. He escaped and then accidentally drowned in the river Nith in Dumfries and Galloway. 'He was not simply a performer,' noted the *Edinburgh Courant*, 'but he was a composer of singular ability, and his style of execution so superior that even the ears of Her Majesty were pleased with an instrument which in less able hands would have been discordant.'[14]

*

Royal patronage and popular acclaim had a decisive impact on the appearance of the Highlander in the British Army. Whereas during the Napoleonic Wars most of the Highland regiments had their traditional clothing substituted for the ordinary trousered uniform of a foot regiment, this changed in the 1820s. In that decade, five Highland regiments wore kilts – the 42nd, 78th, 79th, 92nd and 93rd – while the 71st and 72nd wore tartan trews. The 93rd Sutherlands wore the Government tartan, while the 78th Ross-shires wore a version of it overlaid with white and red stripes and the 92nd Gordons had yellow stripes. The 42nd Black Watch wore a darker shade of the Government tartan to live up to their name, but the 79th Camerons had their own distinct Erracht sett.

The proud elaboration of Highland dress extended to the feather bonnet, which grew in height. This was a strange piece of headgear that evolved from the simple blue beret-like cap with a diced band worn by Highland regiments in North America. It has been argued that these soldiers were influenced by the American Indian tribesmen they fought against.[15] They copied their impressive head-dresses by adding feathers to the sides of their bonnets. These few feathers developed into the mass of plumes attached to a wire frame over a bonnet worn by Highlanders in the Napoleonic Wars. Far from being an awkward piece of headgear, the feather bonnet was claimed to be cool in a hot climate and saved many Highlanders' lives by providing a substantial cushion against any sword blow to the skull, while its height provided a false target for enemy riflemen aiming at their heads. The bonnets were later adorned with ostrich feathers.

The sporran, not worn during the Napoleonic Wars, also enjoyed this post-1822 process of elaboration, evolving from a simple leather purse into a goatskin-covered ornament hung with silver bells and tassels. Ornate dirks and cairngorm shoulder brooches, once only worn by women, added to the fancy outfit. Later, in 1855, when tunics were introduced for regular foot soldiers, Highlanders wore a short doublet with four flaps, known as the Inverness skirt, which, again, distinguished them from other redcoats.

Chapter 8
The Thin Red Streak

Lieutenant FG Currie of the 79th Highlanders sailed through the Dardanelles on the way to the Crimea on 24 May 1854. He was on watch on deck about 6.30 a.m. when the band of the Camerons decided to wake up the local Turks with a rousing rendition of *Highland Laddie*. As the troopship passed through the sun-drenched land, Currie mused in a letter home about former heroes of the ancient world, such as Aeneas and Hector, who had fought across the same ground.

The next day, the engines of the steam ship gave out before they reached the British camp at Gallipoli. She dropped anchor, and Currie along with a group of Cameron Highlanders visited a small town called Pranchi. They went ashore mob-handed, carrying their bagpipes, and headed for an open-air terrace café, where the local inhabitants languidly puffed on long *chibouks* and drank coffee out of small cups. The Highlanders shattered the calm by playing their pipes and dancing a reel on the stage where the Turks sat cross-legged and bemused. 'None of us could speak Turkish, and none of them could understand French or English,' noted Currie. 'The men are very good looking, but not the women; there were a great many children, and pigs and dogs all about the place.'[1]

The 79th Camerons were part of the Highland Brigade commanded by Sir Colin Campbell and dispatched to the Crimea to fight alongside the French and the Turks against the Russians. It was a campaign intended to limit the expansion of the Russian Empire in Eastern Europe and the Black Sea region. The rest of the

Highland Brigade consisted of the 42nd Black Watch and the 93rd Highlanders, officially renamed Sutherland Highlanders in 1861. They were part of the 1st Division commanded by the Duke of Cambridge, one of five divisions that formed an army of just over 21,000 British troops. It was a small contribution to the alliance compared to the French, who fielded three times as many men at the beginning of the conflict.

Private William Nairn had enlisted in the 93rd Highlanders at Edinburgh in 1848. He was just seventeen years old and had marched 112 miles from Aberdeen to Balmoral to be presented before Queen Victoria. When the Crimean War broke out, he joined his regiment sailing from Plymouth to Gallipoli, taking just seven days and three hours to get as far as Malta. At Gallipoli, they disembarked with the other Highland regiments to dig seven miles of entrenchments and fortifications around their base. The next stop was Constantinople, capital of the Ottoman Turkish Empire. There, they occupied Turkish barracks, but these were so overrun by rats that they had to remove themselves to an encampment 'where the dogs turned out to be more plentiful than the vermin in the barracks'.

> We remained at Constantinople until reviewed by the great Sultan, who to my ideas resembled a barber's apprentice, being so puny. The Sultan's wives thought the English soldiers very nice only they lacked beards.[2]

The allied force finally landed on the Crimean Peninsula in September 1854. With no harbour available to them, the troops swarmed ashore on to an open beach thirty miles north of Sevastopol. On the second day of the landing, the clouds darkened and the Highland Brigade was soaked by a heavy downpour. They barely had time to get their clothes dry when they were ordered to advance on the enemy; their mission was the destruction of the Russian naval base at Sevastopol. The Russians drew their line of defence behind the river Alma on the ridge of a hill overlooking the coastline.

The Highlanders were on the extreme left of the allied position and were given the task of taking the Russian fieldworks beyond the river Alma on top of the hill. The 42nd Black Watch was on the right flank of the brigade, the 93rd in the centre, and the 79th

Camerons on the left. When Lieutenant Currie got his orders to advance, the 79th were lying down with shells and round shot landing around them. They marched through a vineyard. Russian cannon balls crashed among them all the time, skidding across the slick earth. The Camerons waded into the river up to their waists, re-formed their line on the far side and resumed their steady advance on the enemy 'under a very hot fire'.[3]

Sergeant Edward McSally of the 42nd Black Watch remembered the advance a little differently, with a faltering start. The sixty-one-year-old brigade commander Sir Colin Campbell rode to the front of his men and shouted, 'Come on Forty-Second'. But no one moved. Campbell then took off his hat and waved it, repeating his command. 'The first few paces were taken rather unsteadily,' explained McSally. 'We had never previously stepped off at the Brigadier's command, and waited for the Colonel giving the word, but he did not do so.' Sir Colin vigorously pointed forward so the Black Watch finally got the message, but others not hearing his words or seeing his urgent gestures 'were late in stepping off'.[4]

The moment of confusion passed, the Black Watch regained a unified pace and advanced steadily through the vineyard and across the river. Although coming constantly under artillery fire, McSally noted the loss of only three men in the ranks around him. The Highlanders now advanced up the slope towards the Russian fieldworks and moved through the British Light Division. 'It was with a feeling of pride we passed through them,' said McSally, 'and found that no body of British troops was interposed between us and the enemy.' They were then given orders to fix bayonets.

One nervous young Highlander dropped his bayonet and ran back to get it. The Lieutenant-Colonel of the regiment thought he had lost his nerve and shouted out to his soldiers, 'Shoot that man, shoot the coward.' They were about to level their guns when the young lad picked up the bayonet and hastily rejoined his mates. 'I wasna' runnin' awa' sir,' he told the Colonel.

A body of Russians then appeared on the right flank of the Highlanders, having been hidden by a hollow in the hill. They had been broken by the fire of the Coldstream Guards and were falling back, but were still a deadly threat. The 42nd took the opportunity to open fire on them, but the Russians stood for a moment to trade volleys and inflicted the worst casualties so far on McSally's Black Watch.

> As our advance continued with its original rapidity we were closing fast on them when their determination to resist so sternly seemed at last to give way, and no wonder. More than half their number were killed or wounded ... some, whom a panic fear seemed to overcome, cast off their accoutrements and knapsacks, dropped their muskets and ran off up the hill as fast as they could.[5]

Some of the Russian wounded fell down holding their guns and fired at the redcoats as they passed by. Word of this quickly spread along the line and the Highlanders took their weapons from them, threatening to smash out their brains if they didn't hand them over. Cheers of victory echoed along the British regiments. The Guards had taken the Great Redoubt in the centre of the Russian position and the Highlanders almost broke into a run to reach the top of the hill.

Lieutenant Currie of the 79th Camerons survived the advance up the slope and enjoyed the spectacle of victory. 'When we got near the top,' he recalled, 'the Russians thought better of it and went down the hill on the opposite side – best Derby – we then opened fire with our rifles and killed numbers of them as they went along the valley in close column, and the Horse Artillery coming up on our left, made some very good practice.'[6]

Private Nairn of the 93rd estimated that the battle lasted the best part of three and a half hours. 'During the last hour of the fighting,' he said, 'I was wounded by a bullet in the left thigh, but did not quit the ranks.'[7] MacSally noted that the teenage boys in their regimental band bravely exposed themselves to enemy fire to quickly remove the wounded from the battlefield.

After the fighting had ended, the Divisional commander, the Duke of Cambridge, rode over to the 42nd to congratulate them on their part in the battle. 'Well done 42nd,' he said, 'you are a lot of bricks!' This was a nickname that stuck with the Black Watch for the rest of the campaign. The Duke received a hearty cheer since the Highlanders appreciated his constant concern for their welfare, but the biggest cheer was reserved for their supreme commander, Lord Raglan. He rode up to shake hands with Sir Colin Campbell.

'I left you on the plain Sir Colin,' he said, 'and I could not believe my eyes when I saw you riding up the hill followed by your gallant Brigade – yours was a decisive movement.'

'Gentlemen,' replied Campbell, 'I have known the Commander-in-Chief a long time. In fact ever since I was a boy he has been kind to me. I trust he will do me one kindness more.'

Raglan nodded his assent.

'I trust that henceforth he will give me leave to wear a Highland Bonnet.'[8]

The Highlanders crowded around the two men, threw their feather bonnets up in the air and shouted 'Scotland for ever'. One Irishman among them joined in and shouted 'Ireland for longer', making everyone laugh. In addition to wearing the feather bonnet, Campbell had a hackle made for it combining the red worn by the 42nd with the white of the 79th and 93rd.

The soldiers spent the night camped out near the battlefield. They ate a supper of beef with an extra ration of biscuits to make up for those that had been soaked in crossing the Alma. They took off their wet clothes and put on dry ones. The next day was taken up with tending the wounded and collecting Russian prisoners. Some of them feared they were going to be shot and begged for mercy. 'If a battle is an exciting thing,' wrote Currie, 'nothing is more melancholy than the day after one.' For miles around the dead and dying were piled in heaps. At one of the Russian forts, the bodies were four deep – Russian and British soldiers side by side.

*

Sir Colin Campbell was renowned for his bad temper, but he emerged as one of the great Highland heroes of the Victorian era. 'He was supposed to have been an unfortunate, friendless officer,' observed *The Times*, 'who, in spite of his gallantry and merits, ate out his heart in disappointment because he had neither money nor aristocratic connexions.'[9] He certainly came from a humble background. His grandfather was laird of Ardnaves in Islay, but chose the losing side in the '45 and lost his estates. He settled in Glasgow, where his son became a carpenter.

Colin was born in Glasgow in 1792 and the real name of his father was Macliver, but his mother's brother, Colonel John Campbell, took charge of his education from the age of ten. Five years later, his uncle presented him to the Duke of York in London, who murmured 'another of the clan'. From that day on, Colin adopted his uncle's name of Campbell and received a commission as an ensign in the 9th Regiment (East Norfolks).

At the age of just sixteen, Campbell joined the Duke of Wellington's army in the Peninsular War, fighting at Rolica and Vimeiro. He took part in the dismal retreat to Corunna, marching in bare feet when the soles of his boots wore away. Safely on board ship after the long and tortuous march, he found that the remaining leather of his boots had adhered to the skin of his legs and had to be painfully cut away in strips.[10]

Campbell contracted malaria during the Walcheren campaign in the Netherlands, which dogged him throughout his life, and, back in Spain, was wounded twice in the thigh leading a forlorn hope at the siege of San Sebastian. His bravery was never in doubt and, after the Napoleonic Wars, he rose steadily to become Lieutenant-Colonel of the 9th in 1835. He sailed all round the world with the British Army, serving in Nova Scotia, Gibraltar, Barbados, British Guiana, Hong Kong and India. He was a senior commander during the Second Sikh War and led expeditions against Pathan tribesmen on the North-West Frontier. He was now in his late fifties and should have been thinking about retirement, yet his most famous moments were still ahead of him. He received a knighthood in 1849.

Having turned sixty, Campbell was promoted to Major-General and put in charge of the Highland Brigade in the Crimean War. At Alma, he distinguished himself by his fearless leadership, having one horse shot from beneath him as he led his Highlanders up the hill towards the Russian positions – a scene later commemorated in a famous painting by Edinburgh artist Robert Gibb, *Forward the 42nd*. But this was a minor event compared to the Victorian legend that was about to unfold a month later at the battle of Balaklava.

*

A month after Alma, the allied forces laid siege to the Russian naval base at Sevastopol. A quick assault would have been preferable, but the British dug in and bombarded the harbour from their trenches. Days of artillery fire followed, and it bothered Lieutenant Currie of the 79th that they were indiscriminately killing men, women and children in the Russian port. 'I hope they will look sharp and finish,' he wrote in a letter to his family, 'I am tired of this work, my insides being all wrong. I am also rather rheumatic, which sleeping out of doors does not improve.'[11]

Illness spread among the Highlanders in their damp, cold trenches and they ached for some action. Good-quality food was hard to come by. 'We thought we had got some oatmeal to make stir-about,' remembered Private Nairn, 'but it turned out to be Russian rusk, which made bread as black as your boot.'

Early on the morning of 25 October 1854, the Russians decided to take the battle to the allies and a relief army advanced from the north towards the British base at Balaklava. The attack caught the British off guard and they had to react quickly to prevent a major breakthrough. Sir Colin Campbell observed a large force of Russian cavalry riding towards Balaklava and roused his 93rd Highlanders and some Turks to meet them on the plain before their base. They had been sheltering from Russian artillery fire behind a hill, but Campbell ordered them to stand firm in front of the Russian attack. 'Remember,' said Campbell, 'there is no retreat from here men. You must die where we stand!'[12]

Seeing several hundred Russian Hussars charging towards them, the Turks begged to differ and ran away. British artillery was brought to bear on the Russian cavalry but still they kept coming. Sir Colin Campbell hastily formed the 93rd into a single line two ranks deep. Private William Nairn stood anxiously in the ranks and was told by his commander not to fire a single shot 'until the enemy were within 175 yards'.[13] Private George Greig was another of the Sutherland Highlanders facing the Russian horsemen and he remembered an earlier volley. 'The first volley fired by the 93rd Sutherland Highlanders was at about 800 yards,' he said, 'but the Russian charge exhibited no check or wavering.' On came the main body of imperial cavalry, the ground trembling beneath them. When they were within 200 yards, the front rank of the 93rd Sutherland Highlanders knelt and both ranks gave them a volley from their Minie rifles, 'which made them pull up in confusion for they never completed their charge'.[14]

It was a formidable display of courage and firepower, but, most importantly for the history of the 93rd, this moment was witnessed by the pioneering war journalist William Russell, correspondent of

The Times. His thrilling report immortalized the scene as the Russian cavalry charged down on Campbell's 93rd.

> The ground flew beneath their horses' feet; gathering speed at every stride, they dashed on towards that thin red streak tipped with a line of steel.

It was that description of the resolute Highlanders that would become the Thin Red Line of legend. Russell described what happened next:

> With breathless suspense every one awaited the bursting of the wave upon the line of Gaelic rock; but ere they came within two hundred and fifty yards, another deadly volley flashed from the levelled rifles and carried terror among the Russians. They wheeled about, opened files right and left and fled faster than they came. 'Bravo, Highlanders! Well done!' shouted the excited spectators.[15]

When the smoke cleared, the Scots Greys, Inniskilling Dragoons and 4th and 5th Dragoon Guards cleared the remaining Russians from the plain. Greig, Nairn and their fellow Highlanders cheered the British Heavy Brigade cavalry as they charged the Russian horsemen to complete the British victory.

An English historian has recently called the stand of the 93rd during the battle of Balaklava 'one of the most insignificant skirmishes in British military history',[16] but thanks to William Russell's newspaper report and a subsequent painting of the event by Robert Gibb, it has become one of the most celebrated moments of the Crimean War, ranking alongside the calamitous Charge of the Light Brigade as a demonstration of British courage in the face of overwhelming odds. If Campbell had formed the 93rd into four ranks or a square, as he should have done to face a cavalry attack, it might not have resounded so much with the British public. It was the fragility of that thin red line that so impressed them, proving the intrinsic superiority of the Victorian redcoat over his enemies. 'No,' said Campbell, as reported by Russell, 'I did not think it worth while to form them even four deep!'

Interestingly, the stand of the 93rd did not feature in

contemporary popular images of the war, which focused on the more significant cavalry action at the battle of Balaklava. It was not until Robert Gibb's painting, *The Thin Red Line*, appeared in 1881, over a quarter of a century later, that the incident became a Victorian icon. Gibb's painting was one of a trilogy of images depicting the Crimean War, including the battles of Alma and Inkerman. Such paintings were commercial enterprises designed to be turned into popular prints that sold widely. Gibb claimed to have been inspired by reading accounts of Balaklava and Alma in Alexander Kinglake's *The Invasion of the Crimea* published in 1863, which drew on Russell's reporting.

The art critic of *The Times* understood the significance of the painting immediately when it first appeared on exhibition at the Royal Scottish Academy. 'Those [soldiers] in the foreground,' he wrote, 'are at the "ready" and are holding their fire in obedience to the word of their officer at their head, whose attitude, with his left hand raised, bespeaks at once confidence and caution ... Taking all in all the picture is a notable delineation of heroism, and appeals strongly and legitimately to the national sentiment.'[17] It still does. Gibb's *The Thin Red Line* now hangs in the Regimental Museum of the Argyll and Sutherland Highlanders in Stirling Castle.

The phrase quickly entered popular speech and was used to good effect in a House of Commons debate on 28 June 1883. Sir Walter Barttelot challenged the suggestion of clothing British soldiers in khaki or 'rabbit colour', as he called it, by saying 'We all knew what the "thin red line" had done in every quarter of the globe.'[18] Rudyard Kipling played with the phrase in his sardonic ballad *Tommy* of 1892 about the British soldier being unwanted in peace but cheered in times of war.

> Then it's Tommy this, an' Tommy that, an'
> 'Tommy, 'ow's yer soul?'
> But it's 'Thin red line of 'eroes' when the
> drums begin to roll.

*

Success at Balaklava kept the Russians away from their besieged naval base, but did little to resolve the campaign. The weather worsened and there was a lack of fresh supplies. Lieutenant Currie's mood darkened as he looked down on the remains of battle.

> The valley below is covered with dead horses and men, and the vultures and dogs make a great noise. The day after the action I only saw one vulture, but today I counted twenty-eight, not a very pleasant sight, but like everything else, you get used to it.

The winter was closing in. Standing around in the bitter cold on guard duty did little to help the soldiers shake off coughs and colds. 'I have been rather seedy,' grumbled Currie. 'We are just in the same state as we landed, no clothes but those we have on our backs, I managed to buy a shirt for which I gave £1, value 5 [shillings].'[19] Civilian traders were not slow to exploit the shortages in the army.

Captain Thomas Henry Montgomery of the 42nd Black Watch considered himself pretty comfortably off, but wrote in a letter of 7 November that 'you must know I have had nothing on but my kilt since I landed'. He was looking forward to the arrival of more ships with 'wine, preserved meats, and everything that one can want',[20] but this was not to be. A ferocious storm was about to wreck the allied supply fleet and make life even more miserable for the Highland Brigade.

Private William Duguid of the 93rd had had a tough life back in Scotland. At the age of nine, he had been apprenticed as a boot-maker to his uncle in Aberdeen, who beat him. He tried to escape with a friend by making a raft and floating away in Aberdeen, harbour but was caught and beaten again. At the age of seventeen, he joined the army for a better life, but two years later found himself in an even bleaker situation in the Crimea. 'November 11th we had the severest storm of wind and rain I ever saw,' he wrote, 'all the tents of the whole Army were blown down and all the ships in the harbour ... our pay and clothing was [all] lost so that we got no clothes and very little money for a whiles ...'[21] By December the weather had deteroriated and 'the whole Army [is] in starvation for want of clothes and bad food'. In February came heavy snow and Duguid and his comrades suffered from frostbite – 'our moustaches and beards were frozen together'.

The deprivations suffered by the British Army during the

Crimean winter of 1854–55 became the theme of William Russell's newspaper reports. Initially thrilled by victories at Alma and Balaklava, the British public grew angry at the logistical failures that left their soldiers hungry and ill. Their discontent forced the downfall of the government as they demanded better care for the troops. Florence Nightingale established a vastly improved military hospital service, and a railway was built from Balaklava to supply front-line soldiers. But this could not prevent a calamitous fall in the number of combat-fit soldiers to just 12,000 in February 1855.

New troops arrived from Britain in the summer and Private George Conn of the 79th Highlanders was one of them. Born at South Cranna in Banffshire, he enlisted at Edinburgh in November 1854, part of a wave of recruits excited by accounts of Alma and Balaklava. His company set sail in March 1855 and arrived in the Crimea in May. He was just in time for a new offensive against the Russian defences at Sevastopol. The attacks focused on two strong points called the Malakoff and the Redan. On 18 June the British took part in a night assault on the Redan but they were caught in a crossfire of Russian guns and suffered heavy casualties. After this failure, they settled down to yet more pounding of the Russian defences with their artillery.

In early August Private Conn and the 79th were caught in a bitter skirmish when Russian soldiers from Sevastopol launched a night raid on their trenches. 'It was a very dark and rainy night,' wrote Conn to his uncle, 'and the Sentries had not seen them advancing until they were on top of them.' Some of the British fell back, but the Highlanders were joined by the Royal Irish.

> When that became known to the Highlanders they with one shout or rather a yell rushed upon the astonished Russians and the clatter of bayonet to bayonet became furious. The Russians wheeled about to retire but they soon found themselves between Highlanders and wild Irishmen which was the worst position they were ever in. [22]

The 79th took 115 prisoners, but had to spend the rest of the night in the trench with 250 dead and wounded Russians.

Having survived this fight, Conn and the 79th were told to prepare themselves for a major assault on Sevastopol. The

Highland Brigade, led by Sir Colin Campbell, had volunteered to be the forlorn hope in an attack on the Russian lines. For Conn, this action would never come. A corporal of the 79th wrote to his sister just seven days after Conn had sent his last letter home. 'I have to acquaint you with the sad tidings of the death of your dear brother,' he wrote, 'he was killed on the spot by the fragments of a shell bursting in one of the trenches yesterday forenoon.'

The stalemate finally ended on 8 September 1855. In an operation that resembled one from the First World War, a three-day bombardment of the enemy positions was followed by a synchronized assault out of the allied trenches towards the Malakoff and the Redan. The French took their target, but the British were not so fortunate. Currie followed his Highlanders along the trenches, ready to follow up the initial attack. At a given signal, two English Divisions scrambled out of their trenches towards the Redan, but the attack was badly planned and they were repulsed, with at least a hundred officers recorded among the many fallen.

Sir Colin Campbell prepared his Highland Brigade for an attack the next morning, but when the time came, soldiers collecting the British wounded reported a strange silence from within the Redan. This was followed by a series of tremendous explosions echoing across the bay as the Russians blew up their own defences. They had had enough. So had Currie. 'Sooner than go through another siege,' he wrote, 'I should leave the army and throw up that most valuable commission, and the enormous pay of 6/6 *per diem*.'

The Russians evacuated Sevastopol and the allies streamed in to see the city they had fought so long and hard for. Walking among ruined buildings with shell-holed walls blackened by smoke, Currie was horrified by what he saw: 'You go into a room in which you find about 400 dead men, some in coffins, and others just dead, in most awful attitudes.'[23] The allies had won the Crimean War and quelled the threat of Russian expansion in the Near East, but it had been a costly campaign. More soldiers were incapacitated by illness than by wounds and the British military administration had failed in the face of severe weather conditions.

The Highland Brigade stayed in the Crimea until February 1856 when the whole army was reviewed by its commanders. Over the next four months the soldiers slowly returned home. Privates Greig and Nairn of the 93rd survived to tell their family and friends about their part in the Thin Red Line. Lieutenant Currie endured a second Russian winter by dreaming of a comfortable posting in India. Sir Colin Campbell was less than happy.

After his sterling performance at Balaklava, Campbell had been given command of the 1st Division. When Lord Raglan died, his commander-in-chief, he hoped to receive the ultimate accolade, but political wrangling within the army and the government denied him this role and it went to a more junior figure. Furiously, Campbell returned to England, but he was convinced by Queen Victoria to continue his service to Her Majesty, even though he was reduced to the rank of colonel. In June 1856, he was promoted to Lieutenant-General. He must have thought this marked the apex of his career, but in just over a year, the grumpy sixty-five-year-old was back on the front line as commander-in-chief in India. His prized Highlanders would be at his side once more and this time they would prove their worth by winning an unprecedented number of medals for valour.

Chapter 9
Six VCs in One Day

When Lieutenant William McBean of the 93rd Highlanders arrived in the Crimea, he feared he was too late to take part in the fighting. He had been left behind at Varna for a good part of the campaign to look after the baggage animals. He had never faced the enemy. But he did have an opportunity to prove his mettle when he stepped forward to settle a fight between Turkish and French troops. The Sultan was so impressed by his fearless behaviour that he awarded him the Order of Medjidie 3rd Class. It was a source of pride, but McBean hungered for more.

Eventually, the thirty-six-year-old lieutenant joined the assault forces in September 1855 and was so keen to get stuck in to the enemy that he volunteered along with ten other Highlanders to creep up towards the Russian defences at the Redan, prior to the main attack. McBean suspected something was wrong as the volunteers entered the fieldworks, finding only dead and wounded. The Russians had left before McBean could get to grips with them. It was all very frustrating for a man of action. But this would change with McBean's next posting – India 1858. There, he would get more than enough front-line combat.

The Indian Mutiny had broken out in May 1857. Up until that moment, Britain's dominance over India was maintained by the East India Company, with armed forces composed mainly of native troops, sepoys. The British Army had only a few regular units posted there. Unrest between the sepoys and their British commanders had been simmering for some time but the spark that set off the Mutiny was provided by the introduction of a new rifle cartridge. The rumour took off that this was greased with animal fat, incorporating that of cows, sacred to Hindus, and pigs, unclean to Muslims. As the paper cartridge had to be bitten before loading, this proved offensive to the native soldiers.

Some British officers understood the reluctance of their men but others would not tolerate any refusal to use the cartridge, declared the sepoys mutineers and imprisoned them. At Meerut, the mutineers broke out and massacred any European officers and their families they could find. Political agitators seized on the Mutiny to encourage a general uprising against British rule and the fighting spread to Delhi and other cities where more European men, women and children were butchered. At Cawnpore, over two hundred European non-combatants were guaranteed safe passage by the rebels but then cruelly murdered. It was this savagery directed against women and children that enraged the British and determined their merciless response to the Mutiny.

Colour Sergeant George Wells of the 79th Cameron Highlanders was part of the force sent from Britain to restore order. His ship set sail in August 1857 and by the time he arrived in India, the original events were past, but he attended the site of the massacre in Cawnpore.

> I visited the place where the blood thirsty wretches committed such vile and cruel deeds upon our poor and unfortunate women. The house where they were committed has since [been] levelled to the ground and there was a tree that grew close by this house [where] they were in the habit of tying the women and cutting off their breasts. There is also a well close by where the sepoys threw them down after they tortured them in every conceivable shape they could think of.[1]

The women prisoners were not in fact tortured as Wells says, but they and their children were slaughtered by rebel swordsmen, who hacked away at them, dismembered their bodies and threw them down the well.[2] The horror of those dreadful moments resonated throughout the British forces.

*

Sir Colin Campbell was at home in Britain on 11 July 1857 when he received the call from the Prime Minister Lord Palmerston to head the British Army in India, following the death of his predecessor during the early months of the Mutiny. He was asked how soon he could leave for India. 'Within twenty-four hours,' he replied. Just over a month later, he landed in Calcutta and began assembling his forces. Among the troops newly arrived from Britain were the 93rd Highlanders, Campbell's Thin Red Liners. They greeted each other like old friends, with the 93rd wildly cheering their old commander.

At the time, the 93rd were characterized as the most Highland of all the Scots regiments with 70 per cent of them speaking Gaelic. They were also the most religious of the Highland regiments with a minister and six elders selected from the ranks. Those other Crimean Highland veterans, the 79th, would join Campbell later in the year.

Campbell's first move was to march into the kingdom of Oudh and come to the relief of the British garrison besieged at its capital city of Lucknow, stoutly defended by Highlanders of the 78th. On the way, Campbell and the 93rd also visited Cawnpore and witnessed the site of the massacre of the women and children – the bloody handprints of desperate children could still be seen on the walls. Campbell's army numbered about 5,000 troops with the addition of numerous loyal Indian warriors, including the aggressive Punjabis.

The 93rd included volunteers from other Highland regiments and one of these was acquiring a strange reputation. James Wallace had come from the 72nd Highlanders. It was noted that he neither wrote nor received any letters and was so taciturn in his manner that he was dubbed Quaker Wallace. In fact he was highly educated and could translate any Latin quotations shown to him. At night, he was heard to recite French poetry to himself. It was suggested that because of his evident education he should be promoted, but he resolutely refused, saying that he had joined the 93rd for one purpose only and when that was accomplished he was happy to die. As the Highlanders marched towards Lucknow, many of them said they would give up a day's drink just to see the mysterious Quaker Wallace under fire.

Early on the morning of 16 November, as Campbell and his Highlanders readied themselves for their attack on the

Sikanderbagh, a fortified palace just outside Lucknow, Dr William Munro, surgeon to the 93rd, had a quiet conversation with one of his Highlanders. Captain John Lumsden was an officer in the East India Company army but had joined the 93rd for the expedition against Lucknow. 'That is the last sunrise that many will see,' he told Munro, 'and God knows to which of us three standing by this fire it may be the last.' Lumsden was a large, powerful man in perfect health, but there was 'at the moment he spoke an expression of sadness, perhaps of anxious care, upon his face, for he had just returned hurriedly to India, having left his wife and bairns at home in Scotland'.[3] The dread feeling did little to discourage him from his path of duty, noted Munro, or to affect his courage when the time came to lead his men into action. But two hours later, Lumsden and another officer present at that meeting would lie dead in the bitter battle for Sikanderbagh.

The Mughal palace was heavily defended by the rebels and was the last major obstacle before the relief army could reach the beleaguered British garrison holding out in the Residency nearby. Inside the compound, soldiers of the 78th Highlanders were protecting the civilians, but doubted they could hang on for much longer.

One of the soldiers' wives, a Scotswoman called Jessie Brown, was sunk in a fever, but then she heard a distant sound that roused her. 'Dinna ye hear it?' she said to her friend. 'Ay, I'm no dreamin', it's the slogan o' the Highlanders! We're saved, we're saved!' Her friend had no idea what she was talking about. 'I felt utterly bewildered: my English ears heard only the roar of the artillery, and I thought my poor Jessie was still raving ...' But then Jessie sprang to her feet and cried out in a voice that could be heard by their Highland defenders, 'Will ye no believe it noo?'

> That shrill, penetrating, ceaseless sound, which rose above all other sounds, could come neither from the advance of the enemy, nor from the work of the sappers. No, it was indeed the blast of the Scottish bagpipes, now shrill and harsh, as threatening vengeance on the foe, then in softer tones seeming to promise succour to their friends in need.[4]

It was the pipes of the 93rd Highlanders and they promised relief to those locked inside the Residency. The sweet droning sound assured them of survival and this heart-stirring account inspired a song called *Jessie's Dream* that became highly popular in music halls.

Two days earlier, Campbell had told his Highlanders that they faced a task greater than that in the Crimea. Not only did they have to deal with a rebel army trained and armed by the British, but they also had to rescue the men, women and children weakened by their ordeal in the Lucknow Residency.

'When we make an attack,' instructed Campbell, 'you must come to close quarters as quickly as possible; keep well together, and use the bayonet. Ninety-Third, you are my own lads! I rely on you to do the work!'

'Aye, aye, Sir Colin,' shouted a Highlander. 'We'll bring the women and children out of Lucknow or die with you in the attempt!'

Corporal William Mitchell of the 93rd witnessed this exchange and provided the most dramatic account of the following action on the 16th.[5] While Campbell let his artillery batter the walls of Sikanderbagh to create breaches for them to enter, he told his Highlanders to shelter behind a low mud wall. 'Lie down, Ninety-Third, lie down! Every man of you is worth his weight in gold in England today!'

One Highlander ignored his command and stood up, swearing at the enemy. He was one of the volunteers who had joined from the 72nd and was considered a bad lot. His name was Hope and his Captain bellowed at him to shut up, telling him that foul language was no sign of bravery.

Hope ignored him and carried on swearing, saying that the bullet was not yet moulded that would kill him. The Captain was just about to arrest him as drunk and disorderly in the face of the enemy, when Hope leapt on top of the mud wall. Right then, an enemy bullet struck him. Diverted by the buckle of his sporran, the bullet tore into his belly and his guts spilled. Two more shots struck him in the chest, killing him stone dead. At that moment, Quaker Wallace rushed over to where the dead man lay and stared intently into his face.

'The fool hath said in his heart, there is no God,' declared Wallace. 'Vengeance is mine, I will repay, saith the Lord. I came to the 93rd to see that man die!'

Wallace's mystery thus explained, the assault went ahead.

Punjabis led the race to the breaches in the wall, but when two of their British officers were shot down before them, they staggered to a halt. Campbell then turned to one of his senior officers and said: 'Bring on the tartan – let my own lads at them,' and nearly 800 Highlanders rose with one roar. Their eight pipers played *On with the Tartan* as they ran towards the weakened palace walls and threw themselves through the breaches against the defenders. Not caring if he died or not, Quaker Wallace burst into the palace, coolly reciting verses from the 116th Psalm as he lashed out at anyone before him: 'I love the Lord, because my voice and prayers He did hear …' Shooting and bayoneting any rebel who dared come near, it was said that Wallace killed at least twenty men that day and not one of them touched him.

Corporal Mitchell watched all his Highlanders fight with a fury he had not witnessed before.

> By the time the bayonet had done its work of retribution, the throats of our men were hoarse with shouting 'Cawnpore! You bloody murderers!' The taste of the powder (the muzzle-loading cartridges had to be bitten with the teeth) made men almost mad with thirst; and with the sun high over head, and being fresh from England, with our feather bonnets, red coats, and heavy kilts, we felt the heat intensely.[6]

As he climbed in through the breach, Mitchell was hit by a bullet at point-blank range. It struck his belt buckle and knocked him off his feet. His fellow officers rushed past him, thinking he was dead. Some of them had bought their own non-regulation broadswords, which performed better than the shorter army blades that broke easily. All the time, they encouraged their men by shouting 'Give 'em the bayonet!' A thrust into a rebel belly was called 'giving him a Cawnpore dinner'.

Campbell had instructed his Highlanders to fight in groups of three. The centre man of each group was to make the attack, while the other two defended him with their bayonets right and left. 'We were not to fire a single bullet after we got inside a position,' recalled Mitchell, 'unless we were certain of hitting our enemy, for fear of wounding our men.' But as the close-quarter fighting deteriorated into a brutal brawl, strict instructions were forgotten. The wire frame of the extravagant feather bonnet worn by the Highlanders proved surprisingly useful, saving lives by absorbing the blows of *tulwars* (sabres) aimed at their skulls. Other soldiers were saved by their greatcoats being rolled tightly across their chests, absorbing the impact of enemy bullets.

The 93rd pipers played throughout the desperate room-to-room struggle, following their soldiers as they advanced through the palace. 'I knew our boys would fight all the better when cheered by the bagpipes,' said Pipe Major John Macleod, 'with the national music to cheer them.'

The Punjabis were excited by the music too and later adopted the pipes. The ferocity of the Highlanders was matched by the Punjabi soldiers who followed them into the breach, plus Irishmen of the 53rd Light Infantry. No prisoners were taken and at the end of the battle over 2,000 rebels lay dead inside the Sikanderbagh. The 93rd lost two officers and twenty-three men dead, plus seven officers and sixty-one men wounded. Outside the palace, the Highlanders and the Irishmen of the 53rd lined up before Sir Colin Campbell to receive his thanks.

'This morning's work will strike terror into the sepoys,' he said. 'Ninety-Third, you have bravely done your share of this morning's work, and Cawnpore is avenged! There is more hard work to be done; but unless as a last resource, I will not call on you to storm more positions today.'

The soldiers lauded their leader, then a lone voice came from the ranks: 'Will we get a medal for this, Sir Colin?'

'Well, my lads, I can't say what Her Majesty's Government may do; but if you don't get a medal, all I can say is you have deserved one better than any other troops I have ever seen under fire.'[7]

In the event, the 93rd Highlanders were awarded six Victoria Crosses for that one savage day of fighting at Lucknow. Captain William Stewart and Lance Corporal John Dunlay were the first Highlanders to enter one of the breaches at Sikanderbagh. With a few men, Stewart led an attack on two rebel guns that were halting their advance and captured them. Colour Sergeant James Munro later rescued Captain Stewart when he was badly wounded and carried him to safety, subsequently being hurt himself. Private Peter Grant defended his colonel by killing five rebels with one of their own swords. Private David MacKay captured one of the rebel standards and was nominated for the award by his fellow soldiers. He was shortly afterwards severely wounded. Sergeant John Paton led his men into a breach under heavy fire. It had been a remarkably intense battle that had demanded the highest courage of all involved.

Victory at Sikanderbagh did not end the fighting at Lucknow and the 93rd Highlanders had to stir themselves for a final surge towards the Residency. Having safely evacuated the exhausted garrison of men, women and children, Campbell then had to make the difficult decision to withdraw before the numerically superior enemy, leaving only a token force behind. The city of Lucknow was surrounded by twelve miles of fortified walls and it was impossible for his small army to capture it. That task would come later – along with the chance for Lieutenant McBean to win the medal he missed at Sikanderbagh.

*

In March 1858 Sir Colin Campbell returned to Lucknow to deal with unfinished business. With him this time were all three Highland regiments that had performed so well in the Crimea – the 91st, the 79th Cameron Highlanders and the 42nd Black Watch. It was a much bigger army, including 164 artillery pieces, and Campbell was prepared to take the city itself. A few days before the assault, Sir Colin gathered his 93rd Highlanders together and read them a letter he had just received from the Duke of Cambridge. It said that as a consequence of the death of their regimental colonel the post had become vacant and had been awarded to Campbell. 'I know that it is the highest compliment that Her Majesty could pay to the Ninety-Third Highlanders,' declared the Duke, 'to see their dear old chief at their head.'[8]

The soldiers hurrahed their new colonel until they were hoarse. Not only was it an enormously popular appointment because Sir Colin had taken a special interest in the welfare of their regiment, ensuring always they were never needlessly exposed to danger, but also because he shared their day-to-day existence, camping out like a private soldier and eating the same rations.

Very early in the morning in the second week of March 1858, Campbell and his troops advanced through the suburbs of Lucknow, eliminating rebel strongholds along the way. Some of the sepoys hid themselves in the cellars of buildings and would emerge only when they thought the main force had passed. This caused the Highlanders a few casualties until they realized what was going on, and they hunted down every sniper. Campbell then brought up his siege guns and mortars to bombard the city.

Colour Sergeant George Wells of the 79th Cameron Highlanders was part of the initial advance on Lucknow. He was ordered to act as a picket, looking out for rebels. He hoped this meant he could lie down and get some rest.

> I was miserably mistaken for the flies were in millions and would not allow you to lie down during the day and what with the mosquitoes at night and the roar of the cannon it was next to impossible to have 40 winks ...[9]

He gave up and took to the roof of a bungalow where he watched British mortar shells dropping on a palace inside the city. The rebels returned fire and one shell plunged over the bungalow to set fire to houses behind it. Wells and his men got a rest the next day, but after that they were told to assemble for the news that the final assault on the city was imminent.

Their target was an iron bridge across the river Gumti. When his Captain asked Wells if he had made out his will before leaving the camp, he said he had no fear for his own life but believed that many Highlanders would die in the assault on the iron bridge as the rebels had a gun battery trained on the approach to it. The Captain smiled but said nothing. Despite this sense of foreboding, Wells and his troops were ordered to march towards the iron bridge. At the last moment, they received orders to return to camp. Wells considered it a 'lucky job that our plans had been altered ... [as] we would not have come off scot free'.

On 16 March Wells and his troops mustered again for an assault on the city. They marched out in the same direction as the iron bridge but to the relief of them all turned down a lane towards a pontoon bridge made of barrels that crossed the river and allowed them to enter the Residency, just outside the main city walls. As Wells passed through the ruins caused by the British bombardment, he saw the body of a woman clad in military

equipment. Female fighters had been noted at the battle of Sikanderbagh, but whereas this made some Highlanders hesitate, others
had dealt with them just as ruthlessly as the male rebels.

Crossing the river by the pontoon meant the 79th could now
capture the enemy artillery covering the iron bridge. This decision
by Campbell not to sacrifice his soldiers in a direct attack on the
bridge saved many lives. By the time Wells got to the bridge, his
men found one rebel sepoy hidden among the rubble.

> It would appear that he had hidden himself some way or
> another in a cellar and he fired no less than three shots upon
> the 79th, but I am happy to say with no ill effects upon our
> men. He was then brought forth from his hiding place, his
> firelock taken from him and broken. We then took his ammu-
> nition out of his pouch and very politely blew him up with his
> own ammunition.[10]

The Highlanders moved around the walls of the city shooting down
any men they came across. They then set up camp inside a mosque,
which the rebels proceeded to shell with their artillery. The British
brought up their own guns and Wells claimed he was hard of
hearing for the next couple of days thanks to the blast of these
weapons. As the 79th Highlanders made their advance, many of
the rebels were busy abandoning the defences of the city. Some of
them attacked the small garrison at Alambagh that Campbell had
left behind after his first relief of the Residency. Failing to take that,
many deserted the city altogether. More skirmishing followed, but
mercifully Wells and his soldiers were spared a contested assault
on the city walls. Lucknow was theirs for the taking.

It was during the fighting around Lucknow that Lieutenant
William McBean of the 93rd Highlanders finally got his opportunity to show what a ferocious warrior he was. Regimental surgeon
William Munro recorded the moment McBean came under attack
in the Begum Kothi palace outside the main city walls:

> One of our officers (McBean), as brave a man as ever lived,
> and yet as simple as a child, found himself almost alone, and
> surrounded by the enemy. But he wielded his sword so
> dexterously, and made such good use of his revolver, that after

a desperate struggle, in which he killed eleven of his foes, he stood unharmed.[11]

Towards the end of the struggle, other Highlanders ran up to help McBean, but he told them to back off as he finished off the last rebel with his sword. 'At length McBean made a feint cut,' noted Forbes-Mitchell, 'but he instead gave the point, and put his sword through the chest of his opponent.' The divisional commander witnessed the extraordinary fight from the ramparts of the city, and recommended him for the Victoria Cross. At a later regimental parade, a general pinned the medal on his chest, saying it was for his 'conspicuous gallantry displayed at the assault of the enemy's position in Lucknow'.

'Tutts,' replied McBean, 'it didna tak' me twanty minutes.'

An Indian Maharajah later offered him a large sum of money to become his personal bodyguard, but McBean refused, preferring to stay in the army and eventually becoming Brevet Colonel of the 93rd.

In total, the 93rd won seven Victoria Crosses during the Indian Mutiny, and the 78th and 42nd won eight each. Noticeably absent from this roll call of glory was the 79th Cameron Highlanders. 'The 79th had two things to thank God for,' said one of their colonels disdainfully, 'one that they never had a man with the Victoria Cross, the other that they had never had a Staff College man.' The Camerons believed it was a soldier's responsibility to do his duty during war and peace and he should not be rewarded with medals for doing it. Thus their CO never put forward any names despite acts of bravery. This regimental policy held fast for the rest of the nineteenth century until the Camerons received their first VC in 1900 during the Boer War.

The high rate of medals won by Highland regiments during the Indian Mutiny led some observers to question whether Highlanders were paying the price for glory in blood by being constantly thrust into the most difficult of military situations. But Campbell was careful not to put his soldiers at unnecessary risk, cancelling at least one direct assault – by the 79th on the iron bridge at Lucknow – because of his concern.

After the taking of Lucknow, Highlanders enjoyed other less official prizes. The temptation to loot rich merchants' houses around the bazaar was too great for many of them. Lieutenant Douglas Wimberley of the 79th made a note of some of the rich pickings. 'Twenty men came across 20 bags of 1000 R[upee]s each, and each one took one,' he said. Bandsman MacGregor snatched a quantity of jewellery, while Corporal Leary and Corporal Macnab found a bag of gold. Leary had a handsome bracelet made out of his gold, while another Highlander gave 70 rupees to one who had missed out on the booty so he could console himself with a glass of grog.[12]

Corporal Mitchell was put on guard duty outside a palace harem, along with other married members of the 93rd. He struck up a conversation with what appeared to be an old woman but was in fact the palace eunuch, who spoke perfect English. Some of the younger harem girls came out to chat to Mitchell and his Highlanders, teasing him about his fair hair and their kilts. During his twenty-four hours on guard, Mitchell said he learned more 'about the virtues of polygamy and the domestic slavery, intrigues, and crimes of the harem than I have learned in all my other thirty-five years in India'.

The suppression of the Indian Mutiny continued into the summer of 1858, when the last rebel leaders were either killed or captured and executed. It had been a brutal campaign, with atrocities committed freely on both sides. The result of the conflict was that the rule of the East India Company was brought to an end and all the conquered Indian territories were formally incorporated into the British Empire. Queen Victoria became Empress of India in 1876.

Sir Colin Campbell came out of the war a national hero for avenging the crimes of Cawnpore. He was promoted to General and raised to the peerage as Baron Clyde in July 1858. He left India in 1860 and was given the rank of Field Marshal in 1862. A year later he died, and was buried in Westminster Abbey. He had served his Highlanders very well, commanding them in two major conflicts that made them heroes of British dominion and added further laurels to their reputation around the world, so much so that Scotsmen not fighting for the Queen wanted to emulate their style and fighting spirit in other countries. In America, this saw the birth of the New York Highlanders – one of the most extraordinary Highland groups to fight outside the British Empire.

Chapter 10
New York Highlanders

The Scots were very welcome in the United States of America. 'They bring us muscle and brain and tried skill and trustworthiness in many of our great industries,' wrote American entrepreneur Neil Dow in 1880.[1] When the first national census was taken in 1790, the Scots were the second biggest group of immigrants after the English, with over 220,000 of them making up 7 per cent of the population.[2] As waves of Irish immigrants fast overtook them in the nineteenth century, Scots continued to make their mark in the new country, often taking up senior positions in government and business.

The Cameron brothers were born to a Scottish immigrant in Pennsylvania and did spectacularly well. As a boy, Simon Cameron was apprenticed to a printer. At the age of just twenty-five, he bought the *Republican* newspaper. From there, he was appointed state printer, made a fortune in railroad construction and banking, and became a US senator for Pennsylvania in 1844. He gave his support to President Abraham Lincoln and became his Secretary of War.[3] Simon's younger brother James was less of a shooting star but he would make his mark in a different way. James Cameron became the first battlefield colonel of the New York Highlanders.

New York's community of Scottish immigrants and Scots-Americans formed the 79th New York State Militia in 1859. Many of its first recruits came from a Highland Guard formed by members of the New York Caledonian Club and the Saint Andrew's Society of New York. The state authorities were not keen on encouraging militia units that reinforced ethnic differences and insisted they wore regulation trousers, but the New York Highlanders ignored that – they wanted to emphasize their special fighting qualities and went out of their way to avoid such restrictions. They were allowed to call themselves the 79th in honour of the Cameron Highlanders of the British Army. American Scots had been reading newspaper accounts of their heroism in the Crimean War and the Indian Mutiny and were eager to be associated with them. The choice of the Camerons may well have been an attempt to flatter the then Secretary of War, Simon Cameron. Certainly, it caught the attention of his brother James.

At the regiment's first parade in Manhattan – to the sound of droning bagpipes – the New York Highlanders sidestepped state orders and wore kilts. Their dress uniform consisted of a traditional Highland doublet in blue with red shoulder straps bearing the number 79 engraved in brass. They wore a blue Glengarry cap, a kilt of Erracht tartan, a white-hair sporran, and red-and-white checked knee-length socks with red gaiters, worn with a dirk. All officers were issued with a traditional broadsword. It was a magnificently theatrical costume.[4] With the outbreak of the American Civil War, the militia unit grew quickly from the original four expatriate companies into the standard ten companies of a regular regiment. The officers and some of the original members still wore kilts but the new recruits were issued tartan trews instead. The *New York Times* described their departure for war in June 1861:

> As the sun was going down, one Sunday evening, Seventy-ninth New-York (Highlands) regiment, clad in the ancient and picturesque costume of the Scottish Highlanders, passed down Broadway amid the plaudits and farewells of [the] multitude. They were over a thousand bayonets strong; and there never marched to the field a thousand men braver, prouder, more intelligent and patriotic.[5]

After their march down Broadway, the New York Highlanders took the railroad from Jersey City to Washington DC. They paraded before President Lincoln and their officers were introduced to James Cameron, who shortly afterwards was elected their Colonel. The regiment's pipe and drum band proved so popular it was seconded to the White House to perform for the President at official events.

On 1 July the Highlanders moved on to a military base outside the city they called Camp Lochiel. They believed their Colonel was descended from an ancient Scottish chieftain and were happy to foster this association. They practised drill and on 7 July 1861 were ordered across the Potomac to meet a Confederate army threatening the nation's capital.

The Highlanders formed part of a Union army of 32,700 soldiers commanded by Brevet Major General Irvin McDowell. The Confederates, led by Major-General Pierre GT Beauregard, numbered only 22,000 but took up a strong position near Washington at the railroad junction of Manassas in Virginia. With his back to the capital, McDowell marched out to meet the danger, but on 18 July his soldiers had the worst of a skirmish. The stage was now set for the battle of Bull Run – the first major combat of the American Civil War.

Both sides were largely composed of inexperienced volunteers and the slightest setback played badly. In their march towards the enemy, the Union soldiers demonstrated a marked lack of discipline. The New York Highlanders annoyed their Colonel by spending too much time chasing after food. On one occasion they overturned some beehives and were punished by being attacked by a swarm of bees. The seriousness of the forthcoming combat only got through to the troops when they were ordered to pack away their kilts and trews and wear regulation blue jackets and trousers.

Union commander McDowell delayed action at Manassas to bring forward more supplies, but it proved a costly error. While the Union army postponed its attack, General Joseph E Johnston brought in 12,000 reinforcements to the Confederate army, making both forces roughly equal and depriving McDowell of any advantage of numbers.

Early on the morning of 21 July, McDowell readied his troops for action. At 5.30 a.m., a shot from a 30-pounder Parrott gun heralded the attack. McDowell saw the Confederate left flank as their weakest point and directed his main assault against it. The New York Highlanders formed part of the Third Brigade of the Union First Division under the command of Colonel William T Sherman. Their task was to launch a diversionary attack at a stone bridge across a branch of the Bull Run river, and they would have taken it if they had advanced immediately at the beginning of the battle when it was lightly defended, but, like their general, they dithered. Their officers were 'green' and spent the first hours of the battle watching the fighting from trees in a wood not far from the bridge. It was a hot summer day and many of the Highlanders wandered off to look for water.

William Todd was a volunteer in Company B of the 79th Highlanders. 'Never having been actively engaged in battle,' he recalled, 'we knew little of the experience in store for us.'[6] By midday, the Union attack had forced the Confederates from their positions and they were falling back, giving McDowell the idea they were defeated. Sherman's brigade and the New York Highlanders were ordered to join in the triumphant advance by crossing the stream north of the stone bridge to manoeuvre all the way behind their own forces and attack the Confederate right flank. Some Highlanders were afraid that the battle would be over before they got a chance to fight, but other, more experienced men told them to hold their tongues. It was true the Confederates had fallen back, but they had since rallied and formed compact lines of riflemen directed at the advancing Union troops.

The New York Highlanders took shelter in a sunken road, but Confederate artillery shells dropped among them, killing and wounding a few and making many of them feel nervous for the first time. Sherman's brigade was ordered to attack the enemy on the brow of Henry House Hill and the New York Highlanders marched with them. Colonel Cameron placed himself on the right of the regiment and boldly led the way, shouting 'Come on, my brave Highlanders!'

'All feelings of fear or even of nervousness at once vanished,' recalled Todd, 'every man felt himself a hero, and our only thought was to get at the enemy and drive him from the field.' Halfway up the hill the Highlanders received their first volley from the enemy and many fell. The line crumbled and the officers had to hastily re-form them and deliver their own fire. But a second volley from the Confederates slammed into the Highlanders and this time their Colonel Cameron dropped to the ground, hit in the chest by a rifle bullet. Shellfire staggered the 79th and confusion swept through their ranks when someone shouted that they were firing at their own men on the crest of the hill. Uncertain, frightened and bleeding, the Highlanders received two more volleys before their nerve finally broke and they ran back down the slope to take shelter from the enemy fire.

In fact, the stand by the Confederates on Henry House Hill, led by Brigadier-General Thomas J Jackson, proved to be the turning point of the battle. It was said to be like a 'stone wall' and their example helped rally the Confederate army. Both sides traded artillery fire, but by the middle of the afternoon a Confederate counter-attack proved decisive and the Union line buckled. Thousands of Union volunteers fell back across Sudley Ford and the stone bridge. During the retreat, a Confederate cannon ball overturned a wagon on a suspension bridge to block their passage. It triggered panic among the withdrawing Union soldiers and turned their retreat into a rout all the way back to Washington.

Defiant Highlander William Todd disputed the general description of panic-stricken Union troops and said that many units withdrew in good order. Although bloodied and bruised, the Highlanders took pride in a solitary prisoner and he marched with them resplendent in his gaudy Zouave uniform of red cap and baggy blue and white stripes. But the action of Confederate cavalry hunting down Union troops caused consternation to Todd and his Highlanders who had to abandon the road. 'We deployed as we ran and zig-zagged as much as possible to disconcert the aim of our pursuers, who as soon as they saw us leave the road began firing their carbines.'

Todd and his men escaped by keeping off the road and passing through woods. The retreat went on into the night and Todd briefly lay down for a rest but was awakened by the threat of being captured by the 'Rebs'. Rain fell in the early hours on the exhausted men. Todd stumbled along with other soldiers, hardly able to stop himself falling asleep as he walked. It was through half-closed eyes that he gratefully saw the Stars and Stripes fluttering above a Union fort. In their baptism of fire at Bull Run, the New York Highlanders lost 198 men dead, wounded or captured. It was the greatest loss sustained by any regiment in the Union First Division and included the death of their much respected colonel.

*

The next commander of the 79th New York Highlanders was Isaac Ingalls Stevens. A short man with dark shaggy hair and beard, he was, like Colonel Cameron, another strong character, who had made a name for himself fighting the Indian tribes of the Northwest and had become the first governor of the state of Washington in 1853 – all achieved while he was only in his early thirties. In July 1861 he volunteered his services to Simon Cameron, Secretary of War, expecting the rank of brigadier-general in the regular army, but there were political complications in his background and the Union military establishment did not approve of him.

Defeat at Bull Run and the death of Cameron's brother changed this to some extent and Stevens was made colonel of the 79th New York volunteers. He arrived at their quarters near the Potomac River in front of the capital, on 11 August 1861. Having just lost their commander in a bloody defeat, their morale was low and they did not like the look of this new colonel imposed on them by government. Like any independent-minded Scots, they wanted to choose their own leader. On top of that, they had just been refused leave to New York and they blamed Stevens for it. The result was chronic disobedience. The Highlanders refused to take down their tents to move to a new camp and many proceeded to get drunk.

Stevens walked among the Highlanders to impose his will on them. When some of his officers tried to take down the tents, they were roughly handled by the soldiers, who threatened to shoot them. In the face of this mutinous threat, Stevens stepped forward and started to dismantle a tent himself. The mutineers were impressed by his cool courage and took the tent down, but they still remained opposed to his general orders. Eventually, Stevens was forced to call in armed assistance from other units and they advanced on the camp with loaded muskets and drawn sabres. Stevens spoke sternly to the Highlanders:

> I have spent many years on the frontier fighting Indians. I have been surrounded by the red devils, fighting for my scalp … and have been in far greater danger than that surrounding me now … Now I shall order you; and if you hesitate to obey instantly, my next order will be to those troops to fire upon you. Soldiers of the 79th Highlanders, fall in![7]

With artillery levelled at them, the 79th relented and their ring-leaders were arrested. The entire regiment was punished by having its colours taken away – a mortifying act. With resistance crushed, Stevens imposed a strict regime of daily inspections and long drills, but he also promoted the more able men within the regiment to show that he could be fair as well. When a trader broke the rules by selling whisky to his troops, he had the man tied to a tree. Stevens's no-nonsense discipline impressed his superiors and he was given command of the First Brigade in the Army of the Potomac, being finally commissioned to Brigadier-General. The Highlanders warmed to the tough-talking officer and when he was given a mission that took him away from them they asked him to 'Tak' us wi' ye'.[8]

Stevens appealed to his superiors and after some wrangling in the War Department the 79th were allowed to follow their colonel along the East Coast towards Sea Islands, off the coast of South Carolina. The plan was to establish a blockade of the coast against Confederate traders and launch an assault on Savannah or Charleston. The area fell without resistance and Stevens occupied Port Royal Island. Amid the elegant white-columned mansions of Southern plantation owners he set up his headquarters at Beaufort. The 79th Highlanders enjoyed the period of rest and serenaded Stevens's wife with their bagpipes when she visited him. They played baseball and cricket and welcomed back some of their com-rades captured at Bull Run with a rendition of *Auld Lang Syne*. They picked blackberries from the cotton fields and a few Highlanders made pets of young alligators. Pleasant though it was, Stevens found himself involved with managing the local slave population and wondered at the value of his continued service in the army. He longed for action and in June 1862 he got it.

The Union commanders resumed their plan to move against Charleston. This involved a complicated advance across swamps and rivers and Stevens feared it would give the Confederates too much time to prepare their defences. The first stage of the attack involved a landing on James Island. There, Confederate troops from Charleston had reinforced the fortifications on the island at the settlement of Secessionville. The Union troops dug in around the fort and bombarded it but, impatient to push on to Charleston, their commanders urged a frontal attack on the Confederate fort –

much against Stevens's advice. He knew the 79th Highlanders were now faithful to him but they were not regular troops trained to storm a fixed position.

On 16 June, of all the troops available, Stevens and his 79th Highlanders were selected for the dubious honour of leading the suicidal assault. At 2.00 a.m., before sunrise, they advanced through woods towards the fort at Secessionville. To complete the attack they would have to charge across a 200-yard stretch of cotton fields and clamber over two ditches in full view of the guns of the defending troops. Stevens wanted to soften up the defences with an artillery bombardment, but his commander insisted on a surprise dawn attack.

The presence of four thousand Union troops did not go unnoticed, and when they burst out of the woods, six Confederate artillery pieces and numerous sharpshooters were waiting for them. The 79th Highlanders were joined in the attack across the cotton field by the 8th Michigan. Bellowing their Highland war cries, the 79th sprinted across the open land to reach the parapet before the fort. Some of them dropped into the ditch to fire at the heads of any rebel gunners they could see.

For a moment, the Highlanders were unsure what to do next. They cheered the arrival of some reinforcements but the pause in firing allowed the defenders to reload with grapeshot and pour rapid rifle fire into their assailants. Retreat was not an option as this would make the 79th even more vulnerable to the sharpshooters above them. The officers hastily conferred and after a few minutes, according to William Todd, 'we mounted the parapet, with the intention of entering the fort and carrying it at the point of the bayonet'. But as they reached the top of the earthwork, the Confederates stood firm and poured a withering fire into them. Fatally wounded Highlanders tumbled back into the ditch.

'To persist in the attempt to carry the fort,' recalled Todd, 'with the handful of men now remaining would be madness.' They looked back to their own lines, hoping more reinforcements were coming, but their commander refused to send any more men into the inferno. It was a treacherous act to push them ahead without full support. They had little choice but to retreat across the open, bullet-raked ground. As the Highlanders wavered, a Confederate soldier ran up on the crest of the parapet and tried to take a

Scotsman prisoner. He grabbed him by the feet and dragged him into the fort, but the Highlander fought back, seized the rebel by his hair and yanked him over the parapet and took him as *his* prisoner. This was the only triumphant moment of the battle. With no support, they had to endure the intense gunfire that followed them back across the exposed cotton field and ditches.

Stevens met his men at the edge of the woods and apologized for the lack of support from their overall commander. Inside, he was seething with anger. So many of his men had been wasted to no good effect. Astonishingly, the New York Highlanders were re-formed and a second assault proposed. A wounded officer tied a handkerchief around his bleeding head and willingly led them back across the cotton field. Their advance was uncontested, because they knew the Confederate gunners were holding their fire until they got closer. Reaching the ditch nearest the fort, the Highlanders ducked down behind the earth bank.

> The enemy now opened with grape and canister – yes – and with scrap iron too, for bolts, pieces of railroad iron and other missiles flew all about us. As one wag remarked while he picked up something from the ground: 'They're firing a whole blacksmith shop at us! Here's the hammer, the anvil will come next!'[9]

The Highlanders huddled in the ditch while their artillery fired back. They lay down for an hour until the firing ended, common sense prevailed and they were ordered back to camp. The attack on the fort had been a superbly courageous act, but a newspaper correspondent compared it to the madness of the Charge of the Light Brigade. This was not what the 79th had in mind when they wanted to emulate the bravery of the Camerons in the Crimean War. Over a quarter of their number fell – 110 officers and men dead or wounded out of 474.

William Todd later heard that some of the captured wounded 79th were looked after by a Confederate volunteer unit called the Charleston Highlanders.[10] It showed there was a greater sense of camaraderie among fellow Scotsmen on either side of the battlefield than there was between senior Union commanders and their own men. They had been too willing to sacrifice the brave Highlanders in a pointless assault.

After the battle at Secessionville, Union troops withdrew from James Island and Stevens considered resignation, but the New York Highlanders surprised him with their devotion. Far from sharing his anger at the waste of their lives in the battle, they praised him for his courage in the face of fire and presented him with a sword in a gold scabbard from Tiffany of New York, silver spurs and a letter of appreciation framed in a silver case. He was deeply moved and thanked them publicly, calling them his 'Beloved Highlanders'. Whisky, usually reserved by the regimental doctor for anti-malaria purposes, was handed out liberally that day.

*

Stevens wrote to President Lincoln saying he believed the campaigning in the South was a waste of time and asked to be given a more significant role. With a new Confederate offensive threatening Washington DC, Lincoln was only too ready to agree and Stevens sailed back north with the 79th Highlanders.

In August 1862, Confederate General Thomas 'Stonewall' Jackson placed his rebel troops in a position near the old battlefield of Bull Run. He was one pincer of an attack planned by General Robert E Lee to crush the Union army of General John Pope before it could link up with a larger Union force. Jackson hastened Pope's advance into the trap by raiding the Union supply depot at Manassas. Stevens and his 79th New York Highlanders were part of Pope's command.

On 29 August 1862, Pope sent forward his troops against Jackson's soldiers protected behind a railroad cutting. They attacked in uncoordinated waves that failed to shift the Confederate forces. Stevens and his Highlanders were part of this offensive. It was a dread moment of *déjà vu* – just over a year earlier the same Highlanders had fought against the same foe in almost the same place.

In the late afternoon, with bayonets fixed, the 79th charged out of woods to throw themselves at the railroad cutting, but they ran into vastly superior firepower. Stevens's horse was shot beneath him. After a terrible fifteen minutes, the weight of casualties was such that the Highlanders had to fall back with their Union comrades to the cover of the trees. As Pope insisted on further attacks, the Confederates were reinforced. But Pope was certain that the

Confederates would break eventually, and the next morning Stevens and his badly mauled New York Highlanders were ordered back into the firing line. Their task was a reconnaissance to test the strength of the Confederate position.

Accompanied by a hundred Highlanders, Stevens saw that Jackson's soldiers were too strongly dug in and argued that any further attacks would incur needless casualties. The slaughter of Secessionville haunted him. But Pope would have none of it and ordered the battle to begin again. Stevens and his Highlanders were ordered to help hold the right flank near Bull Run. General Robert E Lee arrived with more men and Pope was forced to recognize that he faced disaster if he did not withdraw his exhausted troops. Stevens's Highlanders joined the retreat towards Washington and were forced to sleep out in the open that night.

The next day, Jackson tried again to get between Pope and the capital. Pope turned to Stevens and told him to intercept the Confederates on a road near Chantilly. They advanced towards Jackson's troops through an orchard. 'The apple trees were heavy with the yet green fruit,' remembered William Todd, 'and the desire to fill our haversacks was too strong to be resisted ... so "between shots", we shook the trees to bring down some fruit.' But the shaking apple trees indicated to the Confederates where they were and shots rained down on the hungry Highlanders.

As the 79th emerged into a cornfield, a line of Southern grey rose before them, pouring volleys of fire into their blue ranks. Stevens ordered his men to charge. The rebels fell back but then rallied on the edge of a wood. Stevens's son, Hazard, serving as his adjutant, was caught in the hail of shot and struck in the arm and thigh. The New York Highlanders marched on past him. General Stevens paused to check his wounded son was all right and ordered him off the field. He then joined the rest of his Highlanders in the thick of the fighting.

Five times five different standard-bearers of the 79th New Yorkers fell dead. Stevens grabbed the colours from a wounded Scotsman who begged him to let it go – 'For God's sake, General, don't take the colours. They'll shoot you if you do!' Stevens ignored the plea and held the colours high. 'Highlanders!' he shouted. 'My Highlanders, follow your general!'[11]

Stevens charged across the cornfield followed hotly by the New

York Highlanders until they reached the edge of the woods where the rebels stood behind a fence. Seeing the screaming Highlanders running at them, the Confederate line broke and fell back through the trees. At that moment, a summer thunderstorm cracked overhead and heavy rain poured down on the field. As thunder rolled across the battleground, a rebel shot hit Stevens in the side of the head and he fell dead, still grasping the colours of the New York Highlanders.

Stevens's fierce attack threw Jackson on the defensive and though the second battle of Bull Run had been a sound defeat for the Union forces, the subsequent battle at Chantilly halted the Confederate advance on Washington. When it was proposed that Stevens's body be buried on the battlefield, the New York Highlanders protested and ensured that his 'sacred remains' were returned to the capital in an ambulance wagon. They were later buried at Newport, Rhode Island, beneath a monument to his memory. After the war, the flag that Stevens held in his dying hands was sent to his family.

*

In total, the 79th New York Highlanders served in twenty-eight engagements in the American Civil War. After three years they had come to the end of their first term of service and in April 1864 they marched in a final parade before President Lincoln in Washington DC. But they kept on fighting – in major combats at Spottsylvania – until just days before they mustered out on 13 May 1864.

'The past week had been one of anxiety to us all – so near the expiration of our term of service,' recorded William Todd. 'Many who had passed unscathed through all previous engagements had been killed or wounded, and "whose turn next" was often in our thoughts.' Todd was one of the lucky ones and survived his entire period of service. Those men with unexpired terms of service carried on in two companies called the New Cameron Highlanders until the end of the war in 1865.

The New York Highlanders were welcomed back royally to their home city. They were presented with a packed itinerary that included a reception at the Caledonian Club and a banquet at the Jefferson Market Drill Room, dressed with their regimental flags and to the sound of bagpipes. Glengarries were handed out to all the soldiers to replace their army caps.

The brave sacrifice of the New York Highlanders was not quickly forgotten. The militia itself was disbanded by the state in 1876, but a veterans' organization continued long afterwards. In May 1911, on the fiftieth anniversary of their call to war, the *New York Times* recorded a parade of twenty-nine civil war veterans drawn in carriages on their way to a commemorative service at the Scottish Presbyterian Church in Manhattan. Highlanders in kilts from the Caledonian Club marched on either side of them. Other groups joining the parade included the Celtic Society, the New York Scottish and the St Andrew's Societies and clan representatives of the MacKenzies, MacGregors, MacDuffs and MacGuinnesses in their different tartans. A pipe and drum band played *The Campbells are Coming.*

'Heading the parade was a lone policeman,' said the newspaper, 'taller than the tallest Scot. He walked wearily along and seemed not the least interested in his followers. His depressed face showed traces of ancestry in an isle not far from the Highlands. Someone on the sidewalk addressed him as McSweeney, and the policeman smiled faintly.'[12]

The Caledonian Club also hosted annual Highland Games in New York throughout the late nineteenth century where 100 members performed before a 5,000-strong crowd in the Wood and Washington Park. 'Red plaids, dark Scotch bonnets, kilts and flying feathers gave a bright appearance to Jones's wood yesterday,' said one report in 1883. 'After an old-fashioned Scotch reel, which set everyone nearly wild, the circle was cleared and the sports began.'[13] Competitive events included throwing the hammer, running and jumping, sword dancing and playing the pipes, for which prizes and gold medals were awarded.

The most famous Highland association with sport in New York is the former name of the New York Yankees baseball team. From 1903 to 1912 they were known as the Highlanders. This was largely because their new ballpark was constructed in north Manhattan on a high point called Hilltop Park, and they were also nicknamed the Hilltoppers, but it is hard to believe that the Highlander moniker was not in part a fond reference to the city's old militia unit. From 1903 to 1906 the team's president was Joseph Gordon, which led to them being called the Gordon Highlanders.[14] Eventually, the Scottish flavour of the name irritated the city's considerable Irish population and when they moved to a new stadium in 1913 the team was officially retitled the New York Yankees.

Chapter 11
Scandal in the Desert

Highlanders took on Islamic fundamentalists several times in the deserts of North Africa. What was at stake in the late nineteenth century was control of the Upper Nile. The Mahdi, Mohammed Ahmed of Dongola, announced himself a prophet of Islam and led a revolt against Egyptian rule in Sudan. Why this should matter at all to the British was because the uprising threatened their authority over the Egyptian government, which in turn impacted on their control of the Suez Canal – the primary route from Britain to India. For the best part of a hundred years, British foreign policy turned on protecting this imperial crossroads. But for Captain Andrew Scott Stevenson of the Black Watch, the events played out in the Nile campaign of 1884 were a matter of regimental honour.

Captain Stevenson and the 42nd Highlanders were part of a five-battalion force that landed on the Red Sea coast in February 1884. Their mission was to quell the activities of Osman Digna, a local slave-trader and follower of the Mahdi, who had a personal army that included 5,000 Hadendowa swordsmen – nicknamed 'fuzzy-wuzzies' by the British because of their extravagant hairstyles.

Lieutenant-General Sir Gerald Graham was in charge of the 4,000-strong brigade and had no doubts they could deal with a much larger Sudanese force that, just a few weeks earlier, had cut to pieces an Egyptian army led by British officers, at the village of El Teb. The fifty-three-year-old Graham was a physically impressive man, well over six feet tall, who had won the Victoria Cross in the Crimean War by leading an assault on the Redan at Sevastopol.

He liked to be in the thick of the fighting with sword and pistol and expected nothing less from his men.

Shortly after landing, Graham organized his troops into a square to advance into the desert. This was a marching column that could be turned into a defensive formation as soon as the enemy was spotted. Gordon Highlanders formed the front face of the square, the Black Watch made up the rear face, while the other British battalions formed the sides. A squadron of Hussars rode out in front of the Highlanders as they searched for Osman Digna with bagpipes playing. In addition to their single-shot Martini-Henry rifles, the British were armed with several light artillery pieces and crank-operated Gatling machine guns that delivered a high rate of fire.

Graham headed for El Teb, where the bodies of slaughtered Egyptians still lay rotting in the sun. Osman had captured rifles and artillery from the British-led soldiers and armed his 10,000 warriors with them as they waited in trenches for Graham to approach. Captured Egyptian artillerymen opened fire on the British column and scored several hits. This came as a surprise to Graham who was expecting to face only sword-wielding savages. He told his men to lie down in a square and deployed his own artillery. With the Sudanese guns suppressed, the square rose side-on, with the Highlanders deployed on either flank. At that point, a more traditional Sudanese attack was unleashed as Hadendowa warriors hurled themselves at the British square, trading sword and spear blows with bayonets and pistols. The British held their nerve and fought them off.

At some point in the battle, a brigade commander called General Davies ordered the 42nd to charge the enemy. Captain Stevenson, who was not at the battle but arrived a few days later, heard from his scandalized colleagues about what happened next. 'The officers seeing nothing to charge at and knowing the enemy were all hiding in holes just in their front,' noted Stevenson, 'quietly put themselves in the front of their companies and told our men not to move and take command from the Colonel.'[1]

In Stevenson's view this was not a moment of disobedience or cowardice – although it made good sense not to charge entrenched riflemen – but a matter of the proper chain of command. Davies should have informed the Black Watch Colonel who would have then ordered his men to attack. 'Through General Davies'

MAC LACHLAN

Jacobite Highlander of the clan MacLachlan in 1745.
Painted by Robert Ronald McIan.

James Stuart – the 'Old Pretender' – with his half-brother the Duke of Berwick. A less flattering portrait was presented in a reward notice for his capture in 1716: 'He never laughs till he is drunk; plays at cards on Sundays; makes pellets in company with bits of bread, with his fingers, lolls his tongue out, and leans on his elbows.' The top prize for his capture was £100,000 and a statue erected near Westminster Hall.

Wanted poster for Charles Edward Stuart – the 'Young Pretender' – issued during the Jacobite rebellion of 1745, offering a reward of £30,000.

Officer and sergeant of the 42nd Highlanders – the Black Watch – c. 1750. They wear the belted plaid, a traditional Highland combination of kilt and cloak.

Grenadiers of the 42nd (Black Watch) and 92nd (Gordon) Highlanders during the Napoleonic Wars. The bulky belted plaid has given way to the kilt. The sporran was not worn on campaign.

Black Watch at Bay by W. B. Wollen. The 42nd Highlanders are attacked by French cavalry at the battle of Quatre Bras, part of the Waterloo campaign in 1815.

The Thin Red Line, by Robert Gibb, the 93rd Highlanders stand firm before a Russian charge at the battle of Balaklava in 1854.

Sir Colin Campbell (1792–1863), commander of the Highlanders in the Crimean War and, later, during the Indian Mutiny.

Charge of the Black Watch, c. 1900, by Stanley L. Wood.

Sergeant of the 2nd Gordon Highlanders, equipped as a mounted infantryman, 1896.

Remarkable photograph showing the 1st Gordons and 1/2nd Gurkhas posing together – in mutual respect for each other's courage – after taking Dargai in October 1897.

Statue commemorating Argyll and Sutherland Highlanders who died during the Boer War. It stands outside the walls of Stirling Castle, home to the Argyll and Sutherland Highlanders Museum.

79th New York Highlanders, 1861. On the left a private in full dress; in the centre a private in service dress and on the right a sergeant in full dress. Painted by Michael Chappell.

Cape Town Highlander regimental mascot, 'Donald', with keeper Private MacDonald, 1887.

Sir Harry Lauder, an enormously popular music hall star both sides of the Atlantic, lost his son, who had enlisted in the Argyll and Sutherland Highlanders, in the First World War. He later performed for Highland troops on the Western Front.

Exhausted 7th Argyll and Sutherland Highlanders during a break in the desperate fighting near Abbeville in France, June 1940, where the 51st Highland Division was shattered by the German blitzkrieg.

Cameron Highlander of the re-formed 51st Highland Division takes an Axis prisoner after the battle of El Alamein in November 1942.

Field Marshal Bernard Montgomery inspects the 5th/7th Gordon Highlanders prior to D-Day, 1944.

American soldiers watch the arrival of the 1st Battalion Argyll and Sutherland Highlanders at Pusan in August 1950, during the Korean War.

Cameron Highlanders on guard duty at Shaba Camp, Aden, 1957.

In the grounds of Balhousie Castle, home to the Black Watch museum, recent memorials to Black Watch soldiers who died in Iraq.

stupidity, I fancy,' said Stevenson, 'General Graham thought we did not do something we should have done.'

The battle of El Teb was won with hard fighting from the British and surprisingly low casualties, considering the bitterness of the hand-to-hand combat – just thirty-nine men killed and fifty-two wounded. The Sudanese lost over 1,500 killed and many more injured, but few were taken prisoner. Despite the victory, the performance of the Black Watch bothered General Graham and he mentioned it in a speech to them a few days later at Camp Suakin.

'Black Watch, I am a plain spoken man,' he told them, 'and I must tell you I am not pleased with what you did at Teb the other day. You are young soldiers and I am as proud of the reputation of the regiment as any of you. Your officers are a magnificent and splendid body of men. Now I am going to give you another chance and assign you the spot of honour in our front.'[2]

Stevenson and his fellow Black Watch Highlanders were angry at this dressing down, feeling it was an unwarranted slur on their fighting spirit; but it probably goes some way to explaining their ferocity at the next combat in the desert.

*

A few days later, on 10 March 1884, the Black Watch were sent out by themselves ten miles from their base at Suakin to construct a *zareba* defensive position. In the light of Stevenson's comments, one gets the feeling that this was a punishment for their earlier conduct at El Teb. A *zareba* was a field fortification made out of thorny branches, best suited to a land where there were few available stones and the ground was hard to dig up. It was unpleasant, painful labour, pulling the thorn branches into a square, but when the work was finished, Stevenson celebrated by sharing two magnums of champagne with his fellow officers. The rest of the British force arrived the next day.

Early on the morning of 13 March, the Sudanese closed in on the *zareba* and in the moonlight began taking pot shots at the soldiers inside. They mostly fired high, but Stevenson was kept awake by the bullets whistling about his tent and one clanged against a water bottle near his head. The Highlanders kept their cool and did not return fire.

A few hours later, at 9.00 a.m., Graham's little army formed up into two squares and marched out of the *zareba* towards the main body of Sudanese soldiers near the village of Tamai. The Black Watch, as Graham had promised, led the attack. A few snipers harassed the Highlanders as they advanced. Abyssinian scouts were sent out to skirmish with them, but the fire got hotter and the scouts fell back with their wounded into the square fronted by the 42nd. Ahead of them was a *wadi*, a dried-out riverbed holding a large number of Hadendowa swordsmen.

Overly keen to see the Black Watch prove themselves in action, General Graham correctly ordered the Colonel of the 42nd to signal a charge. With a yell the Highlanders bounded forward but came to a halt at the edge of the *wadi*. Seeing a couple of thousand 'fuzzy-wuzzies' spread out before them, the Colonel of the 42nd called up the Gatling guns crewed by the Navy Brigade and they hammered into action. To Captain Stevenson's horror – out of the clouds of dust rising before him and despite the ferocious automatic fire – he saw the Sudanese had broken through and were overrunning the machine guns positioned among his troops.

One warrior threw a spear at Stevenson, which passed over his shoulder. The Captain punched him in the jaw and sent him flying backwards. A second warrior came at him from under a Gatling gun and the Highlander kicked him in the head. Stevenson had no time to draw his pistol and fire. Instead, he pulled his broadsword from his scabbard and fought for his life. A Colour Sergeant and two other sergeants were killed beside him, fighting the Sudanese with their bayonets.

> We fell back crushed as it were by a weight and then my trusty claymore found its way to the hilt into several black devils. I clove a piece out of one of their heads just as one does an egg for breakfast and saw his white brain exposed. I was mad with rage and fury and had I not been a strong man I must have been thrown down and killed.[3]

Stevenson killed five Sudanese warriors with his own blade and helped finish off several others. Miraculously, he received no wounds at all. As he fought, he thought of his wife and daughter at home. He wondered if he would 'be killed at once or die a lingering death', but these thoughts were banished by a more basic instinct and he 'fought like a demon and only wanted to kill, kill, kill these awful plucky demons'.

The 42nd fell back under the onslaught but then rallied, formed a line, and charged forward to recapture the Gatling guns. The Colonel of the Black Watch shot two Sudanese, but then his pistol misfired. Another warrior threw a stone at his head, knocking off his sun helmet and wounding him. Some of the Sudanese tried to pull the kilts off the Highlanders. When one grabbed the green ribbons on Stevenson's kilt, he killed him.

As the desperate hand-to-hand fighting ceased, Stevenson looked around him, expecting to be the only officer left standing. To his great pleasure, he saw all his comrades, bloodied, limping, but still alive. One officer was as 'cool as if he was partridge shooting'. A young lad from Argyllshire had only just joined the battalion the day before, looking smart in his new trews, and stood 'armed with a spear crying to be at the niggers again'. Stevenson took up a spear towards the end of the fighting and finished off several wounded Sudanese – 'it went into their hearts like lightning and their blood flowed out on the sand'.

Elsewhere in the battle, General Graham had his horse shot beneath him and ended up fighting alongside his men with sword and revolver. The combat lasted about half an hour before the British fought off the Sudanese and re-formed their ranks. They took the high ground above the village of Tamai and used their Gatling guns and artillery to clear the battlefield. Victory was theirs, but it had cost the lives of five officers and over 100 men, with more than 300 wounded, many slashed badly by the Sudanese swords. The fact that they had broken into a British square later became the subject of a poem by Rudyard Kipling:

> You're a pore benighted 'eathen but a first-
>   class fightin' man;
> An' 'ere's to you, Fuzzy-Wuzzy, with your
>   'ayrick 'ead of 'air –
> You big black boundin' beggar – for you
>   broke a British square!

Most of the casualties were Highlanders and Stevenson was not so sure that it was the fighting skills of the Sudanese that broke their formation at Tamai. The conventional account of the battle has it that the 42nd charged ahead, breaking their square, because in the confusion of the fight they alone heard Graham's order to attack. The breaking of the square was then to be an accusation thrown at the Black Watch. In any bar-room encounter a soldier could be assured of starting a brawl by asking for 'A pint of Broken Square' in their earshot.[4] But Captain Stevenson had a different explanation for the fatal incident. He blamed it on the malicious command of General Graham.

'After the action was over,' he wrote, 'we found that when Graham ordered the 42nd to charge, he did not order the 65th on our right to do the same, therefore when we got to the gully there was no square and the Arabs came in on our right ... Thus we lost 65 men and nearly all our Sergeants. Who is to blame for this?'[5]

Was this Graham's ultimate punishment for their reluctance at El Teb? Had he sent them ahead to certain destruction because he doubted their loyalty? This shocking revelation comes from Stevenson's personal correspondence. But it was not to be the only accusation to come from the pen of a Highlander concerning the reckless deployment of Scottish troops in battle.

Victory at Tamai did little to reduce the power of Osman Digna and the Mahdi, but it did provide some positive headlines in British newspapers. With honour restored, Graham and his army were withdrawn to Cairo in April and disbanded. A few months later, General Charles Gordon, a hero to the Victorian British public, was killed when Mahdist forces took the city of Khartoum. His death cried out to be avenged, but it was a good ten years before the British returned to conquer Sudan.

*

The Mahdi died a few months after the death of Gordon of Khartoum, but if the British hoped this would bring an end to the Islamic fundamentalist hold on Sudan, they were wrong. His successor, the Kalifa Abdulla, took over his followers and maintained their grip on the region. For ten years the British let it go, but in 1896 imperial strategy demanded that French opportunism in the Nile Valley should be firmly dissuaded, while the Italians, having been badly defeated in Abyssinia, needed a helping hand. Once more, British authority in Egypt was at stake and the passage to India was threatened.

With methodical determination the British spread their rule along the Nile in a three-year campaign, building a railway alongside the river to keep their forces supplied. By the beginning of 1898, the British were in a strong position to force a final confrontation with the Sudanese. General Herbert Horatio Kitchener was in overall command of the army, which was a much more substantial force than that deployed a decade earlier, both in numbers and firepower. Two Highland regiments were deployed – the 1st Battalions of the 79th Queen's Own Cameron Highlanders and 72nd Seaforth Highlanders.

For the ordinary soldiers, the mission was not about regional power play but just one thing – vengeance. This was made clear in the field orders of 7 April 1898 from General Kitchener. As the British approached a Sudanese camp near the Atbara river, he instructed his officers to consider just two words: 'Remember Gordon'. 'The enemy before them,' he said, 'are Gordon's murderers.'[6] They advanced at night in square formation, their way lit by the moon. Captain Granville Egerton marched with the 72nd Seaforth Highlanders. He was sure they were being watched by the Sudanese, but the only sign of enemy presence came near dawn when, eerily, a single dry palm tree was set on fire.

At daybreak, Egerton and his Highlanders saw the banks of the Atbara, fringed with dense foliage. Phantom-like figures rose from the ground, adding to the unease of the moment – they were vultures feasting on the carcasses of animals killed in an earlier raid. Kitchener's army proceeded parallel to the river until the desert sloped down to a bend in the Atbara. There, they saw the Sudanese encampment. It was a wooden stockade protected by a *zareba*. The problem of crossing these thorny fences had already exercised Egerton and his men – some of them considered throwing blankets and animal hides over them, while others suggested pulling them away with hooks and ropes.

While they debated how best to tackle the spiked obstacle, Egerton and his fellow officers sat down and lit their pipes. They watched as Kitchener's artillery laid down fire on the camp at Atbara. Shells burst above the *zareba*, sending down showers of

deadly shrapnel. Rockets joined the cacophony and one Sudanese warrior was later found impaled to a palm tree by a rocket
head. In response to the bombardment, the Sudanese troops
raised their multi-coloured banners and the large number of
these flags indicated to the Highlanders they faced a tough
contest to take the stockade. Very few banners fell in response to
the British shells. If that was not worrying enough then the tacti-
cal decisions made by their battlefield commander made the
situation even more difficult.

General William Forbes Gatacre was in charge of the assault and
he took a fancy to a more complicated plan than was necessary. He
proposed that the Camerons should open the battle by firing on the
move as they advanced towards the *zareba*. The Seaforths would
come behind them and then, when the Camerons halted at the
fence, they would pass through them to take the *zareba*. The officers
of the Highlanders objected strongly to this plan, sensibly saying it
was not a good idea to execute such a complicated manoeuvre in
the face of the enemy fire, but Gatacre ignored their criticisms and
insisted they carry it out.

After three-quarters of an hour the artillery bombardment ceased
and the Camerons moved forward exactly as instructed. They
advanced in a perfect line, firing several volleys before the weight
of Sudanese fire began to tell and casualties dropped from the
tartan line. Doggedly, they carried on until they reach the thorn
fence and halted as ordered to let the Seaforth Highlanders pass
through their ranks.

'It isn't a pleasant operation going through a line firing for all
its worth,' recalled Captain Egerton, 'and then having to push on
to its front.'

> As I jumped into the middle of the thorn bushes a man of the
> Cameron Highlanders just missed blowing my left ear off, and
> I remember saying to him 'For God's sake, give us a chance.'[7]

As Egerton and the other officers predicted, it was difficult to stop
men firing to protect their lives and Highland casualties were
higher than they should have been. Inside the *zareba*, Egerton aimed
his revolver at two dervishes, but both shots misfired. The hammer
of his gun had been bent and was useless. Despite the obvious

agony of clambering through a thorn bush in kilts, the Seaforth Highlanders crashed into the camp. They found piles of dead and dying Sudanese knocked over by artillery shells and the intense volley fire of the Camerons.

Having broken through the outer perimeter, the Seaforths had no time to form line, but simply charged at anyone still standing against them. Some Sudanese hid in pits to fire at the Highlanders, while others clashed with them in fierce hand-to-hand fighting. Soon the area inside the camp was filled with choking clouds of dust and Egerton could barely see fifty yards in front of him. Into this chaos came uniformed Sudanese troops allied to the British whose random gunfire was as dangerous to the Highlanders as it was to the enemy, causing possibly half of their casualties.

The fighting became desperate in the extreme and even acts of kindness could be punished with death. A Cameron Highlander bent over to help a Sudanese woman out of a pit. When he turned his back on her, she picked up a rifle and shot him. Seven bayonets were plunged into her. Another Highlander was speared in the back by a warrior who had pretended to be dead. The Camerons repaid this treachery with their own ruthlessness. One warrior dropped his weapons and threw up his hands in surrender before a Highlander. The Cameron turned to his sergeant for advice. 'Put him out of his misery,' he said. 'We don't want none of these buggers 'ere.'[8] The young Highlander bayoneted the dervish through the neck. Hardly any Sudanese survived the taking of the camp. After half an hour of this brutal struggle, the battle was over. The surviving Sudanese waded through stagnant pools in the dried-out Atbara riverbed to get away from the furious Highlanders, who stood on the bank firing down at them.

It was a victory for Kitchener, but Egerton was furious at the unnecessary losses sustained by his Highlanders. Over ten years later, when he presented a copy of his memoirs of the Sudan campaign to the library of the Seaforth Highlanders, he wrote an additional note on the pages describing the combat. He condemned 'Gatacre's rotten pigheaded idea of this close order formation'[9] and blamed him personally for the high level of casualties.

Egerton compared the losses at Atbara to a later more notorious killing field for Highlanders in the Boer War at Modder River when 483 casualties were listed. That fight had lasted all day. At Atbara, a total of 560 men had fallen in just half an hour – almost 5 per cent of the entire force. The Camerons were the worst hit regiment with sixty men dead or wounded.

To rub salt in the wound, as Egerton and his troops marched out into the desert, he noticed 'all the carefully constructed engines for surmounting the *zareba* which had evidently been abandoned by their carriers'. The Captain visited the field hospital to see his wounded soldiers spread out in the sand, making the most of the little shade provided by mimosa bushes. He also saw the bodies of two of his best friends in the regiment. They were later buried in the desert with a cairn of stones raised above them.

Atbara was a crucial victory in the Sudan campaign of 1898. One of the Kalifa's chief supporters was captured and his army destroyed. But rather than follow it up immediately, Kitchener chose to rest his men for a few months. It was only when the Egyptian summer gave way to autumn that the British general made his move. The climax of the campaign was the battle of Omdurman on 2 September 1898. There, an Anglo-Egyptian army of 26,000 men stood in tight order against a mass charge of 50,000 Sudanese. Equipped with rapid-firing rifles, Maxim machine guns and shell-bursting artillery, the British unleashed a storm of fire. The Seaforth and Cameron Highlanders played their full role in the battle, firing devastating volleys from their magazine-fed Lee-Metford rifles – up to twelve rounds a minute.

Lieutenant Angus McNeil stood with the Seaforth Highlanders and noted how the bullets crashing into the waves of Sudanese made them swerve across the front of the Anglo-Egyptian lines, exposing them to even more fire. 'The steady volley firing of the British Division and the persistent rattle of the maxims continued all along the line,' he wrote in his diary, 'every shot seemed to take effect. The whole plain was a fearful sight – simply plastered with dead and dying men and horses – the wounded attempting to crawl away.'[10]

The impact of some 10,000 rifles plus artillery and machine guns killed and wounded at least 25,000 Sudanese tribesmen – half of their force. It was slaughter on an industrial scale and a chilling prequel to the machine-age destruction that would be inflicted on

European soldiers in the next century. It brought a quick end to the Kalifa and his Islamic realm.

*

Despite the military success of the Highland regiments, the late nineteenth century saw a crisis in recruitment. Regimental recruiting officers reported that many young men were reluctant to leave their homeland to fight abroad, preferring to find a job in the busy factories and dockyards of Glasgow or further south. Conflict over land use in the Highlands continued to poison relations between Highlanders, landowners and central government. There were still some clearances – the infamous process begun earlier in the century when thousands of clansmen and their families were forcibly evicted from land to make way for sheep farming – and many Highlanders emigrated. In the wake of this conflict, political agitators called for Home Rule and disrupted the activities of army recruiters. The agitators even included the recently established Free Church of Scotland, whose members were strongly opposed to the government and its army.

Some Highland regiments had their kilts returned in an attempt to encourage volunteers, but by the 1870s the inevitable result was the amalgamation of several regiments. Under the reforms proposed by Secretary of State for War Edward Cardwell, Great Britain was divided into seventy districts that could each raise a regiment of two battalions. This meant that some Highland regiments were paired to form the requisite two battalions. It was then just a short step to proposing that these regiments be amalgamated.

The esteemed 42nd Black Watch were to be joined with the 79th Queen's Own Cameron Highlanders to form the Black Watch and Cameron Royal Highland Regiment, based in Perth. The 72nd and 91st were to be combined into the Argyllshire Regiment at Stirling, while the 92nd and 93rd would become the Gordon and Sutherland Highland Regiment at Aberdeen. At the great military bastion of Fort George near Inverness, the 71st and 78th would become the Inverness and Ross Regiment (Highland Light Infantry). These suggestions seemed pretty straightforward, but some quirky combinations raised eyebrows, such as bringing together the Lowland 26th Cameronians with the 74th Highlanders to make a Cameronian Highland Regiment. The Englishness of one Highland regiment, the 75th Foot Stirlingshire regiment, was so pronounced that it was to be paired with the 39th Foot and given a base in Dorchester.

In 1880, a new Secretary of State for War, Hugh Childers, wanted to press ahead with the suggested amalgamations but his proposals were met by a storm of protest in the press. The idea of submerging the revered name of the Black Watch into the Queen's Own Royal Highlanders flew in the face of military *esprit de corps*, argued one Ross-shire correspondent to *The Times*. The old names were what soldiers died for. 'To these and every other Highland regiment sweet memories are attached,' he insisted, 'which would soon die out if their names were to be robbed in this fashion.' It was these names that maintained the bond of service between the older and younger generations of soldiers.

> To know that a man belongs to Seaforth's or Lochiel's regiment, to know that his father and his grandfather and generations before them have commanded in these or other Highland regiments, gives him a pride and an interest that I believe nothing else can give; and I fear if the War Office adhere to the line they are at present taking they will find the change has had but little advantage and will do much harm.[11]

Another correspondent, an officer, suspected a conspiracy at the War Office to destroy the regiments' *esprit de corps*. The bureaucrats had little understanding of the value of distinctions in regimental dress, but they were symbols, he protested, 'which for regiments have a deep – we may almost say a holy – meaning to soldiers, for they commemorate or are associated with some gallant deeds ...'[12]

When the War Office finally plucked up the courage to suggest that the 79th Cameron Highlanders might like to give up their distinctive Erracht tartan in favour of the Black Watch sett, the regiment telegraphed a defiant 'no' from their posting on Gibraltar. They were not short of supporters and their most ardent protector was Queen Victoria herself, who had adopted the regiment in 1873. Childers was somewhat taken back by the intensity of this reaction and left the Camerons well alone, but he was intent on making changes and may well have been influenced by another letter in *The Times*, which proposed a more commonsense approach to the Black Watch and amalgamation.

'Beginning with the 42d, who will not give up the red hackle, so gloriously won, nor willingly see it given to strangers,' suggested a soldier correspondent, 'it seems only rational to bring back to its old second battalion, the 73d, which will doubtless be glad to resume the dress in which it gained its earliest honours and mess-plates ...'[13] The historical good sense of this pairing was taken up and the 42nd and 73rd, originally raised as a second battalion for the 42nd back in 1780, came together at Perth. Similarly, the 72nd and the 78th, both first raised by Mackenzies of Seaforth, were happily united at Fort George. The 91st and 93rd were combined to form the Argyll and Sutherland Highlanders at Stirling, while the predominantly English 75th joined the 92nd Gordon Highlanders at Aberdeen. The latter pairing meant that the Gordons had to give up their much loved number '92' and they held a mock funeral for it, burying a flag bearing the number. But the next morning, a resurrection was proclaimed with a motto added to their flags which read: 'Ninety-Twa No' Deid Yet!'

Some of the absorbed regiments were non-kilted, but they all ended up with kilts as a result of the Childers reforms. The unhappiest union was that between the 74th and 71st in the Highland Light Infantry. They were based outside the Highlands near Glasgow and were denied the kilt. On top of this, the 74th hated the 71st and continued to refer to themselves as the 74th until after the Second World War.

All of Scotland north of the Forth and Clyde became the recruiting region for the kilted regiments. The Seaforths had all the country north of Inverness. Sadly, this meant that the Sutherland Highlanders lost their association with this part of the country as they were now paired with the Argylls in Stirling and recruited mainly from there. The Gordons recruited from the north-east of Scotland; of course, this was never traditionally regarded as a Highland region, but it did mean they also raised soldiers from Shetland who came in by boat to Aberdeen. The Black Watch retained their traditional recruiting area in Perthshire but this was extended away from the Highlands to include Dundee and Fife. The Camerons kept their recruiting ground in the heart of the Highlands but because it was so thinly populated they were allowed to raise their second battalion from throughout Scotland.

Reorganized and re-kilted, the Highland regiments were ready now to face some of their stiffest tests yet in the battle to maintain the British Empire against rebels and competitors.

Chapter 12
Shoulder to Shoulder
with Gurkhas

There is a remarkable black-and-white photograph in the Gurkha Museum in Winchester. It shows Gordon Highlanders and Gurkha soldiers standing and sitting next to each other shoulder-to-shoulder, alternating Highlander with Gurkha in five sturdy rows. Straight-faced, they pose against a bleak, stone-strewn landscape of mountains on the North-West Frontier of India. At a time when European soldiers looked down on anyone beyond the Mediterranean as a 'nigger' or a 'wog', this display of inter-racial kinship is astounding. The photograph was taken shortly after the soldiers had fought together at the battle of Dargai in October 1897 and testifies for ever to their mutual respect for each other's fighting skills.

The Highlanders and the Gurkhas have a special relationship within the British Army. Both originate in the highlands of their countries – the Gurkhas coming from the mountains of Nepal – and both have fierce reputations for hand-to-hand combat. The Gurkhas have adopted many of the traits of Highland regiments, including pipe bands and the wearing of tartan and glengarries. Although coming from completely different cultures, there is a wordless understanding between them that was captured perfectly in an encounter described by John Masters in *Bugles and a Tiger*, his memoir of life on campaign in the North-West Frontier in the 1930s.

An officer in the 4th Gurkha Rifles, Masters noticed an Argyll and Sutherland Highlander sit down for a chat with one of his riflemen. The Gurkha showed him his *kukri*, the famous curved knife of Nepal, and denied that it could be thrown as a boomerang. Masters was puzzled as to how the two soldiers managed to communicate for the best part of an hour as neither of them spoke each other's language. He crept close to them to overhear their conversation.

> Each soldier was speaking his own language and using few gestures – it was too hot on the rocks for violent arm-waving. I could understand both sides of the conversation, the Gurkhali better than the 'English', and it made sense. Questions were asked, points taken, opinions exchanged, heads nodded and lips sagely pursed. When [they] moved on, the two shook hands, and the Jock said, 'Abyssinia, Johnny!'[1]

John Masters also received a lesson on the importance of the kilt from a Highland major leaning against a urinal with his kilt raised: 'Join a Highland regiment, me boy. The kilt is an unrivalled garment for fornication and diarrhoea.'[2]

The Gurkhas were first recruited to the East India Company's army in 1816, following their defeat in a war with the company. It was in 1857 during the Indian Mutiny that they proved their loyalty and the Highland regiments got the full measure of them. They were at Lucknow when the Highlanders stormed the rebel strongholds. 'Jung Bahadoor and his Goorkhas had also done good service,' noted Captain Douglas Wimberley of the 79th Cameron Highlanders. 'They advanced from the Charbagh Bridge over the canal on the south side of the city towards the Residency, seizing the enemy's positions one by one, and so covered the left of Sir Colin's own advance.'[3]

The Gurkhas were not the only native troops to impress the Highlanders during the Indian Mutiny. The Sikhs of the Punjabi regiments raced the Scots to attack the rebels and on one occasion stepped in to save the life of Sir Colin Campbell. *The Times* journalist William Russell observed the incident: Campbell was inspecting his troops towards the end of the fighting at Lucknow when he noticed a half-dead Gazee rebel rising to slash at him with his sword. 'Bayonet that man!' he ordered.

The Highlander made a thrust at him, but the point would not enter the thick cotton quilting of the Gazee's tunic; and the dead man was rising to his legs, when a Sikh who happened to be near, with a whistling stroke of his sabre cut off the Gazee's head at one blow, as if it had been the bulb of a poppy![4]

Gurkhas and Sikhs joined with the 72nd and 92nd Highlanders when they marched out of Kabul to avenge the British massacre at Maiwand in Afghanistan in 1880. In a gruelling march to relieve British forces trapped at Kandahar, they crossed over 280 miles of treacherous terrain in just three weeks. To avoid the 110-degree heat, they began each day at 2.45 a.m. and had to contend with a shortage of water, sandstorms and raiding Afghans. The Seaforths and Gordons formed the rear guard and frequently did not get into camp until long after dark. Once they got to Kandahar, the Highlanders, Gurkhas and Sikhs immediately went into action, routed the Afghans and recaptured some of the guns lost at Maiwand. Their commander, Major-General Frederick Roberts, was mightily impressed by all his soldiers. 'I looked upon them all as my valued friends,' he later wrote, 'all were eager to close with the enemy, no matter how great the odds against them.'[5] But it was at Dargai that the fighting talents of the Gurkhas and Highlanders came together most brilliantly.

*

The mountainous North-West Frontier between Afghanistan and British India has always been a hot spot for rebellion and banditry. In August 1897, Afridi tribesmen captured forts along the strategically important Khyber Pass. This success encouraged another tribe, the Orakzais, and soon the entire border region was ablaze. Sikh soldiers of the British Indian Army did their best to hold their positions, but were overwhelmed and slaughtered. Gathering their forces, the British administration decided to punish the tribesmen by invading their summer homeland in the Tirah Maidan valley.

The task force was led by Lieutenant-General Sir William Lockhart and numbered nearly 12,000 British and 22,000 Gurkha and Indian troops. It was formed into two divisions of two brigades each, in which two British battalions were paired with two Gurkha or Sikh battalions. The Gurkhas and Sikhs had already been in action against the Afridi while the 1st Gordon Highlanders had become acclimatized to hill climbing in previous operations. The rest of the English battalions found the rugged terrain very hard going and many succumbed to cholera and dysentery. The Tirah Maidan had never been penetrated by British forces and the rebel tribesmen presumed they would be safe behind its high valleys and narrow passes.

The British concentrated their forces at the railhead of Kushulgarh. To reach enemy territory from there would require a week-long eighty-mile march through a desolate land largely devoid of water and food. To supply Lockhart's two divisions required an enormous baggage train of over 40,000 mules and camels. The advance began in October 1897 and the ground became rougher and rougher and the tracks more precipitous until the narrow paths rose so steeply that the Gurkhas in front looked 'like flies crawling on a wall'.[6] Abruptly, their procession was halted by enemy fire coming from the village of Dargai, perched on top of a cliff one thousand feet above a track leading along a mountain ridge. The Orakzai snipers hid among the huge boulders and it was clear that the position would have to be taken before the British column could move on.

On 18 October, the 1/3rd Gurkhas and the 2nd King's Own Scottish Borderers were charged with taking the heights at Dargai. It was a formidable physical objective, involving climbing a steep rock-strewn slope in full view of the enemy. Light 2.5-inch mountain guns were used to provide cover. The Gurkhas fired their .303 Lee-Metford rifles in two volleys and then climbed in single file to a ridge – beyond that they faced a sprint across dead ground. With enough men gathered, they took a deep breath and bolted over the crest into a hail of fire. Seeing the Gurkhas hurtling towards them, the Orakzais hastily withdrew and left them to take the Dargai Heights.

It seemed a straightforward operation to allow the British column to advance unhindered, but it depended on the Gurkhas and Borderers holding on to the heights. There was not water enough for this and they had to evacuate their hard-won position. Thousands of gathering Afridis had heard the earlier gunfire and rallied to the Orakzais who now flooded back to the mountain top, knocking the British back to square one. Falling back, they came under heavy gunfire and the 1st Gordon Highlanders and 15th Sikhs were called in to help cover them.

Soon, they were under fire themselves and their Major Jennings-Bramly was killed. But the Highlanders stood steady until nightfall, repelling an attack within just a few yards of their fixed bayonets, and then carried their dead and wounded over rocks to their camp eight miles away at Shinawari. 'I walked beside one poor fellow who was badly hit,' said an officer of the Gordons. 'He grasped my hand as firmly as he could, but never complained, though the jolting of the stretcher must have been agony.'[7] To help their Scots comrades, men of the King's Own Scottish Borderers came out a mile from their camp to bring them water.

It was a disheartening action and all the worse because the British commanders decided they had no alternative but to take the Dargai Heights again on the 20th. The 3rd Gurkha Scouts and the 1/2nd Goorkhas (the traditional spelling of their unit name) were to lead the attack, with the 1st Dorsets, 2nd Derbyshire, and 1st Gordons in support and reserve. The march up the narrow path towards Dargai began early in the morning at 5.00 a.m. It demanded a zigzag climb for half a mile up the side of a valley protected from enemy fire. Yet it was demanding work and the combat-fit men had to pause every so often to catch their breath. By 11.00 a.m., the Gurkhas were huddled behind the ridge that had protected them two days earlier. The Gordons offered covering fire from the boulders beneath them.

When ordered, the Gurkhas charged over the crest into the dead ground between them and the base of the cliff beneath Dargai. This time, there were even more rebel tribesmen firing at them from behind stone *sangars* (fortifications). In ten minutes, the Gurkhas suffered sixty-seven casualties and their brave attack faltered. Next, the Dorsets ran into the storm of bullets. Only two of their officers and a handful of soldiers reached the halfway mark across the open ground, lying down among the bodies of wounded and dead men all round them. Captain A K Slessor of the 2nd Battalion the Derbyshire Regiment was waiting on the slope beneath the fighting but soon saw the effects of it.

Presently wounded men, chiefly Gurkhas at first, began to come down past us, some supported by their comrades, some borne on blood-stained stretchers; then a dhoolie [cart] containing a Gurkha officer, dead; and still we sat waiting. Before long dead men were being dragged down the steep slope by the legs with scant ceremony. After all, it did not hurt them, and the path had to be cleared.[8]

When a group from the 2nd Derbyshires went over the top to join the fighting, all but one were dropped by the enemy. After three hours of combat, Gurkhas, Dorsets and Derbys were all huddled behind the ridge. They could make no headway against the Afridi and Orakzai sharpshooters, hidden among the rocks above them. The British could barely poke their head above the ridge without receiving bullets through their sun helmets. To make matters worse, the lead mule bringing more ammunition for the British up the slope stumbled and fell backwards, carried over the precipice by the weight of the ammunition boxes, followed by two more mules. The situation was dire.

It was then that the Gordons were ordered into action, supported by the 3rd Sikhs. On the precipitous mountainside, their commander, Lieutenant-Colonel HH Mathias, made a laconic speech – 'Highlanders, the General says the position must be taken at all costs. The Gordons will take it.'

They had just climbed the steep side of the valley to bring themselves level with the other soldiers, but with hardly a pause for breath they scrambled over the ledge towards the rebel tribesmen. Slessor and his men were told to move aside to let the Highlanders through.

Roused to fierce enthusiasm by their trusted leader's stirring speech, and by the familiar skirl of the pipes, the Highlanders leapt to the assault. Up they came, a long thin string of men with stern, set faces, stumbling, scrambling up the steep in a frenzy of courage not to be gainsaid, amidst spasmodic gasps from the pipes, and cheers from any who had breath to utter, a sight for those who witnessed it to remember all their lives.[9]

Everyone was impressed by their fearless determination, especially the campaign commander Sir William Lockhart, who praised the initial rush of the Gordons in his dispatch from the battlefield.[10]

Slessor felt the Gordons had the slight advantage over his men in that they had fought over the same ground two days before and knew it could be taken. Also, a fusillade from eighteen British mountain guns exploded over the cliff top just at the moment the Highlanders crested the ridge; but they still faced thousands of rebel rifles directed at them as they ran across the killing zone.

Colonel Mathias personally led the next stage of the advance. Rather than attacking in small rushes, he ordered his men to press forward in full battalion strength, so hundreds of Highlanders surged across the open ground. Even then, five leading officers and forty-one soldiers went down almost straight away. Major Macbean was shot in the groin but dragged himself to a boulder and cheered on his men. The pipers played *Cock o' the North*. One of them, George Findlater, was shot through both feet and fell to the ground. He crawled to a rock, propped himself up and carried on playing his pipes. For that act, he won the Victoria Cross.[11]

Colonel Mathias – a veteran of the Nile campaign of 1884 – made it across the exposed slope, but was feeling his age when he paused for a rest. 'Stiff climb,' he gasped to his Colour-Sergeant. 'Not quite … so young … as I was … you know.' The younger man slapped him on the back cheerily, knocking any remaining wind out of him. 'Never mind, sir! Ye're gaun verra strong for an auld man!'[12]

The Gurkhas watched the Highlanders with open-mouthed admiration – taking a position they had sacrificed so many of their men for. Lieutenant Tillard of the Gurkha Scouts later recorded their wonder at the kilted warriors.

> Then followed a scene it is hard for me to describe, it makes me shake with excitement even now. The Gordons advanced at once without any hesitation, each man trying to get in front of everyone else, the pipes playing and men cheering. They were greeted by the same deadly fire as before but they never stopped or wavered although many of them were down. It was one wild continuous rush of men all eager to get at the enemy. The sight was magnificent and the excitement so intense that I for one, although I was shouting at the top of my voice felt the tears springing up into my eyes and could not keep them back.[13]

Seeing the Gordon Highlanders rush fearlessly towards the cliff beneath Dargai, the Gurkhas, Sikhs, Dorsets and Derbys joined in the attack. The Highlanders climbed up the rock face and when they reached the summit of their target, the Afridis and Orakzais had fled. The Dargai Heights were theirs, and what a victory it was – celebrated across Britain as yet another display of the fierce bravery of the Highlander. Four Victoria Crosses were awarded in total, one of them to Gordon Private Edward Lawson, a Northumbrian, who carried his wounded Lieutenant to cover and then, despite being shot twice, continued to rescue another soldier. Colonel Mathias was recommended for a VC, but was debarred because he was a commanding officer. Seven Distinguished Conduct Medals were awarded.

Exhilarated by their triumph, the Gordons were not slow to recognize the contribution of their fellow soldiers and volunteered to carry down the wounded and dead of the Gurkhas. It was a gesture never forgotten and explains the warmth of the joint photograph taken shortly afterwards. The Gurkhas had lost the most men in the battle, with two officers and sixteen men killed and forty-nine wounded. The Gordons lost one officer and two men killed, six officers and thirty-five men wounded.

The victory at Dargai captured the imagination of the public in Britain in the year of Queen Victoria's Diamond Jubilee. Two heroic paintings showing the Highlanders and Gurkhas in action were exhibited at the Royal Academy in 1898 and both featured Piper Findlater, wounded but playing his pipes against a boulder. One of the paintings, entitled *The Cock o' the North*, by Richard Caton Woodville, was turned into a popular Christmas print. Two more Dargai paintings were exhibited in that year, also featuring Findlater, and it was no surprise when he was invited to play at the Royal Tournament. Colonel Mathias's words became a catchphrase and a note appeared on an umbrella stand at the Army and Navy Club in London, reading: 'Do not leave your umbrella in this club. The Gordons will take it!'[14]

Findlater caused controversy when, because he could find no work thanks to his injuries, he took up an offer to play at the Alhambra Music Hall. His regiment was furious but the scandal provoked the government into raising the pension associated with winning the VC from £10 to £50 per annum. Although he was said to have played the regimental march throughout the fighting, he later confessed he had no recollection of what he played.

Best-selling *Flashman* author George MacDonald Fraser was an officer in the Gordon Highlanders just after the Second World War and he remembered a lively conversation in the sergeants' mess in which everyone had a different opinion of the tune played at Dargai. In the end, it was accepted that the Regimental Sergeant Major at the time was asked by Findlater's Colonel what he played at Dargai. The RSM was absolutely certain it was the regimental march. But 'it was only later that it occurred to [the Colonel] that the RSM had not been within half a mile of Findlater during the battle, and couldn't know at all. But *Cock o' the North* the RSM had said, and *Cock o' the North* it has been ever since, and always will be.'[15]

*

The daring deeds of Highlanders on the North-West Frontier were performed in some of the last old-style Victorian campaigns of empire that provided a British audience with reasons to be proud of their fighting men. As the twentieth century approached, technology changed the way war was conducted. A new intensity of firepower was unleashed and warfare became far more costly and far less glorious. This was already to be seen in colonial warfare, with machine guns and repeating rifles inflicting tremendous casualties. The introduction of high-velocity rifles with a considerably extended flat trajectory meant that gunfire became more accurate and deadly over a longer range. The British were to be on the receiving end of this in the Boer War in South Africa in 1899, and it came as a shock that revived bitter memories of the kind of losses last sustained in the Crimean War.

As in that war, several Scottish battalions were organized into Highland Brigades. In Lord Methuen's advance on Kimberley in November 1899, the 3rd (Highland) Brigade consisted of the 1st Gordon Highlanders, 2nd Royal Highlanders (Black Watch), 1st Argyll and Sutherland Highlanders, 2nd Seaforth Highlanders and 1st Highland Light Infantry. For Lord Roberts's offensive against Bloemfontein in February 1900, the 3rd (Highland) Brigade, under the charismatic leadership of Major-General Sir Hector Macdonald, included the 1st Argyll and Sutherland Highlanders, 1st Highland

Light Infantry, 2nd Seaforth Highlanders, and 2nd Royal Highlanders (Black Watch). Highland battalions were also attached to other mixed brigades.

In their battles against the Boers, the Highlanders faced an enemy different to their usual colonial adversaries. The Boers were skilled sharpshooters, armed with high-velocity rifles such as the German-supplied magazine-fed Mauser. When shooting from well concealed trenches, these riflemen could make mincemeat of the traditional volley-and-bayonet tactics of the Highlanders.

The terrible impact of this modern warfare was described by Corporal James H Noble of the 1st Argyll and Sutherland Highlanders at the battle of Magersfontein on 11 December 1899. It was one of three defeats in a few days that made up the notorious 'Black Week' for the British forces. Part of Lord Methuen's advance to relieve Kimberley, the combat was intended to deliver a knockout blow against the Boers positioned in the Magersfontein hills before the town. The Boers dug into trenches at the foot of the hills and commanded the flat ground approaching them. Barbed wire, traditionally used by farmers to fence off their land, was fixed up before the trenches. On the 10th, Methuen, assuming the Boers were on the hills, subjected the hill tops to a fierce artillery bombardment; but the shells had little effect on the Boers sheltering below and gave them good warning of the coming attack.

The 1st Argyll and Sutherland Highlanders, part of the 3rd Highland Brigade, commanded by Major-General Andrew Wauchope, were ordered to their attacking positions at dusk. Around 9.00 p.m., a storm crackled above the soldiers, drenching them in rain as they lay down on the flat terrain. At half-past midnight, the Highlanders were told to move off towards the enemy lines. So as not to get lost in the darkness, they were told to advance in Quarter Column formation, which meant that a mass of 3,400 men moved forward in a dense column. They had little idea of the location of the hidden trenches before them and by 4.00 a.m. they were only 400 yards away from the Boers – that is, within easy range of their deadly Mausers.

'It was just commencing to break daylight,' recalled Corporal Noble, 'when Colonel Goff was giving us orders (in a whisper) to extend when one shot was fired by the Boers followed immediately by an incessant storm of bullets, for a time all was confusion till some person (unknown) gave the order to retire.'[16] The Highlanders were caught in their close formation and every bullet struck home. 'The blow was so unexpected,' said Noble, 'that the whole Brigade staggered and fell back.'

The 2nd Black Watch fixed bayonets and charged at the Boer trenches. Private James Williamson was among them. He and his mates pulled up the barbed-wire fence in front of them and rushed on to the trenches but the weight of fire was too much.

> The bullets were coming down on us like hailstones, so we had to stick there, about 30 yards from the trenches, as soon as I lay down I got a Mauser bullet through my left foot which made me wilder so I started firing back but my luck was out that day, for they peppered at me as if I was the only man firing at them.[17]

A second bullet severed a muscle in his left leg, a third thudded into his back, but he kept on firing. A fourth bullet struck his right shoulder, making him drop his rifle. He picked it up, but got a fifth bullet in his right leg and then a sixth that broke his right arm. Williamson could do nothing more but lie on the ground a helpless spectator of the fighting around him.

Brigade commander Wauchope was killed almost immediately as he desperately ordered his men to spread out. The majority of the Highlanders withdrew, shocked by the hail of bullets but determined to rally and attack again. 'By firing volleys and advancing by rushes,' said Noble, '[we] managed to get within about 900 yards of the position, but could make very little impression on the enemy who were so cunningly entrenched.'

British artillery helped out by sending a barrage of shells into the Boer trenches, having finally worked out where they were, but this fire also hit the few Highlanders who attempted to break through the enemy lines. By midday, the majority of Highlanders were helplessly pinned down in the open ground beneath a baking sun. Wearing kilts beneath their khaki jackets, their legs were exposed and got burned by the sun, leaving them to blister the next day. They remained in this position until 4.00 p.m. when the assembly was sounded and the Highlanders retreated from the battlefield. At least one observer claimed that some of the Highlanders were so panicked that their officers had to threaten them at gunpoint, but other first-hand accounts tell of an orderly withdrawal.

The next day, the Boers signalled a truce, allowing the British to remove their wounded and dead. Wauchope was buried first, followed by his officers and other ranks. The pipers played *The Flowers of the Forest* and Noble recorded the funeral service was 'a very impressive one, many giving way to tears'. The Highlanders had suffered a heavy toll, with 202 men killed and 496 wounded, although Noble reported a higher figure of 870 casualties for the brigade, with 98 coming from the Argyll and Sutherland battalion.

Lord Methuen expressed his regret for their losses to the Highlanders in a speech, declaring their advance was carried out perfectly but was betrayed by someone shouting the word 'retire' when the order 'charge' would have seen the Boer lines taken. He made no mention of his catastrophic failure to locate the position of the enemy trenches, which led directly to so many deaths.

Methuen's evasion of responsibility for the defeat infuriated Corporal WT Bevan of the Argyll and Sutherland Highlanders. 'Why did the Brigade advance in quarter-column formation?' he asked. 'It was not fighting, it was simply suicide. Men were hung on the wire like crows, and were simply riddled with bullets. We hear that our brave general [Wauchope] remonstrated with Lord Methuen before we left camp about the plans, but Methuen only told him to obey orders.'[18] Bevan's criticism was later published as a letter in a London newspaper and reflected a growing discontent among British soldiers at the incompetence of their commanders. The disasters of 'Black Week' and the consequent uproar in British newspapers led to the replacement of Sir Redvers Buller as Commander-in-Chief by Lord Roberts, but Methuen kept his job.

Many letters appeared in Scottish newspapers detailing the realities of the war. 'We were under fire about fifteen hours,' wrote one Highlander to his parents about fighting on the Modder River. 'The whistling of the rifle bullets all around you, and the crack, crack, crack of the Maxim all day long was a strain on the nervous system. It makes one a bit nervous when you hear the least crack of anything. I hope I won't have to go up again because I will be very nervous after getting shot once.'[19] The arrival of this letter was a relief to the soldier's family as he had been presumed killed.

Other men described the desperate tactics they faced. 'The Boers threw all their dead horses in the river,' wrote one private. 'Thousands of them came floating down, and we had to drink it, and it did stink, but we were glad to get it.'[20] Some men just got angry. 'One chap of ours was shot dead whilst assisting a wounded comrade, and the dirty beggars even shelled our ambulances. I saw it myself, so I know it is true.'[21]

Despite the grim truth of modern warfare appearing throughout the national press, there was still room for heroic moments involving tough Highlanders with an old-fashioned approach to fighting. Nine Victoria Crosses were won by Highland regiments in the Boer War, one of them by Lance-Corporal John Frederick Mackay of the 1st Gordon Highlanders, who nearly became the first man to win two VCs.

Under fire at Doorncop near Johannesburg, on 20 May 1900, Mackay rushed forward several times to help his wounded comrades, despite putting himself at risk of being shot. He carried one man to cover and it was a miracle he survived unscathed. He was recommended for the VC by Lord Roberts in June, but in the meantime he had acted heroically in combat at Wolverkrantz in July and was recommended for a Bar to his medal. Unfortunately, the rules stipulated that a Bar could only be added if the award of the initial VC had already been approved, which it had not. Mackay got his VC without Bar and ended his career in the army as a Lieutenant-Colonel.

With its soldiers in khaki exposed to rapid fire from modern weapons, the Boer War gave a taste of the conflicts to come in the rest of the twentieth century. As Highlander Private Chonlarton put it in a letter to a friend, 'It is pure warfare we are having now.'[22]

Chapter 13
Khaki Aprons

Gordon Barber was extremely tall and strong, but gentle with it. He was born in Cheshire and worked in business in Liverpool, but he was fascinated by military history and in 1912, at the age of twenty, he joined the Special Reserve of Officers. In August 1914 he received a commission in the 1st Battalion of the Queen's Own Cameron Highlanders. It was the first month of the First World War. By October, he was on the Western Front.

The complex trench system that would dominate the war had not yet evolved, and Lieutenant Barber and his men slept in dugouts on straw with little to protect them from the rain. Early on, Barber got a reputation for looking after his men. His parents sent their eldest son parcels of cigarettes, but smoking too many of them made him feel ill and he passed most of them around the Highlanders in his platoon.

On 30 October 1914, near the Belgian village of Zonnebeke, Barber was making his way back from lunch served in a cottage near his dugout when a German high-explosive shell landed near him. It blew him off his feet. One piece of the deadly shower of shrapnel pierced his right foot and he saw blood come through the white spat covering his boot. His men rushed up to him and a doctor dressed his wound straight away. They discovered he also had three more shrapnel wounds – one piece had smashed into his left breast pocket next to his heart. Fortunately, the metal splinter had embedded itself in a tin of foot-ointment and penetrated no further.

Barber was carried two miles across the muddy landscape to a collecting station where he was given morphine to reduce the excruciating pain in his foot. A horse-drawn wagon then took him three miles to Ypres, although the wagon was too short for the very tall Highlander. Three other wounded officers rode with him and they all groaned with pain as the wagon bumped over the rough road.

In Ypres, Barber was placed in a grand school building that had been turned into a field hospital. His foot hurt like hell and he was given more morphine, but he was put out to discover that his haversack containing 100 cigarettes had disappeared. With only a few loose cigarettes left, he passed the time chatting to a fellow Cameron officer with a bullet graze on his head. Two other men near him died from wounds to the stomach. A day later, with his wound freshly dressed, he was put on a train to Boulogne and went home on board the *St Patrick*. His wound continued to give him great pain and he was given repeated doses of morphine.

It took the best part of a year for Barber's wounded foot to heal, but once better he was sent back to Belgium in December 1915 where he was promoted to captain in the Cameron Highlanders. He was quietly philosophical about the risks he faced and expressed this in his diary.

> We are, I am convinced, all of us frightened, and not unnaturally so. I don't think it really is fear of Death itself; it isn't fear of being wounded, or not altogether … No, what we are frightened of is that we won't see those near and dear to us again: and this thought makes us appreciate our relatives and friends as they should be appreciated.[1]

In spring 1916, Barber and the Cameron Highlanders were transferred to France to take part in the great Somme offensive. He noticed the change in warfare from his first days at the front. His trench was now part of a massive fortified system that stretched from the Belgian coast to the Swiss border. It was no hastily dug parapet but was carved deep into the ground with retaining boards on either side and was linked by communication trenches to a further maze of support trenches. The dugout he slept in was buried twenty feet below ground. Beyond the trenches was a forest of barbed-wire entanglements. The weapons had changed too. He now had to contend with trench-mortars, rifle-grenades, aerial torpedoes, and mortar-launched mines.

For most of the time, Barber's life in the front line was 'a truly monotonous existence'. 'When in the trenches,' he wrote in his diary, 'you look filthy and feel filthy, and are usually frightened if there is any "strafeing" on; but when things are quiet one can enjoy existence after a fashion.'[2] On one occasion, Barber complained about a horrible smell in his dugout, but to combat it a Highlander put down too much chloride of lime and it ending up gassing them. With eyes burning, they had to evacuate the trench.

In early June, Barber came home on leave and told his family and friends all about his experiences, some funny and others not so amusing. Despite his fear of life on the Western Front, he had kept his sense of humour. At the end of the month, Barber was sent to the Somme sector. Here, his diary entries came to an end. He was about to take part in one of the most notorious operations of the First World War.

On 1 July 1916, waves of British troops – many of them new recruits – were ordered out of their trenches to attack German lines defended by machine guns. In just one day, 60,000 soldiers were either killed or wounded. It was industrial-scale slaughter and fulfilled the dread of modern warfare experienced by those soldiers who had barely survived the increased firepower of the Boer War.

Two weeks later, Barber advanced in the second phase of the battle of the Somme. The 1st Battalion of the Cameron Highlanders was incorporated in the 1st Division, one of the more veteran divisions in the front line, being made up of regulars, including the 1st Battalion of the Black Watch. Their target was the Bazentin Ridge in the middle of the Somme battlefield. Rather than alerting the Germans with a long bombardment, a short five-minute barrage preceded the infantry attack. It worked, catching the Germans by surprise.

In the dark at 3.25 a.m., the first waves of British soldiers crawled across No-Man's Land. Accurate artillery fire on the German positions plus more sensible infantry tactics made for a quick, effective assault that captured the villages along the ridge by the end of the day. It was in marked contrast to the carnage of the first day of the Somme. Barber was part of the action and the success lifted the spirits of his Highlanders, who must have hoped it heralded a break-through.

Sadly, the triumph of the Bazentin Ridge was short-lived, as the Germans relentlessly counter-attacked. This was attritional warfare at its worst and the battle would drag on for months. Just over a week after the victory at Bazentin, Captain Gordon Barber was killed on the Somme. His father took comfort from the last letter he received from him.

> If I fall it is God's will, and is best for me. Don't think of me as dead, but rather as living the great and glorious life of that happy band of warriors who have fought the good fight and fallen in the Faith.[3]

Barber's father privately published his war diary in Liverpool in 1917 as a memorial to him – 'a dear son, a brave soldier, and a kind and generous friend'.

*

The massive deployment of manpower in the First World War demanded larger formations of soldiers. Secretary of State for War, Field-Marshal Lord Kitchener – victor of the Sudan – was under no illusion that this was a different kind of warfare to the colonial conflicts of the previous century fought by individual regimental battalions. Brigades of Highlanders had been assembled for the Crimean War and in South Africa to fight the Boers, but Kitchener believed the war begun in 1914 would last at least three years and needed seventy divisions to fight it, each made up of three brigades.

Regular battalions of Highland regiments, like Barber's Camerons, were allocated to different divisions and mixed with English regiments. At the Somme, the 1st Black Watch and the 1st Camerons fought side by side in the 1st Brigade of the 1st Division, but so many more Scotsmen volunteered for the Great War that in the Argyll and Sutherland Highlanders alone there were up to eleven battalions serving on different fronts during the war.

In 1908, the Territorial and Reserve Forces Act created a citizen reserve army of fourteen divisions. One of these was recruited from the Highlands and this became the Highland Territorial Division. In May 1915, it was retitled the 51st (Highland) Division and among its twelve battalions included Seaforth, Gordon, Argyll and Suther- land, and Black Watch Highlanders. A second Highland Territorial Division was raised in August 1914, numbered the 64th, but it remained on duty within the United Kingdom, providing reinforce- ments for the front-line division. Highland battalions also served in the 52nd (Lowland) Division, the 9th (Scottish) Division and the 15th (Scottish) Division, and established fine reputations on the Western Front and in the Middle East; but it was the 51st Highland Division that would draw most attention in both world wars.

In addition to the regular regiments and the extra battalions raised for the Highland divisions, there were Scottish territorial kilted regi- ments raised south of the border, such as the London Scottish and the Liverpool Scottish. The London Scottish can trace their origin back as far as the Napoleonic Wars when the Highland Armed Association of London and the Loyal North Britons were volunteers recruited to oppose the threat of French invasion. They were dis- banded soon after, but in 1859 the Highland Society of London, along with the Caledonian Society, helped form the London Scottish Rifle Volunteers. So as not to indicate any clan preference, they were clad in a hodden grey kilt chosen by their commander, Lieutenant-Colonel Lord Elcho. A traditional 'neutral' colour worn by Highland hunters, it was a very early form of camouflage. London Scottish volunteers served in the Boer War alongside the Gordon Highlanders and were the first Territorial infantry battalion to fight the Germans in 1914. The origin of the Liverpool Scottish also goes back to 1859 and they too sent volunteers to fight alongside the Gordon Highlanders in South Africa.

The Boer War was immensely influential on the evolution of the British Army in the first decades of the twentieth century. Its sol- diers had proved highly vulnerable to the accurate rifle fire of the Boer guerrilla fighters and this hastened a move towards a more modern approach. Not the least of these changes was the adoption of the khaki uniform, which became the official service dress of the British Army in 1902. Scarlet jackets were preserved only for cere- monial purposes. This transformation had an impact on Highland military uniforms. The government proposed the abolition of the kilt and the equipping of all Highland regiments in standard combat dress. When the Highland Society of London heard rumours of this, they began an active campaign to oppose it. The Secretary of State for War was visited by the President of the Society and several clan chiefs.[4] Questions were asked in the House of Commons.

'May I ask whether it is the intention of the War Office,' said the MP for Gateshead, 'that the distinctive tartans of the kilt are to be abolished in the Highland regiments in future, and whether this is being done by the War Office in revenge for Bannockburn?'

'Of course the distinctive tartans of the Highland regiments will be preserved,' replied the Secretary of State to loud cheers from the House.[5]

It was a victory for the Highland Society. The kilt was retained but several major changes were made to the appearance of the Highland soldier. He kept the characteristic round skirt front to his jacket, but wore a khaki apron over his kilt. It was a plain cloth garment secured at the waist – the compromise always desired by the government, providing standard camouflage for all its troops. He wore hose and gaiters or spats. The 'hairy purse' was replaced by the plain service leather sporran, but this was rarely worn. The Glengarry cap of dark blue was worn with a diced band around the edge for the Seaforths, Gordons and Argyll and Sutherland Highlanders, but plain for the Black Watch and Cameron Highlanders. This was later replaced by the smaller Balmoral bonnet with a khaki field-cover and then the looser, flat khaki tam o'shanter, big enough to take the large badges favoured by Highland soldiers.[6]

That the kilt was still very much part of the fighting spirit of the Highlander on the Western Front was proved by an incident during the build-up to the battle of the Somme in May 1916. To prevent the Germans from observing that the 51st Highland Division had extended its front prior to the attack, units of the 152nd Brigade were ordered to remove their kilts and Balmoral bonnets and wear ordinary khaki trousers and field service caps. This outraged the men, according to Captain Sutherland of the 5th Battalion Seaforth Highlanders, who, suspecting 'some Sassenach plot to strip them for ever of the kilt, grumbled very much and protested to their officers'.[7]

*

It was in the final stage of the battle of the Somme in northern France that the 51st Highland Division established its formidable reputation. The weather had deteriorated and delayed an attack from October into early November 1916. The target was German positions on the north bank of the river Ancre between Beaucourt and Serre. The 51st Highlanders were given the task of clearing Germans from the ruined village of Beaumont Hamel that had been heavily fortified. The 51st Highlanders had been nicknamed 'Harper's duds' after their HD initials, the name of their commander Major GM Harper, and the belief that they had not performed as brilliantly as expected in the earlier phase of the battle. The 51st Highlanders now had the opportunity to prove their critics wrong.

The early morning of 13 November 1916 was dark and misty as Highlanders crept into their advance positions in the trenches just 250 yards from the enemy lines. Weeks of rain had transformed the clay soil into a swamp with treacherous water-filled holes scattered across No-Man's Land. At 5.45 a.m. – an hour before sunrise – the battle began with the detonation of a massive mine near the enemy lines. Captain Sutherland and the 5th Seaforth Highlanders scrambled over the top of their parapets alongside the other Highland battalions of the 51st Division. Because of the wet ground, they were not running or walking towards the enemy, recalled Sutherland, 'but wading knee-deep and sometimes waist-deep through the morass of sticky mud and water and neck-deep shell holes'.[8]

An artillery barrage was supposed to have cut the barbed wire around Beaumont Hamel, but when the 5th Seaforths moved towards a German trench to the east of the village they found the fences still intact and were held up by heavy fire from German machine guns. A creeping artillery barrage was timed to advance just before the Highlanders, but because of the uncut wire, the shells went too far ahead, giving them little cover. The persistent early-morning fog did not help either and soon the Highland advance was broken into scattered groups with officers using compasses to find their direction.

One Seaforth Highlander had opened a bottle of fine whisky just before Zero Hour and then lightly replaced the cork in case, he claimed, it was needed for emergencies. As he pressed on across No-Man's Land, he realized that one stray bullet could shatter the precious bottle in the left pocket of his greatcoat and so he advanced with his right shoulder forward to protect it.

Eventually, Sutherland's men took their section of the first line of enemy trenches. They found the entrances to German dugout shelters and threw grenades inside them. By this time, the Highlanders were plastered with mud from head to foot and were annoyed to see the Germans looking clean in their dry uniforms; they took out their irritation by kicking them in the backside as they took them prisoner. As the 600 prisoners of the Seaforths were led back to the rear, Sutherland claimed a story went round about a padre from the nearby Naval Division who was said to have told the Seaforth officer to hand the Germans over to him. When the officer refused, the man of peace, it was said, punched him, knocking him unconscious into a shell hole, and then took the prisoners.

Elsewhere on the battlefield, the Gordons and the Black Watch dealt with strong resistance at a position called 'Y' Ravine. For the 5th Seaforths and 8th Argylls, the fighting got tougher when they reached a third line of trenches, with German machine guns and snipers inflicting several casualties. Two tanks were sent in to help, but got stuck in the mud. Instead, it was left up to a couple of Highland bombing parties to creep through the trenches and eliminate German resistance. By the end of the afternoon, the 51st Division had captured Beaumont Hamel and a total of 7,000 prisoners.

The fighting continued for several more days, but the 51st had done enough to establish their reputation. 'All the world looks upon the capture of Beaumont-Hamel as one of the great feats of the war,' wrote their Corps commander, 'and to those who know the ground and defences it must always be a marvellously fine performance.'[9] A statue commemorating the courage of the 51st Highlanders now stands on top of a stone cairn on a ridge in Beaumont Hamel Memorial Park and is affectionately known as the 'Jock on the Rock'.

*

The reputation of the 51st Division attracted volunteers from far and wide. Sergeant HE May, a London policeman, was in a protected occupation, but he escaped from London and journeyed overnight to Scotland where he volunteered in 1917. The corporal who trained him spoke Gaelic and shocked him with his swearing. May was transferred to the Gordon Highlanders and fought at Ypres. With so many English and other nationalities joining Highland regiments to get away from their ordinary life – and possibly difficulties – Highland regiments began to resemble the French Foreign Legion as a refuge for troubled men or men looking for adventure. One Lancashire soldier told a Scottish comrade, 'Ah've been a Jock longer than thee!'[10]

May was later a victim of a gas attack, which revealed the inadequacies of Highland uniform in modern warfare. 'A deluge of gas shells,' he recalled. 'Eyes swollen and red; throats parched; flesh inflamed and almost raw where the mustard variety of gas had burned it – a serious disadvantage of a kilt.'[11]

It was at the third battle of Ypres that two 51st Highlanders each won the Victoria Cross. Alexander Edwards was born at Lossiemouth on the coast of the Moray Firth, the son of a fisherman. He was twenty-nine years old when he joined the 6th Battalion of the Seaforth Highlanders in September 1914. He demonstrated a natural skill for leading men and was soon promoted to sergeant. He survived the fighting at the Somme in 1916 but was sent back home to recover from a throat infection. In the meantime, other members of his family had already proved their fearless character. His younger brother John had won a Military Medal, and his cousin George was awarded the DSO for capturing two hundred Germans – both were also in the ranks of the Seaforths.

With news of these family honours ringing in his ears, Edwards returned to the front line in July 1917. The third battle of Ypres was to be the last great combat of attrition fought on the Western Front, lasting over three months and culminating in the assault on Passchendaele, the alternative name for the battle. It was intended to be one final massive blow against a weakened German Army but turned into weeks of agonizing fighting across a waterlogged battlefield. Edwards took part in the attack on the first day on 31 July. He was acting Sergeant-Major of C company in the 6th (Morayshire) Seaforth Highlanders, part of the 152nd Brigade of the 51st Highland Division. Their mission was to advance down the shallow slope of Pilckem Ridge and take enemy positions on the banks of the Steenbeek stream.

The weather was horrendous and Edwards's battalion was soon

bogged down in muddy fields. Around locations dubbed Macdonald's Farm and Kitchener's Wood, they came under heavy fire from German machine guns hidden among the ruined buildings and splintered trees. A British tank clanked forward to knock out any resistance in the farm, but machine guns in concrete pillboxes continued to inflict heavy casualties on the Highlanders. Edwards's commanding officer was hit by one bullet and Edwards decided to creep forward by himself to locate the deadly gun.

He slid into a shell crater that gave him a good view of the rear of the pillbox. Armed with two revolvers, he aimed one at the open door of the concrete emplacement. His first bullet silenced the German firing the gun and other bullets finished off the rest of the crew. Having knocked out this obstacle, Edwards went back to order his men forward, but was struck in his right arm by a sniper's bullet. Realizing that this man also had to be dealt with, Edwards ignored his wound and, in the words of his medal citation, 'crawled out to stalk him'.[12]

Edwards hunted the sniper across open ground and along his line of fire, until he got near enough to finish him off. Despite bleeding heavily, Edwards continued to lead his men as they came close to the Steenbeek. They dug a shallow trench for shelter against the rattling German machine guns the other side of the bank. Edwards wanted to complete his mission by crossing the stream and taking the enemy guns, but had little choice except to sit tight as bullets tore up the mud around him. In the meantime he kept up the morale of his troops by shuffling along the trench and talking to them all, cheerily using their nicknames.

As Edwards waited in his trench, another Highlander had already distinguished himself in a remarkable solo attack on the enemy machine gun emplacements the other side of the stream. Private George McIntosh was also in the 152nd Brigade but was a twenty-year-old territorial in the 6th (Banff and Donside) Battalion of the Gordon Highlanders. His unit was to the right of Edwards's Seaforths. Earlier in the morning they had dug in about 200 yards away from the Steenbeek. As they did so they came under a hail of bullets from machine guns across the water. While his comrades took cover, McIntosh ran towards a narrow bridge over the stream.

The sight of a single figure charging towards them armed only with a revolver and one grenade surprised the Germans, but not enough to stop them firing. Their bullets ripped into his haversack and tattered his kilt, but he was not harmed. He pushed on from crater to crater until he reached the machine gun nest. The astonished Germans threw up their hands in surrender but McIntosh tossed in his Mills bomb, killing two and forcing the rest to run. He then calmly took hold of the two light machine guns, one on his shoulder and one under his arm, and walked back to his own line.

'Throughout the day,' said his VC citation, 'the cheerfulness and courage of Private McIntosh was indomitable, and to his fine example in a great measure was due the success which attended his company.'[13] He later explained his action by saying 'somebody had to gae forrit' and he knew he could throw a Mills bomb further and more accurately than anyone else in his unit.[14]

Meanwhile Sergeant Edwards found himself opposite several enemy strong points, and any attempt by British soldiers to storm across the Steenbeek was met by withering fire. A unit of King Edward's Horse had tried and been shot to pieces. When Edwards heard that the major of this cavalry squadron was lying badly wounded in the open, the Highlander ran out from his shelter to find the wounded officer and carried him back. By now, Edwards's right arm was swathed in blood-stained bandages but still he refused to give up.

Under the cover of worsening weather with the stream turned into a torrent by the rain, the Germans launched a counter-attack, but the Highlanders would not be moved and exploited the failed assault to make their own rush on the remaining bridges across the Steenbeek. Edwards led his Highlanders to capture two enemy strong points, but due to a lack of support had to give them up and return to his lines. In this fighting he received a further wound to his right knee from shrapnel. The next day, Edwards was ordered to report to the field hospital and finally accepted his removal from the front line in silence. The following month, he was awarded the VC. He later explained his motivation on that day.

If I had not gone on, it would not have given the boys much encouragement ... The wound on my arm was worst ... The sleeve was cut from my tunic, my hosetops were down over my boots and I was covered with mud. Oh, what a game ...[15]

'This very gallant NCO,' said the London Gazette, 'maintained throughout a complete disregard for personal safety, and his high example of coolness and determination engendered a fine fighting spirit in his men.'[16] Recovering from his wounds, Edwards was sent on leave to Scotland where he received a hero's welcome in Lossiemouth, being carried shoulder high through crowds of well-wishers. At Buckingham Palace, he received the Victoria Cross from King George V. But that was not the end of the war for Sandy Edwards.

Fully recovered from his wounds, he returned to the front line in France during the bitter fighting following Germany's last-ditch Spring Offensive. In five days of combat to halt the German advance in March 1918, his battalion suffered almost 400 casualties. One of them was Edwards himself, who was reported missing in action near Bapaume. His body was never found. A sundial memorial was later raised to him next to the final green at Moray golf course. Alongside his name is inscribed that of his cousin George, who won the DSO and was also killed on the Western Front. Together, as boys, they had loved playing on the links near the sea.

Having helped stem the German spring offensive of 1918 in France at the cost of nearly 5,000 casualties, the 51st Highlanders were called on again to hold the line in Flanders and suffered a further 3,500 dead, wounded and missing. A final German assault in the Champagne region was resisted and the Highlanders joined in the Hundred Days of Allied fighting that led to ultimate victory on the Western Front in November 1918. This brought 6,000 more casualties – a total of over 27,000 men of the 51st having been killed or wounded in the war. It was a heavy price to pay.

A year after the end of the war, the French President, Raymond Poincaré, visited Glasgow University to give a speech of thanks to the Scottish soldiers who fought on the soil of his country against the Germans. In his speech, he listed all the major battle honours of the 51st Division and the numbers of their casualties.

'To the mothers and widows of those heroes,' he concluded, 'I give the assurance that their image will ever be engraved in the memory and the heart of my country, and that the French women will take care of their graves as if they were those where their husbands and children are sleeping.'[17]

Chapter 14
World-wide Highlanders

As the British Empire spread around the world, Highlanders followed in its wake. Some of them had been on the front line, winning the battles that extended dominion, others came as farmers and traders. When they settled in far-flung lands, they liked to re-create a little bit of Scotland around them. For some this meant raising a Highland regiment. It was the beginning of a military heritage that would ensure an enduring affection for the Highland soldier among millions of people around the globe. However, the enthusiasm that some Scots emigrants first brought to the project was not always matched by those around them.

John Scott was a forty-one-year-old ex-soldier living in Cape Town in South Africa when he got the urge to lead his own band of Highlanders. Born in Aberdeen, he had tried three times to enlist in the army as a teenager before he was finally accepted. He served with the Royal North British Fusiliers (later the Royal Scots Fusiliers) in South Africa, seeing action in the Zulu War at the battle of Ulundi in 1879. Standing in the corner of a red-coated square, he and his comrades faced a wave of Zulu warriors banging their shields while the British poured volleys of rifle fire into them. Scott left the army just before the 1880 Boer War. Five years later, he was a respected member of Cape Town society when he got dragged into a dispute within the local Scottish community.

A volunteer Scottish company already existed in Cape Town, but when a decision was made to stop wearing the Highland doublet as part of their uniform, many local Scots became angry and proposed to set up a breakaway unit. They approached John Scott as a professional military man, and he agreed to become commander of a new corps called the Cape Town Highlanders. Some 150 local Scots agreed to join the unit and Scott keenly promoted a parade in which these new recruits would appear before the citizens of Cape Town. When the day arrived, a large crowd gathered to watch the new Highlanders march before them, but only three officers and sixteen men stepped forward. It was mortifying.

Undeterred, Scott formed his handful of men into a single rank and put them through some basic drill. They marched back and forth for an hour and then retired to a small room in the old Exchange Buildings. Some of the spectators shouted out their doubts as to the future of the unit, declaring there were not enough men for two Scottish corps in the town. Scott wondered whether they were right, but when he asked the crowd for volunteers he was pleased to receive many more names. By the time a second parade was called, there were a much more respectable 160 volunteers. The Cape Town Highlanders were up and running and by the end of the year they had an impressive new uniform.

Captain Scott and his fellow officers created a uniform that combined the Gordon tartan for their kilts with the sporran, spats and hose of the Sutherland Highlanders. A dark blue Glengarry with blackcock tail was worn with a dark green doublet without facings. The regimental badge took the shape of the Scottish Star with a thistle in the centre and 'CTH' in the garter. Officers wore trews, and there was a small drum and pipe band. The appearance of so many young men in kilts thrilled the local population, and some enterprising Scot even held classes to teach Gaelic. 'When toasts were exchanged in bars,' reported a local newspaper, 'the traditional Gaelic "Slainche Mhor" was given by people who had never been within 7,000 miles of Oban.'[1]

Within the year, the Cape Town Highlanders were called into action. The City Council had closed a burial ground on Signal Hill used by Malay immigrants. When the Malays came to bury one of their children, the police tried to stop them and were pelted with stones. Thousands of angry immigrants gathered around their burial ground, and at the sound of the firing of three guns, the CTH volunteers hastily pulled on their uniforms and marched out to confront them. They had, in fact, mistaken the signal, which was actually from a ship warning of fog; but the Highlanders turned out with pipes playing *The Campbells are Coming*.

The Malays were given a Riot Act warning and dispersed within a few minutes. A few days later, the Cape Town Highlanders took their first church parade at St Andrew's Church, and such was the excitement caused by their appearance that they recruited more volunteers, bringing their numbers up to 300 men. The next year, on the occasion of Queen Victoria's Diamond Jubilee, the Cape Town Highlanders turned out 400 men led by their newly imported regimental mascot – a Highland stag called Donald harnessed in black leather with silver mounts.

The first real fighting seen by the Cape Town Highlanders was in the Bechuanaland campaign. When Galishwe, a native ex-convict, had objected to his cattle being shot to prevent an outbreak of rinderpest, the incident ignited rebellion against the South African government. To the sound of bands playing *Auld Lang Syne*, the Cape Town Highlanders crowded on board a train and left for action in February 1897. They expected to be away for only a couple of weeks. After five and half months of trekking through snake-infested grassland with the Bechuanaland Field Force, Galishwe was tracked down, wounded and starving in a cave. Most of the Field Force casualties came from disease. Only two Cape Town Highlanders were wounded.

A more serious test came in 1899 with the outbreak of the Boer War. The Cape Town Highlanders were mobilized. Their parade dress was now khaki jackets worn with kilts, although blue jackets were worn for guard duty – and that was their first job, guarding key buildings in Cape Town. They envied the professional Highland Brigade as it marched off to fight the Boers under Major General Wauchope, but their first task on the battlefield was to send representatives to attend Wauchope's funeral after his men had been decimated at the battle of Magersfontein in December. News of the British Army's 'Black Week' shook the confidence of the residents of Cape Town.

By January 1900, the colonial volunteers, who had been originally dismissed as amateurs by the British Army, seemed a useful pool of men with good knowledge of the South African terrain. Several members of the Cape Town Highlanders were transferred to the bodyguard of Lord Kitchener, the new commander-in-chief, to form a squadron of Kitchener's Horse. With the surrender of the Boer command in February, the campaign entered a new phase of guerrilla warfare in which Boer commandos struck throughout the region. A company of the Cape Town Highlanders was sent to garrison the town of Jacobsdal, not far from the battlefield of Magersfontein.

On the morning of 24 October 1900 a dust storm swept through Jacobsdal, covering everyone in a thin layer of powdery sand. The Cape Town Highlanders were looking forward to an evening concert organized by the townspeople, but then came rolls of thunder, and rain lashed the little community. As outsiders huddled among the clapboard buildings, some seventy Boer guerrillas took advantage of the atrocious weather and smuggled themselves into the town. Their target was the 15-pounder gun guarded by the Cape Town Highlanders. With the concert cancelled, the Highlanders retired to their tents, but as dawn broke the next day they were abruptly woken by the sound of gunshots. A solitary sentry had challenged the Boer guerrillas as they made a grab for the gun. It was still pouring with rain and, in the confusion, the Cape Town Highlanders stumbled into the crossfire of snipers. Some were shot down in their tents and others piled biscuit boxes around them to make hasty defences.

The fighting continued throughout the morning as both sides scrambled around, looking for the best positions to fire pot shots at the enemy. Just after midday, a column of horsemen was spotted riding towards the town. If there had been more Boer guerrillas, the Highlanders would have had it. Fortunately, they were Colonial troops bringing up supplies. Rather than take cover, the horsemen bravely rode into the town and pitched in with the Highlanders. The 15-pounder gun was put into action but by the time its shrapnel tore into the enemy's holdouts, the majority of the Boers had taken to their horses and ridden off, leaving their commander dead with a bullet in the head.

The Cape Town Highlanders had been blooded. Ten of their number were dead, with nine seriously wounded, four dying later, and several more reported wounded. It brought home the cost of the war to Cape Town, and its grateful residents erected a memorial to the Highlanders' sacrifice at Jacobsdal.

When the First World War came, it was viewed by many as yet

another challenge to the British Empire. Colonial forces from around the globe rallied to the Union flag. The Cape Town Highlanders were no exception and several of their members volunteered for service abroad. They joined the South African Scottish, one of four battalions in the South African Infantry Brigade offered to the British Army by South African Prime Minister General Louis Botha. The kilted battalion also included soldiers from the Transvaal Scottish and Caledonian Societies throughout South Africa. They wore the collar badge of the Cape Town Highlanders and their tartan was of the Atholl Murrays, as their honorary colonel claimed descent from a member of the 77th (Atholl) Highlanders. Some 337 of these soldiers were born in Scotland, but the majority were South Africans, with a further 258 being English-born and 92 being Irish or Welsh.

Arriving in Britain in 1915, the South African Brigade expected to be sent across the Channel to the Western Front, but instead were re-routed to Egypt and ended up fighting Senussi tribesmen in Libya as part of the war against the Ottoman Turkish Empire. When these rebels were defeated, the South African Scottish finally arrived on the Western Front in 1916 where they served beside other Highland battalions, including the Black Watch, Seaforth and Camerons, in the 9th (Scottish) Division. They fought at the Somme, where they distinguished themselves at the attack on Delville Wood, but suffered heavy casualties, with a total of 502 men of the South African Infantry Brigade killed in three weeks of fighting.

The South Africans took part in the great battle of Ypres in 1917 but suffered so many casualties that they were withdrawn from the line for a rest. Along with the rest of the 9th Division, they were caught up in the German Spring Offensive of 1918. They held their part of the line at Marrieres Wood against fierce attacks but were hit by friendly fire from British artillery. Despite this, they held on for all they were worth, until they numbered barely 450 men left in a single composite battalion, with not even a single company left to represent the South African Scottish. It had been a dreadful slaughter and even the Kaiser was heard to comment, 'If all divisions had fought like the 9th I would not have had any troops left to carry on the attack.'[2]

The survivors of the South African Scottish were re-formed with reinforcements from Britain, and the South African Brigade ended the war as the easternmost troops of all Empire forces in France. The little world into which the Cape Town Highlanders had been born had gone for ever. The carnage of the twentieth century would claim more of the regiment's members in the Second World War in North Africa and Italy, although in both theatres they fought under their own regimental name. In Italy, from 1943, they were combined with the First City, another kilted South African Scottish unit originating from Grahamstown volunteers in Cape Province before 1835. Other kilted South African regiments fighting in the Second World War included the Transvaal Scottish and the 1st Anti-Tank Regiment, South African Artillery (Pretoria Highlanders).

In 1947, when Queen Elizabeth II celebrated her twenty-first birthday in Cape Town, the CTH formed the guard of honour, and forty-eight years later, when the Queen returned to meet the country's first black President, Nelson Mandela, they proudly repeated the duty. The Cape Town Highlanders are now a reserve infantry unit in the South African National Defence Force. Their drum and pipe band still delights audiences around the world, playing a fusion of Celtic music and African drumbeats.

*

In Asia, the evolution of Highland units followed the trade routes of Empire. In Calcutta there was a substantial community of Scottish merchants. In 1913, at a crowded meeting in the Theatre Royal, Norman McLeod stood up before an enthusiastic audience. 'The percentage of Scotchmen in Calcutta is very large,' he said, 'and it is almost a shame that Scotland does not take a specific and active part in protecting the very large interests represented by their countrymen.'

McLeod argued that a Volunteer force would not interfere with the working lives of those involved but would in fact add to their strength of character. 'Scottish and Highland Regiments have played a magnificent part in the wars of Empire,' he concluded. 'Scottish Volunteers have always been to the front in the movement and if you emulate their example it can only lead to success.'[3]

JB Ross of the Mercantile Bank of India in the appropriately named Clive Street had a letter published in the local newspapers appealing for volunteers. 'There is no reason why Calcutta, the second city of the Empire,' he wrote, 'should not be able to maintain a Scottish corps and thus rival other parts of the Empire where corps such as London Scottish and Toronto Highlanders do much to uphold the traditions of "Caledonia stern and wild".'[4] Ross was Secretary to the Scots of Calcutta and his appeals worked so magnificently that on 1 August 1914 nearly 300 local men stepped forward to enrol in the Calcutta Scottish Volunteers. Their uniform consisted of a kilt of Hunting Stewart tartan with a scarlet doublet, a white goat-hair sporran with six black tassels, green and white hose, a Glengarry with green and white diced border, and a white sun helmet.

In 1920 the Calcutta Scottish became part of the Army Auxiliary Force of India and was deployed on internal security missions. In 1926 they were called out to quell rioting in the city. They stood guard on important buildings and patrolled the streets at night. Early one morning a shot shattered the silence, and masonry and bricks showered down near a patrol. 'Nerves have been on edge owing to the darkness,' noted one of the Highlanders, 'and something bordering on panic follows the explosion. Confused orders from the patrol leader and a dash for cover from bombs, until sanity is restored by the discovery that the commotion was due to the sergeant's rifle having gone off accidentally.'[5]

The amateur character of this work was underlined by numerous jaunty reports gathered in the regiment's journal, which is filled more with sporting engagements than front-line action. It was in many ways an excellent club for its members. In 1947, with the independence of India, the Calcutta Scottish was disbanded.

The Singapore Volunteer Corps (SVC) established a Scottish company in 1922, alongside other companies representing European, Chinese and Malay inhabitants of the city. Their Major DG McLeod ensured they had a splendid uniform including a kilt in Hunting Stewart tartan and a sporran of white hair with six small black tassels mounted with a metal top and bells. An earlier sporran-top of patent leather had to be abandoned because it became sticky and unserviceable in the tropical climate. Their original plain blue Glengarry was changed to a knitted Balmoral with green and red diced band and a large red toorie (pompom). White spats were exchanged for khaki spats.

Like their Calcutta cousins, the Singapore Scottish were mainly deployed for ceremonial duties or internal security. In November 1922 the SVC were called out in the so-called battle of Lavender Street, in which twenty Chinese gangsters fought off a raid by the local police. The SVC brought in Lewis guns and light artillery to support the police, but by the time they arrived at the shoot-out, the Cantonese gang leader was dead and the rest had surrendered. Unfortunately, a Scottish volunteer sent a letter back home saying what the SVC had intended to do with their overwhelming fire-power and the lurid account got published in the *Dumfries and Galloway Advertiser*. A Scottish father was just about to send his daughter out to Singapore to get married when, he said, he was so shocked by the account of this 'hell spot' that he sent a letter to her fiancé saying that 'if he wished to marry his daughter he must find a job in a more civilized country!'[6] It was a case of Chinese whispers getting out of hand.

The Singapore Volunteer Corps survived until 1965, when with the independence of Singapore, it was renamed the People's Defence Force and became a combat-ready unit of the Singapore Army. Other southern Asian tartan-wearing Scots companies were raised within the Bombay Volunteer Rifles, the Rangoon Volunteer Rifles, the Shanghai Volunteer Corps, the Hong Kong Volunteer Defence Force and the Malay States Volunteer Force.[7]

Australia had little need to raise local militia troops throughout much of its early history and its Scottish immigration population was not exceptionally large. Of the 150,000 convicts transported to Australia, only just over 8,000 came from Scotland and most of these were being punished for burglary committed in and around Glasgow and Edinburgh.[8] The majority of law-abiding immigrants were Lowlanders, with some 39,000 Scottish men and women arriving between 1832 and 1850. Early senior administrators came with the British Army and Royal Navy and several of these were Scots – including three of the first six governors of New South Wales. Three Scottish regiments served in Australia during the colonial period but none of them was a Highlander.

The oldest Scottish regiment native to Australia was the New South Wales Scottish, raised in 1885 in Sydney. In 1898 the Victoria Scottish Regiment was raised in Melbourne and, a year later, the Cameron Highlanders of Western Australia were formed to keep order during the gold rush. They all responded to the call to arms sounded by the British Empire during the Boer War and sent volunteers to South Africa. The South Australian Scottish Regiment was raised in 1912 and the Byron regiment, named after a district in New South Wales, has been dated to 1914. All these units wore tartan and Highland dress.[9] They continued to serve the Empire and their country in the First and Second World Wars and afterwards in Korea and Vietnam. Although there are no Scottish regiments left today in the Australian Army, pipes and drums are played proudly by Australian Scots on ANZAC Day.

In New Zealand, four Scots volunteer units were raised in the late nineteenth century: the Christchurch Highlanders, Dunedin Highland Rifles, Wanganui Highland Rifles and Wellington Highland Rifles. In 1911, all these military personnel were transferred to the New Zealand Territorial Forces. But in 1937 the Scottish societies of New Zealand campaigned to resurrect a Scottish unit and the result was the formation of the kilted New Zealand Scottish Regiment in 1939. Only men of Scottish descent were accepted into its ranks and an affiliation with the Black Watch was authorized. It came as a disappointment that the unit was not sent on active service, but many of its soldiers served in Italy. In 1949 it was reformed as the 1st Armoured Car Regiment (New Zealand Scottish).

*

By far the biggest Scottish population outside of Scotland is located in Canada. In 2006 a national census reported that 4,709,859 Canadians regarded themselves as of Scottish origin. With only an ocean to separate them from a landscape and climate similar to their own, Scots have been making their mark on the country since the seventeenth century. Early on, they named a territory after their own, when Nova Scotia was claimed on behalf of the kingdom of Scotland in 1621. In the early eighteenth century men from Orkney joined the Hudson Bay Company and settled in the province of Manitoba, while many of General Wolfe's Highlanders who defeated the French at Quebec stayed on. They married French women and some of their families today are completely French-speaking but with Scots surnames. From 1770 to 1815, 15,000 Highland farmers arrived in Nova Scotia and Upper Canada. Many of them spoke only Gaelic and maintained their Highland traditions.

After 1815, it was mainly Lowlanders that came to Canada, in enormous numbers – some 170,000 before 1870, almost 14 per cent of British migrants. A third of Nova Scotians could claim to have come from Scotland. These hard-working Scots quickly prospered in business and trade and the first two Canadian Prime Ministers were born in Scotland. Scots immigrants continued to pour into the country in the twentieth century, with 240,000 arriving just in the years before the First World War. Many of the later immigrants avoided the familiar areas along the Atlantic coast and struck out to settle in Ontario and the west of the country.

With such a strong Scottish heritage, it is hardly surprising that Canada should have the largest contingent of Highland military units anywhere in the world outside their homeland. These include the Black Watch (Royal Highland Regiment) of Canada, the Stormont, Dundas and Glengarry Highlanders, the Pictou Highlanders, the North Nova Scotia Highlanders, the Cape Breton Highlanders, the Cameron Highlanders of Ottawa, the Argyll and Sutherland Highlanders of Canada (Princess Louise's), the Queen's Own Cameron Highlanders of Canada, the Calgary Highlanders and the Seaforth Highlanders of Canada.[10]

One of the most venerated of the Canadian Highland regiments is the Black Watch of Canada, which was founded in 1862. The outbreak of the American Civil War was the trigger for the raising of many militia units since Britain was sympathetic to the Southern states and feared its long Canadian border might be vulnerable to a Federal attack. Six companies of the 5th Battalion of the Royal Light Infantry were formed in Montreal, each of them commanded by prominent local Canadians, all with Scottish family names. The following year, three more companies were added, including a Highland Rifle Company. Despite their Highland character, these were light infantry units and so were dressed not in kilts but in trousers.

In 1866 and 1870 the Canadian Scottish militia units faced their first real challenge when Irish Fenians based in the United States sent raiders across the border. The militia turned out to patrol the frontier and the show of strength dissuaded the Fenians from any major action.

Within the Scots community in Montreal there was a strong desire to turn their light infantry soldiers into a kilted regiment and this eventually bore fruit in 1880, after funds had been set up to raise the money for the expensive uniform. Wealthy business friends of the regiment helped boost the funds and by 1895 they added feather bonnets with the red hackle. They were now called the Royal Scots of Canada and slowly but surely they acquired every uniform detail of the Black Watch, their parent regiment in Scotland.

During the Boer War, the Royal Scots of Canada contributed a greater proportion of volunteers to the British forces in South Africa than any other Canadian regiment. They were rewarded for their loyalty by being officially allied to the Black Watch in Britain in 1905. It is a connection valued by both regiments, and many former soldiers have left their Scottish unit in Perth to emigrate to Canada and there rejoin the ranks of the Canadian Black Watch.

In 1914 the Canadian Minister of Militia immediately promised to raise an expeditionary force of 25,000 Canadians to send to Europe to assist Britain. Over a thousand men stepped up in the Canadian Black Watch for service abroad and they were designated the 13th Battalion, Royal Highlanders of Scotland. Within six months, they voyaged across the Atlantic and were entrenched on the Western Front. Three more battalions followed, full of Scottish Canadian volunteers.

On the afternoon of 22 April 1915 during the second battle of Ypres, the 13th Black Watch were positioned on the front line in Belgium with Turco (French North African troops) on their left and the Toronto 15th Highlanders on their right. The enemy were only seventy-five yards away in their trenches and they unleashed a heavy bombardment for two hours that shook up the Turcos and the Black Watch. Then, for the first time in the history of warfare, came a new danger. Clouds of yellow-green chlorine gas billowed across the battlefield. Overwhelmed by the poison gas in their lungs, the Turcos panicked and fled. Behind the clouds of chlorine came lines of German soldiers. Despite this horrifying assault, the Canadian Highlanders held firm and fired at the Germans as they streamed past them in pursuit of the Turcos towards their target of capturing St Julien.

'At first a faint, sour pungency, that dried our mouths and set us coughing', was how one Canadian described the first whiffs of the gas attack, but then it took a terrible toll of the soldiers in its way.

'Row after row of brawny Canadian Highlanders lay raving and gaspy [sic] with the effect of the horrible gas,' recalled Private Harold Baldwin, 'and those nearing the end were almost as black as coal. It was too awful – and my nerves went snap!'[11]

At great risk to themselves, a company of Highlanders in the rear tried to stem the flow of retreating French troops. Captain Guy Drummond spoke French to them but was killed almost instantly by the heavy artillery fire. Eventually, the Highlanders rallied 200 of the Turcos and they rejoined the company at the front who stood their ground despite their ranks being thinned by heavy shelling. Several times the Germans tried to shift the Black Watch but they would not move and the fighting continued into the night.

The next day, the Canadian Highlanders withdrew 300 yards to shorten their line and get a better field of fire. Germans dressed in captured French uniforms tried to bluff their way through but were shot down. The Germans pressed forward on three sides of the Highlanders, but the Canadians only intensified their resistance. One of them was Lance-Corporal Frederick Fisher. He grabbed his machine gun and ran forward to cover the withdrawal of some comrades. Four of his team were shot around him, but he kept on blazing away. With four more men he then returned to the firing line to cover the advance of other Highlanders. But this time his luck ran out and he was cut down. For his bravery, Fisher became the first Canadian in the war to be awarded the Victoria Cross.

Almost surrounded and running short of food and water, the 13th Black Watch held on throughout the day. It was only at 10.00 p.m. that they were finally ordered to withdraw. Carrying their wounded with them, they conducted a fighting retreat, allowing fresh troops to fill their gap in the line. The next day the Germans released more poison gas, forcing the Toronto Highlanders to join their comrades. Several battalions of British soldiers passed through the remnants of the Canadians as they licked their wounds. On the 28th, with a draft of reinforcements, the 13th Black Watch rejoined the attack and stayed on the battlefield until 4 May, when they were finally pulled out.

In those bitter days at Ypres the Black Watch won a terrific reputation for tenacity and courage. They had helped hold the line and prevent a disastrous defeat in the face of the first chlorine gas attack of the war. When news of their brave stand reached Scotland, the parent regiment proudly added their name to their recruiting poster, saying: 'With which is allied the 13th Canadian Battalion, RHC'.[12] Recognition of their contribution to a strong tradition did not come any better than that.

All Canadian Highland battalions performed well in the First World War and won several more Victoria Crosses. Piper James Cleland Richardson was a recent immigrant to Canada with his family from Lanarkshire. His father became chief of police in British Columbia while James joined the 72nd Seaforth Highlanders of Canada in 1914. During the battle of the Somme in 1916 his Highlanders were part of the 1st Canadian Division advancing on a position called Regina Trench, between the villages of Courcellette and Grandcourt. Bogged down by barbed wire, the assault ran out of steam but Piper Richardson struck up his pipes and marched up and down the line for ten minutes in the face of enemy fire. Inspired by his bravery, his comrades resumed the attack and broke through the wire. He was later killed in the same battle, while retrieving his pipes, but he was awarded a posthumous Victoria Cross for his inspirational playing.

The Black Watch of Canada went on to win battle honours at the Somme, Arras, Vimy, Passchendaele and Amiens. In the Second World War they joined the British and Americans in Normandy in 1944 and fought their way across Nazi-occupied Europe. The contribution of all Highland units from around the world to the success of allied forces in both world wars was remarkable testimony to the enduring fighting culture of the Highlander.

Chapter 15
Vengeance for St Valery

Andrew Meldrum was a bricklayer's apprentice when he saw the Second World War come to Scotland. He was building a swimming pool at the Royal Navy base at Rosyth when he saw the first German air raid on British soil. He and his mates took cover as nine Junkers Ju-88 bombers swooped low to attack ships in the Firth of Forth. One bomb came perilously close to hitting a passenger train on the Forth Bridge, the main link between Edinburgh and the Highlands. The bombers struck two small battleships and killed sixteen naval personnel, but were chased away by RAF Spitfires that shot two of them down. It was 16 October 1939. A month later, Meldrum received his call-up papers. He reported to barracks in Perth and became No 2758507, Private Meldrum, 2nd Battalion, Black Watch.

For the next six years Meldrum would serve in every major theatre of the war from France to Egypt to Crete to Burma. His remarkable career embodied the wide-ranging demands on the tenacity, bravery and endurance of the Highland soldier in the Second World War – as one regimental curator put it, 'the 2nd battalion had all the shit jobs'.

Meldrum embraced the square-bashing, becoming quite skilled at rifle drill and the spit and polish demanded. The Black Watch regularly marched into Perth to show everyone how they were being methodically transformed from civvies into soldiers. A piper led them and they wore their dark tartan kilts, but in reality this was the end of the road for the kilted fighting man. Khaki battle-dress was now the official combat outfit of every soldier in the

British Army. When they went to war, they looked like workmen equipped for the job of defending their nation's liberty. One of the reasons given for the demise of the kilt was the threat of skin-blistering mustard gas, but kilts were still worn by pipers and drummers and sometimes, in the first year of the war, a few die-hard soldiers wore them in the combat zone.

In January 1940 Meldrum was one of a hundred Black Watch from the 2nd Battalion drafted to join the British Expeditionary Force (BEF) in France. The Germans had won a quick campaign in Poland and were shifting their attention to the west where their next move was to be against Scandinavia. To the British it was still the Phoney War, and Meldrum was more concerned about the poor state of French sanitation. 'The train which took us down to Abbev-ille had only a hole in the floor for the toilet,' remembered Meldrum. 'I thought this to be very backward and not at all like home.'[1]

Meldrum's task was to help build a field hospital next to a château at Abbeville. The material they were given came from the First World War, right down to the duckboards to cover muddy ground. After four months of this, the war came to France. The German blitzkrieg swept through Holland and Belgium, pushing back the British Expeditionary Force to the coast. The 51st High-land Division was further south, sitting in trenches defending the French Maginot Line, when the German panzers simply drove round them. Private John Clarke was in the 1st Battalion of the Black Watch when he was ordered to fall back with the rest of the 51st Highland Division and fight a rearguard action to protect the BEF as it raced towards evacuation from French coastal ports. Clarke and his Highlanders marched in the dark and dug in during the day to shelter from the constant air attacks. 'The marching by night was terrible,' recalled Clarke, 'as most of us were walking as if in a trance for lack of sleep.'[2]

Meldrum and his hundred comrades in the 2nd Battalion Black Watch tried to link up with Clarke and the 1st Battalion but were forced back by German Stuka dive-bomber raids. They tried to join the 4th Battalion and the rest of the 51st Highlanders, but again were cut off by German aerial bombardment. Back in Rouen, their commanding officer told them to make their way to the fishing port of St Malo from where they could be shipped back home. It was a march of over a hundred miles and by the time Meldrum got there he was feeling ill. His feet were bad and a ticket to that effect was pinned on his jacket as he was carried on to a hospital ship. On the quayside, he saw soldiers of the 51st Division queuing up patiently, fully armed and combat-weary. They had fought their way out. By the time Meldrum got back to Britain, his feet had become badly infected. 'When my wife came to visit me in hospital,' said Meldrum, 'I handed her the entire skin from my left foot which they had removed as it was completely black.'

Meldrum had escaped the Germans, but Clarke was not so lucky. The 1st Battalion of the Black Watch fought side by side with the French at Abbeville to halt the German advance, but they could not hold them back for long. In the meantime, the Germans were cutting off all escape routes along the French coast. The 4th Battalion conducted a fighting retreat but were lucky to get on boats at Cherbourg. The 1st Battalion was falling back towards Le Havre with the rest of the 51st Division when they took up positions at the little port of St Valery-en-Caux late on 10 June.

It was a desperate situation: German tanks and artillery drove up to the heights overlooking the harbour, threatening any Royal Navy vessels that might dare to rescue them. German aircraft howled overhead. General Erwin Rommel, commander of the 7th Panzer Division, offered surrender to Major-General Victor Fortune of the 51st, but he rejected it. Instead, Highlanders built barricades with their bare hands in the streets of the port to block the German tanks. They fought like wild cats.

'They engaged the first tank – shot at it, killing the crew and putting it out of action,' said one London soldier watching the Highlanders. 'Then the second tank slewed round, so they fired at it and put that one out of action. The third tank turned round and drove off.'[3] The Highlanders might have been able to see off tanks, but there was little they could do against Stuka dive-bombers and the long-range artillery battering the fishing village.

They fought on, but running short of ammunition they were told that the Royal Navy would not be able to evacuate them. Even then, Major-General Fortune and his Highlanders wanted to carry on fighting. On the morning of 12 June the French contingent, trapped in the village alongside them, had had enough and ran up a white flag on the steeple of a church just a hundred yards from the 51st headquarters. Fortune was furious and ordered it brought down immediately, not knowing it was flown by the order of the French commander. Captain Ian Campbell, the future Duke of Argyll and a British intelligence officer, was sent to take it down and discovered a frightened Moroccan Major who had climbed into the belfry to hang out the white flag.

Campbell was ordered to confront the French commander and tell him that 'the 51st had no intention of surrendering and would continue to fight, if necessary entirely independently of the French'.[4] They were brave words, but the French commander showed Campbell his own definite orders to surrender, dated two hours earlier. As Campbell returned to the divisional headquarters, he saw German tanks rolling along the streets of St Valery, while shells and machine-gun bullets rained down around him. Despite the courage of the Highlanders, the situation was impossible and Fortune had to accept surrender and order his men to lay down their arms.

The 51st's war had come to an end too early and at St Valery more than 10,000 Highlanders became Rommel's prisoners. When Fortune was introduced to the German commander, he announced his decision to accept capitulation but added that he would not have been standing there if his force had any ammunition left.[5]

Prime Minister Winston Churchill blamed the French for this disastrous loss of men. 'I was vexed,' he later wrote in his history of the war, 'that the French had not allowed our division to retire on Rouen in good time, but had kept it waiting until it could neither reach Havre nor retreat southward, and thus forced it to surrender with their own troops.'[6] But it has also been argued that the 51st had already been sacrificed for the good of the Anglo-French alliance, when Fortune was placed under the command of the French and thus had no authority to abandon his allies and escape to the coast.[7] Certainly Churchill felt a sense of guilt about the French absorbing most of the blows from German blitzkrieg, but when the French urged him to throw the RAF into the battle, he declined, knowing it was not the right place or time to commit all his forces. It seems likely then that the 51st had simply been outpaced by the fast-moving sequence of events.

Churchill was right when he said that the 'fate of the Highland Division was hard'. As the 51st were rounded up by their captors, Private Clarke felt humiliated.

We were lined up on the road where we were searched by the Germans. I don't know about the rest of the lads but I felt about two feet tall as they helped themselves to anything they fancied.[8]

John Clarke and his comrades faced a long march into captivity. Some of the wounded Highlanders fell at the side of the road, never to get up again. Clarke teamed up with two mates and, when they could, they broke away from the column to grab vegetables from the fields and pick up bundles of wood. When they stopped at night, herded into a field, they made fires and roasted the vegetables. When officers discarded their greatcoats, Clarke and his friends picked them up and wore them to gatecrash the officers' enclosure at night. It meant they got a better meal than the other ranks, but they were soon spotted by Black Watch officers who told the Germans, and they were kicked out.

The Germans delighted in mocking their prisoners. On one occasion they stood at the edge of a field and threw a loaf of bread to the hungry Highlanders. One soldier grabbed the bread but then was jumped on by other starving men. 'The Germans kept repeating this all the time,' noted Clarke, 'laughing their heads off at the scene below.' Clarke got his revenge by surviving the ordeal and eventually escaping back to Britain. Just seven weeks after the capture of the 51st Highlanders at St Valery, the 9th (Highland) Infantry Division based in Scotland was retitled the 51st. They too would have their vengeance.

*

When Private Andrew Meldrum was fit again for service, he was sent back to Perth to rejoin the Black Watch. The majority of the 2nd Battalion were in East Africa fighting the Italian Army that had launched an attack on British Somaliland from Abyssinia. At one stage, and vastly outnumbered, the Black Watch covered the withdrawal of the King's African Rifles by fixing bayonets and charging downhill at the Italians in a splendidly old-fashioned Highland assault. Meldrum missed this, but rejoined his battalion in Egypt after sailing around Africa via Cape Town.

The Black Watch moved out into the North African desert but

was not directly involved in the defence of Tobruk, beginning in April 1941. An Australian division took on the brunt of this fighting against General Erwin Rommel and his Afrika Korps. After his brilliant panzer victories in northern France, the fifty-year-old German general had been sent to North Africa to stiffen the resolve of the Italians who had lost thousands of their soldiers as prisoners. Rommel's presence struck dread in the British Army who began to doubt their ability to win against him. The nine-month struggle for Tobruk took on an epic quality as it developed into a personal duel between Rommel and the British.

During April 1941 the 2nd Black Watch carried out patrols and more training in Egypt. Worryingly, one exercise included learning how to swim in full combat gear. Their instructor, a Major, showed them how to keep their weapons dry while crossing a river. With a Bren gun on his shoulders, he boldly jumped into a swimming pool – and sank straight to the bottom. 'He had to be rescued by some of the lads,' remembered Meldrum, 'and after this incident we nicknamed him the "Mad Major".'

Before the Black Watch could be committed to the defence of Tobruk, they were sent to tackle another crisis which was fast developing in the Mediterranean. To help out the Italians yet again – this time they had botched an invasion of the Balkans – Hitler committed his forces to a blitzkrieg attack on Greece. In response, a British army withdrew to Crete and received reinforcements from Egypt in the hope of holding the island. The 2nd Battalion were part of this and were given the task of defending the airfields at Heraklion.

The mountainous landscape of Crete reminded Meldrum of the Highlands, and to avoid some German air raids they hid in caves. The Highlanders dug slit trenches around the airfield and set up minefields ahead of their positions. They were expecting a conventional attack from the sea, but what they got was a new form of warfare – aerial assault by paratroopers. From 20 May, following a savage air bombardment, thousands of German paratroopers dropped on key positions on the island. 'The air was thick with them,' said Meldrum, 'and like sitting ducks, they were slaughtered. I don't think many of them survived.'

A second wave of paratroopers landed in the valley near the airfield. Some of them grouped at a farmhouse but the Black Watch blew it apart. Meldrum went through the enemy dead, collecting their identity discs. The Germans had failed to take Heraklion airfield but elsewhere they were successful, and the Black Watch received orders to evacuate their position and make their way at night through vineyards to ships waiting for them on the coast. Meldrum and his Highlanders caught the last ship off the island. Another ship in the convoy was bombed on its way to Alexandria and over a hundred Black Watch went down with it.

The situation was now looking bleak for the British in the Near East after Rommel repulsed a British attempt to relieve Tobruk. Meldrum and his 2nd Battalion were brought up to strength by the addition of over a hundred Southern Rhodesians and then sent into Tobruk to replace the Australians. The Germans constantly bombed the harbour of the besieged city, but the Royal Navy defied them and kept bringing in supplies. Some of the activities devised by the Highlanders to keep themselves entertained included illegal gambling. Three Black Watch fife players were always trying to raise money for drinks and when they got a skinful were happy to take on anyone who challenged their regiment, including some equally drunk Green Howards.

In November 1941 the British began a major offensive to end the stalemate: their tanks battled against Rommel's Afrika Korps in the desert at Sidi-Rezegh, while the Tobruk garrison joined in the fighting. On 20 November, the 2nd Battalion Black Watch advanced with tank support. The attack was at dawn and every Highlander was given a tot of rum. Meldrum was armed with a Bangalore torpedo to throw over the barbed wire of the enemy positions and blast their way through. He considered it a suicide mission as he felt sure he would end up stepping on the tripwire of a German mine.

When the time came, Meldrum managed to avoid any traps and his mates passed through relatively unscathed. He took three German prisoners, but when he returned he found his commanding officer, Lieutenant-Colonel George Rusk, in tears. Another company of Black Watch, including many of the Rhodesians, had been badly shot up by German machine guns, with over a hundred dead. Their Pipe Major Roy, though wounded in both legs, had kept on playing *Highland Laddie* and other tunes, which kept up their spirits; but it had been a savage mauling and Rusk felt it badly.

Rommel managed to check the initial offensive, but the British held their nerve, pushed ahead again and surrounded some of the German forces, eventually pressing them to withdraw. For the moment, the British had saved the situation in North Africa but the final showdown was to come a year later in 1942. Meldrum and his Highlanders had done their bit and were removed from the theatre to undertake some political manoeuvring in Syria where they confronted the Vichy French. For the moment, Meldrum was out of the line of fire. It was up to other Highlanders to take up the task and finish off the Germans in North Africa.

*

Alex Clark from Aberdeen wanted to join the Highlanders when he was just seventeen years old. His father had been a sergeant in the Gordon Highlanders in the First World War, was wounded and taken prisoner at Passchendaele. Some of Alex's friends had managed to get in, but he was quite small for his age and was not yet shaving. The army got a copy of his birth certificate and refused to accept him, but a year later he was in. It was January 1942 and he had joined the 1st Battalion of the Gordon Highlanders. After three months' basic training in Scotland, he was put on a troopship to Port Suez. From there, the Gordon Highlanders joined the 51st (Highland) Infantry Division and carried out several more months of training, getting used to the weather and the desert landscape. The smooth-faced Private Alex Clark was given the job of company runner, one step behind the Sergeant Major, ready to take his messages anywhere. The officer knew the young lad needed a fatherly hand and liked to keep him close.

The 51st Division was at the forefront of General Bernard Montgomery's plans for a major offensive in North Africa towards the end of 1942. Monty had halted Rommel's attempt to seize Egypt and the Suez Canal and now wanted to finish him off. So too did the Highlanders, whose comrades had been humiliated by him at St Valery. Montgomery had learned his military trade in the First World War and knew the value of a strong artillery barrage tightly followed by an infantry advance. He also wished to avoid any needless slaughter and put meticulous planning into the detail of the assault, ensuring that no soldier's life would be wasted. His men loved Monty – he had given them back their confidence – and they were determined to put on a good show for him.

Major-General Douglas Wimberley was the commander of the 51st Highland Division and he believed that the military tradition of the Highlanders was the key to their motivation. 'Tell a man his father fought well,' he said, 'his grandfather fought well – and when it comes to the bit he won't let you down.'[9] His men returned the compliment by nicknaming him 'Tartan Tam'.

The 51st Highlanders were given an idea of what to expect of fighting in North Africa by the experienced 9th Australians. They were to be one of four infantry divisions to make the initial attack at El Alamein. Besides Alex Clark's 1st Battalion of Gordon Highlanders, were two battalions of Seaforth Highlanders, three Black Watch (not Meldrum's 2nd), one Cameron, one Argyll and Sutherland Highlanders and another battalion of Gordons.

The battle of El Alamein began on the evening of 23 October 1942 at 9.40 p.m. Nearly a thousand British artillery guns opened fire on German positions. Private Alex Clark found it terrifying. When the firing ceased, the bagpipes of the Highland Division sounded[10] and they advanced into the darkness – their mission to take a five-mile corridor of the enemy line so that tanks could follow through.

Enemy guns had not been wholly silenced by the bombardment and Clark crouched down as they advanced, but his Sergeant Major stood up as though he was on a parade ground, firing his rifle as he led his men forward. It made him a prime target – and he was struck by a German bullet.

> My Sergeant Major fell in front of me, and I knew when I saw him, that he was dead. I don't know what came over me – but I picked up my rifle and charged like a banshee shouting at the Germans. I won't tell you exactly what I was shouting, but they'd killed my Sergeant Major. I thought this was a terrible thing that had happened to me, that they could do this.[11]

From that point on, Clark did not care if he was killed or not. He just got on with his job. Later, he was made up to Lance Corporal and then Corporal. Clark never forgot the name of his Sergeant Major – Hugh Sinclair – and visited his war memorial every year to pay his respects.

Clark and the Gordons took their objective and captured thousands of prisoners, but if they thought the battle was over, they were wrong. Rommel's Afrika Korps fell back in good order and Montgomery's army had to chase them across the desert. Some of the fighting included night raids in one of which Clark and another Highlander blew up a German machine gun post with hand grenades. Sometimes they had to clear mines. 'We used to have to use our bayonets to dig in at an angle to feel the metal,' he recalled. 'Then you had to clear sand off the top of the mine and lift it out away to the side.' Generally, this was the job of engineers and specially converted tanks with revolving chain flails that ignited the mines. 'They were great things – but sometimes they got knocked out so readily.'

The battle of El Alamein and the subsequent pursuit lasted until the end of the year. At the same time, the Americans landed in Morocco and advanced rapidly towards the rear of the German positions in Tunisia. In March 1943, Rommel, ill and defeated, was recalled from North Africa. The battle of El Alamein was one of the decisive battles of the Second World War. It lifted allied morale considerably and showed that the so far invincible Germans could be beaten. The 51st Highlanders had played a full part in this triumph and acquired the nickname of 'Highway Decorators', derived from their divisional abbreviation. They would proudly paint a large red 'HD' on the side of buildings or on tin signs wherever they went.

In February 1943, Winston Churchill flew into North Africa and took the salute of the 51st Highlanders as they marched in a victory parade at Tripoli. With helmets to boots all polished, Signaller Aston Fuller from the Royal Artillery was attached to the Highlanders and was swept up in the pride of the moment. 'The kilted pipers, figures erect, lead,' noted Fuller. 'The gallant men march with pride ... gone now is the dust and sweat ... the Division is proud.'[12] The bitter humiliation of St Valery was erased and the reborn 51st had had its revenge against General Rommel.

*

That the fighting was not completely over in North Africa was proved by the award of two Victoria Crosses to Argyll and Sutherland Highlanders in April 1943.

Lieutenant-Colonel Lorne MacLaine Campbell was forty-one years old when he led his battalion of Highlanders into battle at night at the Wadi Akarit in Tunisia on 6 April. They took the enemy position and captured 600 prisoners, but that was only the beginning of his task. When daylight came, Campbell realized that the gap blown in an anti-tank ditch did not correspond with a vehicle lane cleared through the enemy minefields. Under heavy fire Campbell took personal charge of ensuring that a gap was made ready for the Allied anti-tank guns, but as the day progressed German tanks and soldiers increased their counter-attacks.

The Argyll and Sutherland Highlanders held on, determined to keep their bridgehead into the enemy position. Campbell moved among his men, cheering them on. He had already demonstrated his close relationship to them when he led 200 Highlanders to safety in France in 1940, personally scouting out gaps through the German lines at night. Now in the desert, he rallied his troops when they faltered in the face of enemy fire and kept them holding their positions until darkness fell. At one stage he was wounded in the neck by a splinter of mortar shrapnel, but he kept on pushing his men to resist.

'This officer's gallantry and magnificent leadership when his now tired men were charging the enemy with the bayonet and fighting them at hand grenade range,' said the official citation in the London Gazette, 'are worthy of the highest honour, and can seldom have been surpassed in the long history of the Highland Brigade.'[13]

When an officer later saw Campbell with a bandage around his face and asked him if he had been wounded, he replied with typical understatement and a broad grin, 'No, just cut myself while shaving.'[14]

Major John Thompson McKellar Anderson of the 8th Battalion Argyll and Sutherland Highlanders was one of the 200 men Campbell had brought out of France in 1940. Like his Colonel, he believed in leading from the front and showed his courage under fire during a Highland assault on Longstop Hill in Tunisia on 23 April 1943. The high point had to be taken so as to allow the allies to break through the German line to Tunis. Anderson was second in command of the battalion and led them across the open hillside against enemy fire to take their first objective.

The Highlanders suffered heavy casualties, including their commanding officer, forcing Anderson to take over and lead them to take their second objective on top of the hill with just four surviving officers and fewer than forty other ranks. The fighting demanded they capture three machine gun positions and each time Anderson was the first man into the pit. He was wounded in the leg but carried on leading from the front until the hill top was secured and the allies could continue their advance. On a previous occasion, when Anderson won the DSO, he was observed to 'walk calmly along in enemy machine gun and mortar fire'.[15] One mortar shell landed next to him and killed or wounded everyone else close by. He merely scratched his leg and walked on.

*

Victory in North Africa meant the allies could establish their base for an invasion of Italy. The first step in this campaign was the conquest of Sicily, and the experienced soldiers of the 51st Highland Division took part in the operation in July 1943. Corporal Alex Clark was now in the 5th/7th Battalion of the Gordon Highlanders. The British advanced up the east coast of the island and had a tougher time than the Americans on the other side. The Highlanders faced Germans methodically withdrawing before them, fighting hard to give their comrades time to evacuate from Messina. The Italians, in contrast, were mostly keen to surrender to the allies, knowing that their part in the war was rapidly coming to a close. Clark and his Highlanders had been warned to treat the Sicilians as potential enemies, but they got on very well with them. 'We helped them with their harvests,' he remembered, 'taking in the grapes and everything.'

One night, the Gordon Highlanders' band played for the local people in a town square. Captain Hamish Henderson of the 51st Intelligence section had no idea his troops were so far ahead of the front line and was shocked to hear the sound of pipes echoing through the Sicilian hillside. He left his jeep and crept up to the village to see Clark and his Highlanders marching and dancing with the locals who were clapping their hands to the drone of the bagpipes. 'The local Iti civilians thought our Highland pipe bands were just the cat's pyjamas,' wrote Henderson, who later had a distinguished career preserving traditional Scottish music.[16]

'I am just a clown to follow the pipes,' said Clark. 'The pipes were an integral part of our marching. We didn't go marching without our piper. He didn't play all the way, he took breaks but he was always there to drum up and give you a tune.'[17]

At the end of the Sicilian campaign, the 51st Highland Division was sent home and ordered to prepare for another great invasion. Montgomery was to command that operation – the projected invasion of north-west Europe in 1944 – and he wanted with him his veteran soldiers, including the Highlanders. They were by now regarded as an elite formation and were part of what had become a war-winning team.

In a farewell order of the day read to his soldiers in Sicily, divisional commander General Wimberley paid tribute to their performance throughout the campaigns in North Africa and Sicily. It was a revival in their fighting spirit, he said, which began at 'Alamein and the moonlit night, when you went into your first battle, new and untried as individuals, but bearing in your historic tartans and your pipes an inheritance of centuries of gallantry from your forebears, and each bearing Scotland's banner in your hearts'.[18]

It was an attitude to war that was embraced by soldiers not even remotely connected to a Highland regiment. When Britain's new elite force of commandos raided German positions at Vaagso in 1941, their second in command was Major Jack Churchill from the Manchester Regiment and he wanted to lead his men into action in an appropriately martial style.

As their landing craft chugged towards the German gun emplacements on the Norwegian island of Maaloy, Churchill played the bagpipes to his commandos, giving them a stirring rendition of *The March of the Cameron Men*. When the craft hit the stony beaches, he jumped into the water and waved them forward into dense smoke with a basket-hilted broadsword. It was extraordinarily bold and much admired by his soldiers – but he had no personal connection with the Highlands at all.

'Mad' or 'Fighting' Jack Churchill was born in Surrey and served in the Manchester Regiment before the war. It was while he was stationed in Burma that he was taught to play the pipes by the Pipe

Major of the Cameron Highlanders. His eccentricity was already coming to the fore and he worked hard at getting himself dismissed from the army, turning up on parade on one occasion carrying an umbrella. He needed a break from military life and in the 1930s worked as a movie extra, playing bagpipes in a film about fighting on the North-West Frontier called *The Drum*. In 1938 he came second in a military piping contest at Aldershot – the only Englishman out of seventy pipers.

With the outbreak of war, Churchill returned to the Manchester Regiment and fought with them during the retreat to Dunkirk. His other great passion was for archery and he carried his bow and arrows into combat, killing at least one German with an arrow. Churchill was keen to join the commandos and enjoyed their training in the Highlands of Scotland, where he met and later married the daughter of a Scottish shipping magnate. He was in the environment he loved best and proved to be a brilliant combat commander, winning the Military Cross twice.

At Salerno in 1943 he led No 2 Commando in a midnight breakout from the beach. Bellowing 'commando' and waving his Scottish broadsword, Churchill raced far ahead of his troops. Accompanied only by a corporal, he broke into the village of Pigoletti and captured an astonished German sentry. He then used the subdued German to creep up on other sentries and bagged a total of forty-two prisoners, including a mortar team, marching them all back to British lines. For this act, he was recommended for the VC but received the Distinguished Service Order.

In Yugoslavia, Churchill's commandos fought alongside Tito's partisans, but on the island of Brac his luck ran out. In a moonlit assault, playing the bagpipes, he led his commandos forward to storm a hill known as Point 622. In the heavy fighting he became isolated with only a handful of men around him. Down to his last bullets and with the rest of his group dead or wounded, Churchill picked up his pipes and played *Will ye no come back again*. A hand grenade exploded nearby and one of the fragments knocked him out.

Churchill's German captors were haunted by the sound of his lone pipes and treated him with respect, allowing him to play a lament for his dead comrades. Normally, commandos fighting with partisans would have been executed immediately by the Nazis, but the Germans believed he was related to the Prime Minister and kept him in special confinement. Needless to say, he attempted to escape several times, and eventually succeeded in April 1945.

It was only after the war, in 1946, that Jack Churchill's dream finally came true and he joined a Highland regiment – the Seaforths. He then became second-in-command to the 1st Battalion of the Highland Light Infantry, serving with them in Palestine. There, in April 1948, coming straight from a battalion parade, he rushed to help out a Jewish medical convoy that had been ambushed by Arab terrorists.

To calm the situation, Churchill stepped out of his armoured car and, resplendent in full dress uniform, including kilt, white spats and Glengarry bonnet, nonchalantly strolled in front of the Arab mob, with a broad grin on his face. 'People are less likely to shoot you if you smile at them,' he said later.[19] Transfixed by this Highland apparition, the crowd stopped fighting. He offered to help evacuate the surrounded Jews but they refused and were soon after overrun by the mob. Churchill had demonstrated yet again his magnificent bravery and could say, at last, that he was a true Highlander.

Chapter 16
Mutiny and Victory

Bob Boyce had a lucky wartime escape – three times. Just as Andrew Meldrum was taking cover at Rosyth, while German bombers struck at the naval base on 16 October 1939, Boyce could have been sitting on the two o'clock train across the Forth Bridge when a German bomb exploded right next to the bridge, throwing a barge up in the air. Instead, he had chosen an earlier train and was safely at his barracks. It was the day of his call-up. 'It was just as well I had a change of mind,' he later recalled.[1]

Boyce was an Edinburgh lad, twenty years old, when he joined the Gordon Highlanders. One of his first tasks was to escort captured German merchant seamen from Scapa Flow to Edinburgh. When the prisoners' train crossed the Forth Bridge, they were disappointed to see it still standing. German radio broadcasts said it had been destroyed in that first air raid. If it had have been, Boyce would have been dead.

In May 1940 Boyce and his fellow Gordon Highlanders were assembled to reinforce the 6th Battalion in Belgium. They were to travel by train to a Channel port and then sail across to join their comrades, but the 6th Battalion – part of the 51st Highland Division – were having a very hard time of it, being bombarded by German artillery and constantly forced back by Hitler's blitzkrieg. On 1 June they were evacuated from Dunkirk. Boyce and his men joined the survivors at Rotherham in Yorkshire. It was his second lucky escape. He had narrowly avoided being captured alongside the rest of the unfortunate 51st Highlanders in France.

Two years of hard training followed as Boyce and the Gordons prepared for their revenge against the Germans in North Africa. They practised 'combined ops' assaults in landing craft on Loch Fyne. Boyce had to climb up and down a scrambling net carrying a 28lb wireless set on his back. In October 1942 their time finally came and the 6th Battalion made their way to Ayrshire ready to embark for Tunisia and tackle Rommel. But two weeks before their departure Boyce fractured his knee in a training exercise and missed the ship. The 6th Battalion fought the Germans and Italians in Algeria and Tunisia in early 1943.

By the time Boyce was fighting fit, the North African campaign had been won. Amazingly, he had served in a front-line Highland battalion for four years and not once stepped outside Britain. This all changed in January 1944, when he found himself bobbing around in a landing craft in the Gulf of Salerno.

*

It was at Salerno in Italy in September 1943 that a group of Eighth Army veterans refused orders and were tried for the biggest mutiny in British military history. Among them were some 51st Highlanders. These were brave men who had fought successfully against Rommel but now brought a stain on their reputation by refusing to be reallocated to other units in the front line at Salerno. This was not a failure of nerve – far from it – it was a case of men not wanting to leave their mates and fight alongside strangers. They had already proved their courage in North Africa. Several had been recognized for their bravery.

One of these men was Private John McFarlane. Originally enlisting in the Argyll and Sutherland Highlanders, he had been transferred soon after to the Durham Light Infantry, much to his disappointment; but he got on well with his Tyneside comrades and proved his loyalty to them during fighting at Mersa-Metruh. Under enemy fire, he ran out to help a Durham gunner whose arm was trapped under an overturned anti-tank gun. McFarlane gave him morphine and amputated his crushed arm. He then dragged the wounded man to safety. For this exemplary act McFarlane received the Military Medal.

On the morning of 20 September, some 300 veterans of the Eighth

Army, including McFarlane, refused to be reallocated to units of the US Fifth Army fighting on the beachhead at Salerno. They hung around in the hot sun in a field near the beach until 3.30 p.m. when a parade was held for the men unwilling to be posted to other units. A Major Ellison then read out a passage from the British Army's *Manual of Military Law*. He told the soldiers that their resistance was mutiny and as a result they faced death before a firing squad.

McFarlane was proudly wearing the ribbon of his medal on his chest on the day he was asked to leave the 50th (Tyne Tees) Division and join the 46th Division. 'I had no intention of moving,' he recalled, 'because I knew that if I left I was going to be pushed into another unit. I was either going back to the 6th Battalion of the Durhams or nobody. At the third time they put the order to us, I just stood tight ... They could have shot me if they had wanted, I wasn't caring.'[2]

In the end, a hard core of 192 men, including several Highlanders, were arrested and put on trial. They suffered the indignity of being herded around with German POWs and were regarded as cowards by other British soldiers. For many of them, this treatment was beyond their understanding. Private Andrew Mills of the 2nd Seaforths had been captured alongside the original 51st Highlanders at St Valery but had escaped twice, eventually getting back to Scotland via Spain. He then joined the reincarnated 51st and fought in North Africa and Sicily. He had an exemplary record and had only got left behind in Tripoli because he was recovering from being bitten by a poisonous spider. There were eighty-three 51st Highlanders caught up in this incident, separated from the rest of their comrades in Sicily.

The worst part of it was that the men believed they were the victims of an administrative 'cock-up'. The message requesting reinforcements for Salerno had gone to Tripoli rather than the main army reinforcement depot in Algeria. On board ship, the soldiers had thought they were going to rejoin their old divisions, not be sent to fill gaps in other units. It was a chronic misunderstanding of the ties that bind a soldier to his mates and how that is the source of a group's fighting spirit. Also, having proved their worth on the battlefield, the veteran soldiers probably felt their wishes deserved some respect from their superior officers. It was not to be.

The mutineers were harshly punished, all of them being given prison sentences of between seven and ten years. Three sergeants were sentenced to death. In November 1943, army administrative officer Sir Ronald Adam asked to see the court martial transcripts and was appalled, ordering the immediate release of the men. But a stigma hung over them and they were sent to join unfamiliar units, at a time when the rest of the 51st Highlanders were being sent home. For many, the injustice ate away at them and eighty men absconded, eventually being recaptured and spending the rest of the war in prison. They were stripped of their decorations – including John McFarlane's Military Medal – and had their war pensions cut. The decision broke McFarlane's heart and the sense of injustice lingered long after the war. There were calls for the survivors to be granted a pardon, but in March 2000 the Armed Forces Minister, John Spellar, refused their request.

The situation at Salerno was a military emergency and many non-front-line troops were already being ordered to fight the Germans, even men from the Royal Engineers and beach administrative companies. The mutineers' own testimony revealed that while at sea, when they had no knowledge of the situation at Salerno, there was already a conspiracy to refuse to serve there. At Salerno, their unit commander was aware of their grievance at being cross-posted and promised, once the emergency was over, to give them the opportunity to rejoin their previous units, but still the hard core of 192 soldiers refused to serve.

'The inescapable fact remains that the men mutinied on active service in the battlefield,' concluded Spellar. 'By any account, that is a serious offence. To grant a pardon for that offence would be a disservice to the many men, including other Eighth Army veterans, who obeyed orders, whether they liked them or not, and fought on. It would be a particular slight to those who gave their lives as a result.'[3]

*

In the early hours of 22 January 1944, Private Bob Boyce of the 6th Battalion of the Gordons finally got to serve in the front line of a Highland regiment. He was sitting tight in a crowded landing craft heading for the beaches of Anzio. He had rehearsed amphibious landings many times, but this was his very first time in action. His mates on either side of him had fought in North Africa and knew what it was like to face the enemy. Since he had arrived in Salerno, they had made fun of him 'skiving' in Scotland while they were on the battlefield. He now prayed he wouldn't let them down when the fighting started.

As the landing craft churned the shallow water close to the beaches, Boyce expected all hell to break loose – but it didn't. The Gordon Highlanders stumbled ashore with little opposition. This was to change over the next week as tens of thousands of German troops were rushed to the area and set up their artillery overlooking the beachhead. For four months the British were stuck in a quagmire as rain and enemy fire poured down. For Boyce, his first taste of combat was an 'absolute nightmare'.

> Within the first month the stench of death hung heavily in the air and everybody quickly developed the practice of soaking a handkerchief from their water bottle and putting it over their nose and mouth. This was not 100% effective but it made day to day life a little more tolerable.[4]

Boyce was a signaller and wireless operator for his unit and spent much of the time in a slit trench with three other Highlanders. The German assault was relentless – Stuka dive-bombers and 88mm artillery guns during the day and infantry raids at night. The Highlanders slept in two-hour snatches. The constant shelling severed the communication lines with battalion headquarters and Boyce had to fix the cables by crawling out across the mud under sniper fire.

In April, the grim weather relented and reinforcements allowed the allies to break out from Anzio and force the Germans back towards Rome. The city was liberated in June and Boyce got to visit the Vatican and all the other sights. Most of the Highlanders had never been outside Britain before and it was a great treat for them all. On 15 June the battalion celebrated the 150th anniversary of the founding of the regiment. They toasted it with a special issue of wine and their pipe band played *Cock of the North* and *A Gordon for Me*.

From Rome, the 6th Battalion advanced on Florence. The Germans blew up every bridge over the Arno, save the Ponte

Vecchio. The Royal Engineers erected Bailey bridges to allow the allied soldiers over. For two nights Boyce and his mates stayed in a palatial villa at Fiesole just outside Florence. Their host was the former manager of the great opera singer Enrico Caruso, and his five daughters entertained them by singing arias. The house was full of gilded furniture and paintings, but clearly the family were hungry and the Highlanders gave them tins of McConachie's Beef and Vegetables.

The Tuscan idyll came to an end in September with hard fighting on the Gothic Line – German fortifications stretching across the northern Apennines – but the brigade broke through and the Highlanders clambered over the mountains. 'We never seemed to stop climbing,' said Boyce, 'the mountainsides were so steep it made progress very difficult.' They finally halted at the edge of a deep ravine where their company commander told them their target was a German position on Monte Gamberaldi. At 5,000 feet, it was the tallest peak in the region. They spent the afternoon recovering from their climb and began the attack in the early evening of 26 September 1944.

Boyce and the other signallers stood back from the initial assault, but German mortar shells arched over the attacking soldiers and landed among the company headquarters. Boyce became one of the first casualties when mortar shrapnel smashed his radio and dug into his back. But for the wireless equipment shielding him, he would have been killed stone dead. He was carried out by stretcher-bearers while the rest of the Highlanders took the position.

As Boyce lay face down on his stretcher on a mountain path, an elderly Italian woman passed by him, carrying all her possessions on her back. She saw the young man with a bloody gash in his back and knelt down beside him. She put a hand on his forehead, shut her eyes, and murmured a few words of prayer. She then pulled out of her bag a garishly coloured card showing Christ on the Cross and placed it next to his face. 'Mille grazie', he mumbled.

> This Italian woman had a heavy enough cross of her own to bear and it said a great deal for her that she forgot her own troubles to show concern for me if only for a few minutes. I have thought about her many times over the last 61 years and feel eternally grateful for the concern she showed ...[5]

Active combat was over for Boyce but after he recovered from his injury in February 1945 he was seconded to a POW mobile documentation team and spent ten months travelling around Italy and Austria checking on German prisoners. His good luck had returned. It was 'almost too good to be true', said Boyce, as the trip turned into a tour of Adriatic seaside resorts. They spent a day in Venice gliding along the Grand Canal in a gondola, but as they floated by the exquisite palaces, his thoughts went back to his comrades who had not been so fortunate He has since spent holidays in Italy retracing their wartime steps and paying homage to all the Highlanders that did not make it back. 'I have always been proud when asked to tell others I served in the Gordons.'

*

After a rest in Britain, the 51st Highlanders returned to Europe for D-Day in June 1944. They were a key part of the break-out in France and fought for seventeen days non-stop across thirty miles of French countryside against the fiercely resisting Germans. In September, they returned to St Valery as liberators. It was another sweet moment of revenge and they paid tribute to their lost comrades by beating retreat with a massed divisional pipe and drum band. In the autumn, the 51st Highlanders fought across Holland until events further south dramatically dragged them away. Hitler's last great gamble in the west was his Ardennes offensive, the battle of the Bulge, in which he threw in his last elite troops against the US Army. The Highlanders were hurriedly called in to help the Americans hold the line.

The advance resumed in February 1945 with ten hard days of fighting in the Reichswald. Then at last, in March, came the symbolic moment when the 51st Highlanders joined the allied crossing of the Rhine into Nazi Germany. Lieutenant-Colonel Martin Lindsay was with the 1st Battalion of the Gordon Highlanders when he rehearsed his men for the crossing. They practised sending Buffalo amphibious armoured vehicles across the river.

There was great competition between the Highland battalions to look their best for the emblematic crossing. The 5th/7th Gordons wore their pre-war white spats and diced hose-tops with hairy white sporrans for their pipe band, but the 5th Camerons went one better. Their men bought their own kilts for the occasion. It was a stirring sight. But not all rivalry was healthy, however, and Lindsay noted insults traded between his Gordons and another Highland regiment.

'The Black Watch went past as we were sitting sunning ourselves,' wrote Lindsay in his diary for 15 March, 'and there was some baa-baa-ing on the part of our Jocks.' He claimed this was an allusion to a Black Watch NCO stealing a sheep. The Black Watch replied by shouting 'What's for supper tonight, boys?' To which they chorused 'Cheese!' He said this referred to an incident in the First World War when a big round of Dutch cheese rolled off the back of a ration truck one night and some nervous Gordons riddled it with bullets.[6] Both sides laughed at the insults, but the officers were quick to quieten the mud-slinging. 'There was a terrible feud between the Black Watch and the Gordons in the last war,' recorded Lindsay, 'which has fortunately quite died out, and the last thing one wants is to see it start up again.'[7]

When the 51st Highlanders finally took the plunge on the night of 23 March 1945, they faced two days of some of the most bitter fighting since D-Day. One of their senior casualties was Major-General Rennie, killed by a mortar bomb. With a bridgehead established on the far side of the Rhine, the 51st were withdrawn for a rest in Holland and then resumed their advance into northern Germany. They finished their war in Bremen in early May on VE Day. It was the end of a long march for the 51st Highlanders, from defeat in northern France to rebirth and victory in North Africa and more hard fighting in Sicily, France, Holland and Germany. On the way, they had won great acclaim for the courage and endurance of all Highlanders. But it was not the end for some. There was still a war to be won in the Far East, and there Highlanders had to battle the jungle as well as the Japanese.

*

Private Andrew Meldrum of the 2nd Battalion of the Black Watch had already racked up more combat experience than most in the Second World War when he was ordered to take part in some of the toughest fighting of the entire war. From watching German aircraft bomb his native Scotland to serving in France, Crete, North Africa and Syria, he was put on board ship in 1942 and sent to India. He was now expected to fight the Japanese in the jungle of Burma.

Shortly after Meldrum arrived in Calcutta, a terrible monsoon swept into Contai in West Bengal and the Black Watch was sent to help the flood victims. 'It was a sad sight to see cattle drowned and people hanging from trees,' recalled Meldrum, 'some of them already dead ... Pits were dug for the cattle and the humans were burnt on pyres – it was a shattering experience for us. We had to get used to anything happening in this war.'[8]

Time off in India was spent at Darjeeling in the foothills of the Himalayas. They were made welcome at the English Club among the tea plantation owners and enjoyed roller-skating and horse riding. When on leave from their base, they visited locations that featured in earlier tales of Highlanders abroad, such as the Black Hole of Calcutta. They also witnessed the stirring of nationalist unrest and saw Gandhi and his followers make speeches. 'We were not getting as much respect from the natives,' noted Meldrum, 'at least not as much as we had received earlier and even the shoe boys have started charging us more.'

From Calcutta, Meldrum and the 2nd Battalion were sent to the dense tropical forests of Ranchi for jungle warfare training. They marched in full kit, carrying a hundred rounds of ammunition, three grenades and one clip for a Bren gun. They marched fifty minutes and then rested for ten. 'By God, did we sweat!' said Meldrum. 'It was march, march, march until you were almost dropping but I'm glad to say that my feet never gave me any trouble as they had done in France ... I had become a real fighting Black Watch man by now.' Those grim early days retreating before the Germans in the French countryside must have seemed a long way away.

In Ranchi they slept in bamboo huts with roofs of bamboo leaves. They were given anti-malaria tablets but had to be wary of the voracious ants. One Highlander left his boots outside the hut and the next morning found that the ants had eaten the soles off them. Meldrum and his mates learned how to make rafts out of bamboo and use them in night-time attacks. Sadly, one of the Highlanders drowned during one of these river-borne assaults. The importance of teamwork was constantly drummed into the men by their officers.

While at Ranchi, the progress of the Black Watch was being monitored by Major-General Orde Wingate, who had made a name for himself by developing an elite force of British, Gurkha and Burmese troops that used allied air transport to launch long-range raids behind Japanese lines in Burma. They were called Chindits and scored initial successes against the Japanese in 1943. Wingate was keen to expand this force and wanted the Black Watch 2nd Battalion to be part of it. Their training extended to flying in American gliders. One of their pilots was the former Hollywood child-star Jackie Coogan, most famous for his role alongside Charlie Chaplin in *The Kid*. 'I asked him what form of ammunition he had,' said Meldrum, 'and his answer was to show me one automatic, one pistol and one dozen grenades, which he dropped like bombs.' With air training completed, Meldrum was proud to hold his head high as both a Black Watch soldier and a Chindit.

The first mission of the Highland Chindits was in March 1944. The Japanese Fifteenth Army was advancing on India and the British were making a stand at Imphal and Kohima. It was up to Meldrum and the Chindits to disrupt the supply lines feeding the Japanese. They flew out not in gliders, which they had trained for, but in powered Dakotas. They flew over the jungle at treetop level and landed on a steel mat strip constructed by American engineers at a secret stronghold code-named 'Aberdeen'. One of the commanders in the field was a former Black Watch officer, Brigadier Bernard Fergusson (Lord Ballantrae), an early convert to Wingate's special forces. The Black Watch 2nd Battalion was incorporated into the 14th British Infantry Brigade, led by Brigadier Thomas Brodie. It was divided into two columns, each numbered after the old foot regiments of the Highlanders, the 42nd and 73rd that were amalgamated in 1881 to form the Black Watch.

Shortly after landing, the two columns moved out into the forest on foot. Burmese scouts led them through the dense undergrowth, while mules carried their radio equipment. They moved along narrow paths in single file. 'The heat was terrible,' remembered Meldrum, 'in no time at all, the perspiration had us soaking through.' They strained their eyes and ears to detect any sign of the enemy. Coming to the end of a rocky ridge, they set up their Bren guns to cover the passage across a bullock track. Passing along the path into a ravine, they heard gunfire and froze. Word was passed down the column that it was a false alarm and they camped on high ground. Meldrum spent a restless night peering into the jungle.

The Highland Chindits marched night and day and in the thick forest lost track of time. RAF supply aircraft dropped bundles of ammunition without parachutes into a paddy field, one of which nearly struck Meldrum and his mate. As they passed the ammo back to their column, a Japanese patrol fired at them from the top of a ridge. They fired back into the trees and a Japanese soldier fell through the foliage towards them.

'To be honest, I was terrified,' said Meldrum. 'We didn't know where we were or what was taking place around us.' They took shelter behind a tree and lit cigarettes, trying to control their shaking. Eventually the fire-fight ended, but they stayed jittery well after twilight. At one point they were told to break from the forest track and keep absolutely quiet. Meldrum later heard that one of their sergeants had been shot dead in the skirmish. What the Black Watch really missed was the sound of their piper keeping their spirits up.

The Highland Chindits spent five months in the jungle. They destroyed a bridge at Bongyaung and cut the Japanese railroad supply line in sixteen places, as well as destroying several fuel and ammunition dumps. In May, another Black Watch column of 200 men ambushed a much larger Japanese force some 1,000 strong early one morning. The battle lasted five hours and the Highlanders got the better of their enemy. But climate and disease were starting to wear down the soldiers. 'One morning I woke to find that I'd been sleeping with a snake,' recalled Meldrum. 'It slithered away but the monsoon had now broken and the leeches were most troublesome.'

Meldrum's Black Watch column was ordered back to base camp. They marched through the Naga Hills and had to dig steps every few yards. One of the mules carrying their radio equipment slipped and fell into a gully. At times they bumped into other units of Chindits. The one detail that separated the Black Watch from the rest of the Chindits was that they were not allowed to grow beards, but had to shave every morning. Back at base camp, Meldrum stopped taking his anti-malaria tablets and immediately went down with the disease.

As the campaign in south-east Asia turned successfully against the Japanese, there was talk of changing the Black Watch 2nd Battalion into a parachute unit, but Meldrum was sent home before that happened. He was in Kilmarnock for VE Day and his long military career eventually came to an end in September 1945. He was discharged with a gratuity of £90, but lost his first building job on civvy street because he was plunged back into an exceptionally severe Scottish winter and could not stand the cold. Suffering recurring bouts of malaria, Meldrum, who had served his country for nearly six years and fought around the world in most operational theatres, was given an army pension of just ten shillings a week. Like so many of his comrades, he was truly a remarkable Highlander.

Chapter 17
Hollywood Highlanders

Anyone who doubted the huge international appeal of the Highlander in the early twentieth century only had to walk along Broadway in New York in May 1929 to see *The Black Watch* emblazoned in electric lights on the front of the Gaiety Theatre. Just two years after the very first 'talkie', this new movie was noted for its excellent use of sound effects and some thrilling action scenes directed by John Ford. One young actor was delighted to get a small, uncredited part in it – John Wayne – and he played a 42nd Highlander. It was a hit and had a long run on Broadway. 'The bagpipes fill the theatre with their peculiarly stirring strains,' wrote *The New York Times* film critic, 'and whether it is "Auld Lang Syne", "Loch Lomond" or "Annie Laurie", one feels the power of such airs and one harks back to the stirring quality of these melodies during hostilities.'[1]

The Black Watch was based on a popular novel by Talbot Mundy, *King of the Khyber Rifles*. In the original story the military hero belonged to a native auxiliary unit, the Khyber Rifles, but the moviemakers chose to change it to a Highland regiment and broaden its appeal. In the film, Captain Donald King of the Black Watch travels to India at the beginning of the First World War. His apparent cowardice is a cover for a secret mission to rescue British soldiers held prisoner on the North-West Frontier.

Captain King was played by genuine tough guy Victor McLaglen. Born in the East End of London, he was a veteran of the Great War. In fact, at the age of just fourteen he had joined the Life Guards and would have been dispatched to South Africa during the Boer War if his father had not alerted the War Office to their underage recruit. McLaglen then briefly became a professional boxer – fighting the legendary world champion Jack Johnson – before joining the Royal Irish Fusiliers in the First World War, when he ended up as a captain in Mesopotamia, serving as the Assistant Provost Marshal of Baghdad. While possessing more than enough military experience for the film role, he did lack the Highland accent. 'Mr McLaglen does good work as Captain King,' said *The New York Times*, 'but it's a pity that his speech does not suggest more emphatically the Scot.' Other critics were harsher, but the film was originally intended to be a 'silent' and only had the dialogue scenes added awkwardly to it later.

The Black Watch was just the first of several Hollywood movies celebrating the British Empire and the role of the Highlanders in protecting it. The most successful of these in box-office terms was *Wee Willie Winkie*, released in 1937. Taking its inspiration from a short story by Rudyard Kipling, it again ignored the original army setting of the 195th and shifted it to the Black Watch Highland regiment. Repeating the successful formula of the earlier film, it again starred Victor McLaglen and was directed by John Ford. The twist was to switch the original character of a six-year-old boy to a girl and this part was taken by the Hollywood child-star Shirley Temple. The relationship between the petite but feisty nine-year-old and the veteran sergeant played by McLaglen charmed audiences. It culminated in a scene in which Temple visits the fatally wounded soldier in hospital and sings *Auld Lang Syne* to him. When the camera stopped rolling, McLaglen raised himself from his sickbed and patted Temple's hand, saying, 'If I wasn't already dead, I'd be crying too.'[2]

Over 100,000 fans turned up to see Temple and McLaglen attend the premiere of *Wee Willie Winkie* and it confirmed the appeal of the kilted soldier in the movies. Laurel and Hardy were among the most popular comedy acts in the world at the time and they took their turn to wear khaki and kilts in *Bonnie Scotland* in 1935. In this comedy the duo travel to Scotland, believing they have inherited a fortune, but only end up with a set of bagpipes. They join a Highland regiment and sail to India, where, inevitably, they are caught up in intrigue on the North-West Frontier. The cinema trailer proclaimed 'when they go into kilts, the whole country goes into stitches'.

It was not the first time that Laurel and Hardy had used Highland dress to comic effect. Although born south of the border in Cumbria, Stan Laurel lived and worked in Glasgow for much of his teens and his kilted appearances expressed his genuine affection for Scotland. In the 1927 short *Putting Pants on Philip*, Stan Laurel played a Scotsman visiting America. His kilt-wearing gets him into scenes of mischief, including a 'Marilyn Monroe' moment when his kilt is blown up over a subway vent. Eventually, Hardy has to step in and get him fitted for a pair of American 'pants'.

*

Future Hollywood movie star David Niven was caught up in the romance of the Highlander in the 1920s. As a young man, he enrolled at the Royal Military College, Sandhurst. With family connections in Scotland, all was on course for him to join the Argyll and Sutherland Highlanders. He had even been introduced to Princess Louise, sister of King George V, the regiment's honorary colonel, and socialized with Argyll officers who assured him of a warm welcome. All he had to do was to fill in a War Office form stating the preferred three regiments in which he wished to be commissioned. He placed the Argylls first and the Black Watch second.

> Then for some reason, which I never fully understood, possibly because it was the only one of the six Highland regiments that wore trews instead of the kilt, I wrote:
>
> 3. Anything but the Highland Light Infantry.
>
> Somebody at the War Office was funnier than I was and I was promptly commissioned into the Highland Light Infantry.[3]

Niven shielded his disappointment from his mother by claiming that the HLI wore trews because at some point in their past the men had been granted the honour of dressing like their officers. It was, however, a tremendous blow and Niven became increasingly disillusioned with army life. Facing a court martial for insubordination, he resigned his commission and sailed to America, where he found work as a whisky salesman. By 1935, he was in Hollywood and played his first military role in *The Charge of the Light Brigade*. It is interesting to note that had Niven got his wish and been commissioned into a kilted regiment he might well not have become a movie star.

Niven finally got to lead an army of kilted warriors when he starred in *Bonnie Prince Charlie* in 1948, but the actors playing these Highlanders turned out to be East End Londoners. When, at the climax of a battle scene, they had defeated the redcoats, one Cockney extra shouted out to their Jacobite leader – 'Oi! David … we've got their f*****g flag!'[4]

Ronald Colman was another future Hollywood star who wanted to serve in a kilted regiment. Born in Richmond, Surrey, he first worked as an accountant but in his spare time joined a Territorial regiment, the London Scottish. When the First World War came, the London Scottish were the first TA regiment to be sent to the Western Front. Along with 750 comrades, Colman arrived in Le Havre wearing his hodden grey kilt to the sound of the pipers playing the *Marseillaise*. At first the young men served as stretcher-bearers and helped put up camps, but in October 1914 they were taken to the front line in a fleet of London buses. Colman sat on the top deck and nine hours later arrived at Ypres. It was raining heavily and the roads were thick with mud. When the edges of his kilt dried out, Colman said the stiff material slashed across his legs like sandpaper, rubbing his knees raw.

At the battle of Messines Colman was hit by a shower of shrapnel from a German shell. The explosion threw him face down into a beetroot field. Trying not to pass out, he slowly dragged himself back to his lines. Realizing that if a stray bullet hit him, he would be found with his back to the enemy, he rolled over in the mud. His daughter recalled what happened next.

> He had every intention of maintaining the dignity of both himself and of his country, whether or not he made it to safety. Without further hesitation, he turned onto his back, and pulling with his elbows, then pushing with his good leg, he retreated from the field of battle while facing the German lines.[5]

Colman survived the battle but was invalided home and could not re-enlist due to his injuries. Drifting through his early twenties, he ended up on board ship to America and arrived in Hollywood. By the mid-1930s he was fully fit and starring in action movies, culminating in his heroic role in *The Prisoner of Zenda*, engaging in sword-play opposite Douglas Fairbanks Jr. It was during this period that Hollywood acquired an insatiable appetite for movies about the British Empire, and Colman also starred as *Clive of India* in 1934.

The comic side of the Highland character became the business of a music-hall entertainer called Harry Lauder. Born in Edinburgh in 1870, he started out as an Irish comedian, but he was most famous for appearing on stage in full Highland dress with a twisted walking stick. His songs, many of which he wrote himself, made him an international success and he was the first British performer to sell more than a million records. By the first decade of the twentieth century, Lauder was touring all over the world, being photographed having tea with US President Woodrow Wilson and larking about with Charlie Chaplin.

In the First World War Lauder was too old to serve, but his son John was a captain in the 8th Battalion of the Argyll and Sutherland Highlanders. On 1 January 1917, Lauder received a telegram telling him that his only son had been killed in action near Poiziers. It was a tremendous blow for him and his wife, but the performer gained some comfort from learning that the last words of his son were 'Carry on!' He turned this into the inspiration for his immensely popular song *Keep Right on to the End of the Road*, a wartime favourite.

To honour his son, Lauder insisted on travelling to the Western Front to entertain Scottish troops. 'We were seldom far away from the firing-line,' he wrote in his memoirs. With a small portable piano made especially for him, he performed as many as half a dozen concerts a day to audiences of a few hundred to several thousand. At Arras, Lauder was asked to sing to a Highland regiment holding a railway cutting on the line to Lens, a position from which the Germans had just been driven out. When he got there, he set up his piano among shell craters and dugouts.

> Our concert had not been started more than a few minutes when a shell came plump into the cutting and exploded with a shattering roar. I suddenly stopped short in the song I was

singing; I felt queer in the pit of the stomach. After a little while I started again. But another shell followed, hitting a railway bridge perhaps two hundred yards, or less, from where we were standing. 'They've spotted us!' said the officer in charge.[6]

Wearing his kilt and a tin helmet, Lauder ran for shelter. A German aircraft had spotted the gathering and informed the artillery of the location. The shelling lasted half an hour and throughout it Lauder was terrified, fearing most that they might be buried beneath tons of earth in their trench. The Highlanders around him carried on smoking and playing cards and when the barrage was over Lauder emerged to finish off the show.

Lauder performed before a different audience at Aubigny, where he sang for the officers of the 51st Highland Division. They welcomed him to a French château with a beautifully adorned drawing room lit by candles. 'It was crowded with officers in kilts of different tartans,' he recalled, 'reminding me for all the world of a social gathering of Scottish chiefs during the '45 Rebellion.' In 1919 Lauder was knighted for his services during the war.

*

The universal appeal of the Highlander was further exploited in a huge range of merchandising from the late nineteenth century onwards. Food and drink manufacturers deployed Highland illustrations to sell their products. 'Camp Coffee', a chicory-based drink made in Scotland from 1885, famously used a label featuring a Highland officer drinking a cup outside a tent while his Sikh servant stood nearby. The drink was said to have originated when Highland soldiers requested a coffee-style beverage that could easily be brewed up on campaign in India. 'Camp Coffee' continues to be made today and still features a Highlander on the label, but because of recent claims of racism in the imagery, the Sikh is now portrayed sitting next to the Highlander and also enjoying a cup.

Porridge is a traditional food of Scotland and a favourite with Highland soldiers who like it with added salt, but no sugar. In 1888, 'Scott's Porage Oats' was milled and sold in a handy box. From early on in its history, the packaging featured a kilted Highlander throwing an iron ball, and an early advertising line claimed it was

'The Food of a Mighty Race'.[7] This was later changed to the less combative 'The True Taste of Scotland'.

When Highlanders settled abroad, they continued to use images of their homeland to sell their products. Even in sun-drenched California, where Scots farmed citrus orchards at Highland and Strathmore in Tulare County, they produced a series of beautiful labels depicting their juicy fruit against landscapes of Scotland with brand names such as Loch Lomond, Tam O'Shanter, Kiltie and Tartan.[8]

From the eighteenth century Highlanders were depicted in printed advertisements for tobacco and snuff. Life-sized carved figures of red-coated Highland soldiers were placed outside tobacco shops. They were a variant on the more widely spread Indian cigar-store figures. A Georgian tobacconist called John Bowden in Threadneedle Street in London traded under the sign of 'The Highlander and Black Boy'.

'When whisky was first introduced into Scotland,' argued a pamphlet of 1858, 'it appears to have been used only as a medicine, and to have been kept strictly under the lock and key of the medical practitioners ...'[9] The Scottish Temperance League would have liked to keep it that way, but despite a strong abstinence movement even within the British Army, whisky became the characteristic alcoholic drink of Scotland and won an international reputation for its high quality. Blended whisky is often simply called Scotch. Naturally, whisky manufacturers recruited the Highlander as part of their sales imagery. In the case of William Grant & Son, it came from a personal connection with a Highland regiment.

On Christmas Day in 1887 the first spirit ran from the copper stills of William Grant's family distillery outside Dufftown. It remains one of the few family-owned whisky distilleries in Scotland today. Through his father, a Waterloo veteran, William Grant had a strong affection for the Gordon Highlanders and joined their 6th Volunteer Battalion, becoming a Captain and then 'Honorary Major' in 1897 – the nickname by which he was known in his local community. The family association with the Gordon Highlanders has continued and to celebrate the regiment's bicentenary, the company produced a special blend of malt and grain whiskies (the Gordon Highlanders Blended Scotch Whisky) to raise money for the regimental museum in Aberdeen. The colourful label featured

Major Grant wearing a glengarry, surrounded by pictures of some of the regiment's greatest military moments. 'Stand Fast' – the war cry of the Clan Grant, has been used on the labels of Grant's whiskies throughout the firm's history.[10]

In 1893 William Britain began to manufacture model soldiers. Previously, the toy market had been dominated by German-produced miniature figures, but Britain had some experience in casting metal from his previous trade as a brass worker and devised hollowcast lead figures which used less metal and were cheaper than competing German toys. They proved immensely popular with boys in the early twentieth century and among the earliest and most popular ranges of toy soldiers were charging red-coated Highlanders. In their very first year of production, two of their twelve sets of toy soldiers were devoted to the Black Watch and the Argyll and Sutherland Highlanders.[11]

The British affection for Highlander toy soldiers continued into the 1970s with Airfix producing a 54mm plastic kit of a Black Watch soldier of 1815 and a set of 20mm Waterloo Highlanders for war-gaming. This marked the high-watermark of military historical toys. In the wake of the huge international success of the *Star Wars* movie in 1977, toy figure making largely moved away from repli-cating real soldiers to science-fiction and fantasy characters.

In recent years there has been a tremendous revival in the pro-duction of historical toy figures, including Highlanders, but these are aimed more at adult collectors. In 2007, to commemorate the 150th anniversary of the Indian Mutiny, William Britain produced a range of VC-winning 93rd Highlanders from the assault on the Sikanderbagh at the siege of Lucknow. The model soldiers included a splendidly dynamic representation of Private David MacKay punching out a sepoy rebel to capture his standard.

*

The thrilling deeds of the British Empire successfully entertained audiences at the cinema throughout the inter-war years. Between 1930 and 1945, it has been estimated that at least 150 'British' films were made in Hollywood, many of them based on events in imperial history. For George MacDonald Fraser, this seemed entirely natural. 'The British child of 1930 thought the Empire was terrific,' he wrote in his *Hollywood History of the World*, 'giving him and his country a status beyond all other nations – and he had the evidence to prove it on a world map that was one-fifth pink.'[12] For the Americans it made good commercial sense. In 1933, the UK was the leading export market for US films, with Germany ranked as thirtieth. In 1938 the UK had the second largest number of cinemas in the English-speaking world after the US – over 5,000. It meant that films like *Clive of India* (1934), *Lives of a Bengal Lancer* (1934), and *Gunga Din* (1939) pulled in large crowds of movie-goers; but a cloud was hovering over this golden age of imperial celebration.

At the beginning of the Second World War Hollywood continued to make movies praising the civilizing effect of the British Empire. It was their contribution to the British war effort as the island nation stood alone against Nazi Germany. But come 1942 and America's entry into the war, this mood changed significantly. Ardent left-wingers within the Roosevelt government were appointed to the Office of War Information (OWI). The role of this bureaucratic body was not to censor, but to advise Hollywood producers about what were appropriate movies to make; but it was, in effect, an office of propaganda. It argued for movies that expressed a more egalitarian approach to world rule, championing democracy and freedom and most certainly not the rule of empires.

The majority of Hollywood producers were deeply conservative and cared more about the bottom line than the pursuit of world democracy, but the OWI struck back with audience surveys that showed most Americans believed the British treated their colonies unfairly and were only fighting to defend their empire. Further OWI data from abroad revealed that audiences in strategically important countries, such as India, were highly offended by films such as *Lives of a Bengal Lancer* and this could provoke rebellion and instability. Clearly drawing on anti-imperial rhetoric to support its case, the OWI declared that British imperial movies did little to help American foreign policy. Their first victim was the planned re-release of *Gunga Din* in 1942. 'The picture glorifies British Imperialism,' declared the OWI. 'At a time when we are stressing that the current war is a people's war, this is an obviously inopportune comment.'[13] Reluctantly, the studio executives at RKO took a loss on the copies of the movie already printed and shelved it for the duration of the war. A major production of Rudyard Kipling's *Kim* was similarly cancelled.

The determined, politically motivated opposition of the OWI to British Empire films ensured that no such movies appeared until after 1945. By then, the appetite for such spectacle seemed old-fashioned. The Highlander remained a popular figure for world audiences, but he was placed firmly within a Scottish setting rather than winning glory on an imperial world stage. This was vividly demonstrated by the post-war success of the musical *Brigadoon*. Written by Alan Jay Lerner and Frederick Loewe, it was the first hit for this enormously successful lyricist and composer who went on to create many famous theatrical and film musicals, including *My Fair Lady*.

Brigadoon had a long run on Broadway when first performed in 1947 and was then turned into a 1954 movie starring Gene Kelly and Cyd Charisse, directed by Vincente Minnelli. Originally a fairy tale about a German village that comes alive once in a hundred years, the location was switched to Scotland where the cosy world of Highland folklore proved a perfect distraction from Cold War realities. Publicity for the film sold it as a follow-up to *An American in Paris* and it depicted the Highlands as an equally exotic and romantic place for a modern American to explore. Disillusioned with modern city life, Gene Kelly falls in love with an eighteenth-century world of dancing maidens and fierce clansmen. *Brigadoon* established a narrower, folksy vision of Scotland that proved more popular with post-war audiences than the pre-war stories of imperial warriors in kilts. It would signal a shift in the fortunes of the British Empire and its tartan defenders.

A darker movie expressing this new reality was *Tunes of Glory*, released in 1960. Based on a novel by James Kennaway, who had served as a junior officer in a Highland regiment, it was turned by Kennaway himself into an Oscar-nominated screenplay set in a Scottish regimental barracks. Focusing on how two wartime Highland veterans cope in peacetime, it dramatized the clash between two strong characters. Acting Colonel Jock Sinclair was played by Alec Guinness as a hard-drinking hero of El Alamein who had fought his way up from the ranks. In contrast, Lieutenant-Colonel Basil Barrow was portrayed by John Mills as a cool Sandhurst-educated survivor of a Japanese prison camp, who had arrived to take over command of the regiment from Sinclair. The two men battle each other to win the loyalty and support of their Highlanders and the result of their conflict is a shocking tragedy.

Although the kilted Highlander as fictional imperial hero was largely killed off by the Cold War, it can be said that East–West tensions led to his rebirth in the surprising form of an elegant but tough British spy – James Bond. Originally, the character of James Bond was represented as the quintessential Englishman, but when his best-selling status required a back-story for his fans, John Pearson, a former colleague of the author Ian Fleming, was happy to oblige. In his authorized biography of the fictional character, Pearson pretended to interview the British intelligence agent and noted how proud he was of his Highland roots. 'I always feel myself emotionally a Scot,' said 007. 'I don't feel too comfortable in England. When I die I've asked that my ashes are scattered in Glencoe.'[14] Bond claimed to be descended from the clan Macdonald, with three Bonds being slaughtered at Glencoe in 1692. His great-grandfather, according to Pearson, won a VC with the Highlanders at Sevastopol.

In fact, it has been suggested that Ian Fleming modelled his spy character on a true Highland war hero called Fitzroy Maclean. Descended from a Hebridean clan, Maclean first served as a diplomat in the British embassy in Moscow in the 1930s. He had many adventures outwitting Soviet agents in Central Asia and this became the basis for his autobiographical *Eastern Approaches*. In the war, Maclean joined the Cameron Highlanders and added further to his heroic profile by serving in the North African desert with the newly formed SAS. One wartime mission involved the kidnapping of a Nazi consul in Iraq – more than enough material for a real-life Highland Bond.

When it came to portraying Bond at the cinema, Ian Fleming had very definite views about the right actor for the part – he wanted David Niven – but the former Highland Light Infantry officer was too old for the role in the early 1960s. When Fleming was introduced to a young Scottish actor called Sean Connery, he was far from impressed. 'I was looking for Commander James Bond, not an overgrown stunt man,' he said.[15] It was Connery's raw sex appeal, however, that helped make Bond a movie success and added to his Scottish associations. The actor refused to modify his Edinburgh accent and remains the most popular actor to play the part.

Connery later appeared in another block-busting action movie with a Scottish background – *Highlander* in 1986 – but he did not take the main role. A superior science-fiction tale, it told the story of an immortal warrior who assumed the guise of a Highlander. Curiously, the lead character was played by the French-raised Christopher Lambert, while Connery depicted an Egyptian immortal with a Spanish name but a Scottish accent. The time-travelling adventure culminates in an exciting duel in which the sixteenth-century Highlander fights with his sword against the villain in contemporary New York – the whole brilliantly enhanced by a soundtrack provided by rock group Queen. It was a hit with a global youth audience and spawned several sequels.

Scottish historical cinematic epics followed in 1995 with the Oscar-winning *Braveheart*, about William Wallace in the thirteenth century, and *Rob Roy*, based on the Sir Walter Scott novel. Although dressed largely authentically and set in a specific time and place, they took considerable liberties with history. In both movies, the complexities of Scottish civil conflict were dropped for a more easily understood Scots-versus-English clash, even though this was far from the truth in either case. Such a false characterization of Highland history has played into the hands of Scottish nationalists (and their showbiz supporters, such as Sean Connery) who prefer to emphasize Scottish–English strife to suit their own political agenda.

Hollywood movies that push Celtic nationalism at the cost of a true representation of history have had a profound impact, claimed British historian Andrew Roberts. 'Hollywood political correctness has fastened on the Brit, especially the imperialist Brit, as a safe target for sustained abuse and misrepresentation. Outrageously factually inaccurate, these films do have an effect on the way the American public views Britain and the British.'[16] As a result, even in the UK, the Highlander is now viewed more as a purely Scottish hero than a British one. It is a further dislocation of the Highlander from his British identity that has been fostered by several events since the Second World War, among them unpopular regimental amalgamations and the rise of Scottish nationalism. The era of queues forming outside a Broadway cinema screening a Khyber Pass adventure movie called *The Black Watch* seems long gone.

Chapter 18
Cold War Highlanders

Andrew Wilkie Brown had done his bit for Queen and Country in the Second World War. He served with the Argyll and Sutherland Highlanders in North Africa, Crete, Sicily and Italy, but by 1945 he thought his front-line days were over. He had joined up in 1933 as a bandsman, touring the country entertaining civilians with a Highland dance band. As a native of Edinburgh, he found most of his fellow recruits from the West of Scotland difficult to understand. 'One wee chap from Dumbarton, asked me, "Are you not a f*****g Sassenach?" I asked him to repeat what he said. Again I could not understand his query. He then spoke slowly and said, "Are you a bloody Englishman?" I said I came from Edinburgh. He said, "I thought you were English because you talk funny!"'[1]

During the war, Brown progressed from a lowly bandsman to a commissioned officer, a Lieutenant Quartermaster in charge of maintaining supplies of ammunition, food and clothing for his battalion's soldiers. In the last months of the war in Europe in 1945 he fell in love with a young nurse called Babs and within weeks they were married in Edinburgh. Babs had worked in a sanatorium for sufferers from tuberculosis, but once married she transferred to an accountancy office while her husband served abroad in occupied Germany. In January 1946 Brown was delighted to get a posting back to Ayr where he hoped he could now enjoy married life.

But Babs had a persistent cough, which was soon diagnosed as TB. After several months of treatment in hospital, she succumbed to the disease in the summer of 1948 at the age of only twenty-one.

Brown was devastated. In the evenings he consoled himself by playing the piano and in the autumn of 1948 he volunteered for service abroad in Malaya. At the age of thirty-three, his Cold War career had begun.

In the wake of Japanese victories over British and other colonial forces in south-east Asia, local Communist groups had become emboldened and after the war launched a number of uprisings throughout the region. In the newly proclaimed Federation of Malaya, Chinese Communists murdered several British rubber planters. It was the beginning of a long campaign characterized by terrorist attacks and counter-insurgency operations that became known as the Malayan Emergency and lasted until 1960.

Andrew Brown joined the 2nd Battalion Malay Regiment but his commanding officer was another volunteer Argyll Highlander. Within a week of his arrival he joined his regiment in a jungle patrol. They hacked through thick stands of bamboo with Malay *parangs* (machetes) and lived off Gurkha-style rations of rice, sardines, biscuits, tea, curry powder and anti-malaria tablets. They swam in jungle rivers to refresh themselves, but there was danger all around. 'I felt a biting,' recalled Brown after one riverside wash, 'and looked down and found a leech feeding on my testicles.' He told the medical corporal who then informed all his troops. 'Loud laughing resulted and they all gathered round as the Corporal lit a cigarette and with maximum modesty I exposed the leech. A sudden sizzle and all was well.'[2]

Further patrols targeted areas around rubber plantations known to hold Communist bandits. Brown and his Malay soldiers sometimes travelled by boat but most of the time it was a hard slog through dense forest and Brown grew a beard during these long-range missions. They destroyed enemy camps and interrogated captured terrorists. Sometimes they combined their operations with regular British forces.

During this period, the 1st Battalion Seaforth Highlanders was based in Malaya in the Johore region. One ex-rubber planter turned historian of the Emergency declared that 'aggressive patrolling by the 1st Seaforths pushed many of the [terrorist] squads into leaving the area altogether'.[3] In total, the Seaforths killed or captured nearly a hundred Chinese Communists at a cost of fourteen killed and twenty-three wounded. Brown saw little combat but contracted

malaria. Heavy sweating and high temperatures induced halluci-
nations and one night he imagined himself looking down at his
body from the corner of his room. After two weeks in hospital he
felt better but was warned that the malaria would come back
throughout his life.

In February 1950 Brown was recalled to his former battalion of
the Argyll and Sutherland Highlanders. They were based in Hong
Kong and he was offered his old post of Quartermaster. He had
been promoted to acting major in Malaya, but he took the drop in
salary and rejoined the regiment. Their camp was in the New Territories and they patrolled the frontier with Communist China.
They were part of an entire division, numbering some 20,000 soldiers, protecting the wealthy British trading colony.

In June of that same year an army of Communist North Koreans
crossed the 38th Parallel to invade South Korea. The United Nations
responded by sending an international force to help the South
Koreans, headed by the US Army. The Cold War had suddenly
erupted into a major conflict. Three Argyll and Sutherland NCOs
were on board HMS *Jamaica* on a cruise to Japan when their ship
was diverted to patrol the sea off Korea. A Communist shore battery
fired shells at them and one burst above the ship, killing six military
personnel and wounding several more, including one Highlander.
They were the first British casualties of the Korean War. 'Little did
we know then how many would follow,' recalled Brown.

*

The Argylls were the first Highland regiment into Korea. They
were part of the British 27th Infantry Brigade sent to Korea as a
contribution to the United Nations force, fighting alongside American and South Korean troops. The Argyll and Sutherland Highlanders were accompanied by the Middlesex Regiment. All National
Service conscripts under the age of nineteen were removed from
the brigade and replaced by volunteers from other units based in
Hong Kong. The Communists had overrun most of South Korea in
the first weeks of the war and the British force was sent to the south-
east corner of the country around the city of Pusan where a pocket
of resistance was established in August 1950. The Naktong river
formed part of the Pusan Perimeter and the Highlanders were

given the task of patrolling a section of it, just a mile away from enemy guns.

Quartermaster Captain Andrew Brown was flown in ahead of his battalion and had the honour, with a colleague, of being the first British soldiers to set foot on Korean soil. His job was to set up supplies for his battalion, but he could also see that the arrival of the British had a significant impact on the morale of the Americans and he was happy to pose in his kilt beside them for newspaper photographs. By September, the UN force was ready to counter-attack and the Argylls advanced with them north of the Naktong river. The Highlanders crossed the water at night over a rickety footbridge built by US Army engineers. A few miles along the road to the town of Songju, the Argylls were told to silence enemy positions on a piece of high ground known as Hill 282.

At dawn on the morning of 23 August, 'B' Company swiftly took the enemy position on Hill 282, surprising the North Koreans at breakfast. Having achieved their target, the battalion's second-in-command, Major Kenneth Muir, oversaw the evacuation of casualties. Accompanied by cooks, bandsmen and stretcher-bearers, they climbed the hill to remove their wounded comrades. The enemy was now fully alerted and began a counter-attack with mortars and artillery, causing more casualties among the Highlanders.

Despite this, the thirty-eight-year-old Muir returned to the hill top to check the supplies of the soldiers holding it. At this critical moment, US artillery support was removed to another sector, allowing the North Koreans to concentrate their fire on Hill 282. Suddenly, after what had seemed a relatively straightforward and successful operation, the Highlanders were coming under increasingly heavy fire and there was little they could do about it – their 3-inch mortars lacked the range to hit back. As the senior officer on top of the hill, Muir was reassured that an American air strike would come to their rescue at midday, but in the meantime he was ordered to hold the position.

At just gone noon, three American P-51 Mustangs appeared in the sky but rather than dropping their bombs on the distant hill full of North Koreans, they hit Hill 282 and the brave Highlanders still holding it. It was an appalling, unforgivable mistake – Muir had specifically instructed his men to leave out fluorescent ground-to-air recognition panels so that the pilots would know they were friendly troops. Captain Brown was standing with the Brigade staff officers when the tragedy occurred. 'We watched the planes coming over and didn't know they hit the wrong hill,' he recalled. 'When the news came through we were horrified. The Americans used napalm ...'[4]

The sticky, burning petroleum jelly killed seventeen Highlanders and wounded seventy-six. It was a devastating blow, leaving only thirty fighting men to hold the hill; but rather than give it up, Muir ordered the surviving Argylls to retake the crest, while he supervised the removal of the wounded men. Constantly under machine gun fire, he moved among his troops, shouting encouragement to them and handing out ammunition. Major JB Ghillies witnessed what happened next to Muir.

> When his own weapon was out of ammunition he took over a 2" Mortar and used it to no small effect. While firing this weapon he was mortally wounded but even then he expressed the desire to fight on. He said 'No Gooks are going to drive the Argylls off this position.' Major Muir was then carried off the crest.[5]

It was the spirit of the Thin Red Line all over again, although one officer later confided to Captain Brown that if Muir had not been killed then all the Argylls would have ended up dead because of his determination not to shift from the position. For his outstanding bravery and leadership, Major Muir was posthumously awarded the Victoria Cross, one of only four won during the war.

*

George Younger was a National Service conscript when he joined the Argyll and Sutherland Highlanders in Korea. Three decades later, he held the posts of Defence Secretary and Scottish Secretary in the British government. 'Ninety-nine per cent of war is utterly boring,' he recalled, 'and the remaining one per cent is terrifying.' The Argylls had had their terrifying moment on Hill 282 and Younger, having just turned nineteen, joined them as they advanced northwards towards the 38th Parallel. As the winter closed in, they had more than the Koreans to worry about.

In Korea, if you got cold and wet, you stayed cold and wet. I'll never forget the bitter cold there ... a north-west wind from Siberia meant if you boiled water to shave, it had ice on it by the time you finished. Even the anti-freeze in the trucks froze – the drivers had to start them up every 20 minutes through the night to prevent it.[6]

On one occasion, a Brigade HQ driver slept under his vehicle during the night so as to keep the engine going, but the next morning another soldier started the vehicle and, not noticing the sleeping driver, ran over and killed him.

Quartermaster Captain Brown had to keep his Highlanders well clothed in the cold but was finding it increasingly difficult, especially as much of the winter clothing was stolen on its way north from Pusan. Many of the troops only had their jungle kit to wear and this had split, 'leaving many of the Jocks with bare bottoms'. Brown's solution was to order a case of whisky and trade it with his American colleagues. 'I found one bottle produced 100 pair of slacks,' he noted. 'In fact I managed to keep the advancing winter at bay for quite a few in the Battalion.'[7] To make sure his troops got fresh food, Brown obtained a large amount of yeast from the Americans and got his Cook Sergeant to produce loaves of bread baked in 40-gallon fuel drums. He used a few of the loaves to bribe American MPs to let him cross pontoon bridges against the flow of heavy traffic.

The Argylls joined the Commonwealth Brigade, fighting alongside Australians, and came under the command of the 1st US Cavalry Division. They saw action near Sariwon, rapidly advancing through the country until they reached the Yalu river in North Korea. But then came the intervention of Communist China. A massive influx of Chinese soldiers sent the United Nations force reeling backwards in November and the Argylls were caught up in the confused withdrawal. The Aussies had a large consignment of beer and made sure they shared it with the Scots before they fell back. In the chaos, the Highlanders rescued a battery of American artillery completely surrounded by Chinese soldiers.

Brown had another attack of malaria, but as one of his sergeants tried to keep him warm in a tent, with improvised central heating made out of biscuit tins, the canvas caught fire. Brown survived but remained poorly as the Highlanders retreated nearly 200 miles. It was grim news to be crossing back over the 39th Parallel and heading south as fast as they could. In January 1951 Brown received news that his father was seriously ill and he flew home. By the time he arrived in Edinburgh, his father was dead.

The UN forces held a line fifty miles south of the 38th Parallel and in late January launched a counter-attack. In April, the Argylls took part in a successful assault on the Chinese near the border. The snow had melted and Brown rejoined his battalion. It would be their last major action of the war. In mid-April the Argylls were sent back to their base in Hong Kong. Their total casualties were 31 killed and 133 wounded, the majority of them at Hill 282. 'The Battalion was given a difficult job and the forward troops had a bloody time,' concluded Brown. 'We were poorly equipped in transport and the absence of ordnance support made things very difficult ... It was improvisation from day one.'[8]

Brown stayed on in the army as a serving officer until 1970. It was while in Hong Kong that he met his second wife, a nurse, and they were happily married for over forty years.

*

The gap left by the Argylls in Korea was filled by the 1st Battalion King's Own Scottish Borderers (KOSB). Among their ranks was a volunteer from the Black Watch, Private William Speakman. Six feet seven inches tall, he was twenty-four years old and came from Altrincham in Cheshire. On 4 November 1951 the KOSB were involved in heavy fighting north of the 38th Parallel along the Imjin river. Hundreds of Chinese soldiers had dug a trench towards the Commonweath Division defences. Australian and South African aircraft napalmed the advancing Chinese. It seemed as though little could survive this strike, but in the late afternoon Communist troops sprang from their hidden trenches and hurled themselves at the section of the line held by the Borderers. Some units were swiftly overwhelmed, but B Company stood its ground.

In the face of intense enemy fire, Speakman led five other soldiers in a desperate counter-attack against the Chinese. 'There was a bunch of us near the crest of a hill,' he remembered. 'We had boxes of grenades piled up in a ration tent behind us. We kept making trips up to the crest and tossing grenades as they came.' Three of his comrades were hit by shrapnel. A mortar shell exploded near Speakman and the fragments struck him in the leg. 'It felt just as if a stone had hit me.' He was ordered back down the hill to get his wound dressed, but when he saw his medical orderly struck by shrapnel, he was enraged, said 'stuff it', and went back into the close-quarter fighting. At one stage, he was throwing rocks and anything to hand at the enemy. They even grabbed their unopened ration of beer. 'It came in very useful,' said Speakman. 'I saw mortar crews cooling the barrels of their weapons with beer. When we ran out of grenades, we threw beer bottles.'[9]

Although badly hurt, Speakman continued to lead charge after charge against the Chinese, allowing the Borderers to withdraw their own wounded from the position and inflicting huge casualties on the enemy. The fighting lasted four hours and the Chinese lost a thousand dead, while the KOSB had seven killed and eighty-seven wounded. For this action – he called it 'quite a little scrap' – Speakman was awarded the Victoria Cross, the second of the Korean War.

The Black Watch was the only other Highland unit to serve in the Korean War and they took over from the KOSB in July 1952. By then, the fighting had reached a stalemate along the 38th Parallel – the eventual finishing line of the war – but the Chinese still launched mass attacks and the Black Watch were caught in two waves in November of that year on a feature dubbed the Hook. Corporal Derek Halley, a nineteen-year-old shepherd from Crieff, was another National Service conscript when he was plunged into the front-line fighting. With his fellow Highlanders, he had to sit in a slit trench, listening for any sound of the enemy advancing.

> The nights were worse. We spent them on our feet in the trenches, peering through slits, kicking away the rats and trying to keep our equipment clean … [the rats] would emerge from the sandbags and scurry around us, defying our ever more desperate measures to rid ourselves of the things. We tried pouring petrol over the holes and setting light to them, even threatening the entire hootchie [dugout] until, on one occasion, we were all but engulfed in the flames.[10]

'Korea was worse than anybody could imagine,' says Halley. 'I have since read about the conditions in the First World War and at least they got breaks from the trenches. We didn't. We only had five days away from the front line in 10 months – and we were just teenagers on National Service!'[11]

The comparison with the Great War could be attested to by Black Watch Private Anthony Laycock, who was caught up in fighting at the Hook in May 1953. He remembers nightly patrols into No-Man's Land and on one occasion his patrol narrowly avoided an ambush, but as they withdrew a Chinese machine gun opened up on them. 'When I reached our own dannet [free-standing circular] barbed wire, I tried to climb over but fell smack into it,' he recalled. 'The more I panicked, the more I got tangled.' Bullets ricocheted around his head and he shouted out, 'Don't leave me lads.' A Black Watch soldier dropped on one knee and fired some covering shots, while a National Serviceman from Falkirk grabbed Laycock and yanked him out of the barbed wire. 'I had lots of cuts and a badly torn pair of trousers, but it was better than being dead.'[12]

*

Highlanders fought in several other Cold War confrontations. In 1951 the Gordon Highlanders found themselves hunting Communist guerrillas in the jungle of Malaya, while the Argyll and Sutherland Highlanders served in Borneo. One of the least known points of conflict was in Aden, and that responsibility fell to the Queen's Own Cameron Highlanders.

Private Alfred Blake was born in Bermondsey in south-east London in 1937. His older brother saw action in World War Two at Dunkirk and when he received his call-up for National Service in 1955, his brother told him to sign up for the infantry. 'He said it would be more interesting,' remembers Blake. 'He was right about that.'[13] Blake was one of a handful of southerners who was told to report for service in Inverness. 'I'd hardly been out of London, only as far as Southend.' When he got off the train at Inverness, the Regimental Sergeant-Major was waiting for him. 'I couldn't understand a word he said'. But after three months of training, his London ear was attuned to Scots and he never felt prouder than when he put on the kilt of the Queen's Own Cameron Highlanders. 'Of course, we wore nothing underneath it and were told not to go on the top deck of buses.'

Blake was sent with the 1st Battalion for peacekeeping duties on the 38th Parallel in Korea. 'It was so cold, we lived in a tin barracks with a boiler to keep us warm and six foot of snow outside.' They were given jungle training in anticipation of being sent to Malaya for the Emergency, but a more urgent call came up following the Suez Crisis in 1956. He was dispatched to the British Protectorate of Aden to defend it against incursions by Soviet-backed Yemeni tribesmen to the north.

The 1st Battalion of the Camerons was sent up country to build a military camp at the village of Dhala, twelve miles south of the border between Aden and Yemen. Amid the beautiful high-rise brick buildings constructed by the local population, they raised their tents. 'We had to dig down into the ground first, because every night the Yemen tribesmen fired at us and bullets went through our tents, so we had to keep down low in our trenches.'

On the morning of 4 February 1957, the nineteen-year-old Blake and 4 Platoon went on a patrol into the mountains. It was a stark landscape with sharp stones strewn across the sun-blasted terrain. 'It was like something out of the Khyber Pass,' he recalled. They rode in the back of a three-ton truck for the first part of the journey, then got out and switched their tam o'shanters for the soft hats of regular field wear and proceeded on foot. Blake was carrying a Bren gun and felt the weight of it in the heat.

At 2.00 p.m., about three miles away from their camp, on the way back, they sat down with some Arabs to have tea, but the officers became apprehensive about the meeting. A few minutes later, as they passed through a narrow *wadi* used as a camel track, bullets suddenly ripped up the ground around them. The soldiers in front were hit first; section commander Corporal William Burnett was shot and killed outright. Private Henry McKenzie – just eighteen years old – was hit several times in the chest but managed to fire his weapon as he fell to the ground dead. 'This young Cameron Highlander upheld the tradition,' said a Battalion report, 'a Cameron can never yield.'[14]

Private Blake was hit in the foot and the impact of the bullet blew off the sole of his boot. A second bullet smashed into his knee and he went down. A third bullet ricocheted off a rock and went into his backside.

'I opened up with my Bren gun,' said Blake. 'They weren't far away, on high ground. I went through one magazine, but that was it. I couldn't move. I couldn't get another magazine.' One of his mates was in a worse way. Corporal William Smith got a bullet in the back that exploded out of his stomach taking his guts with it. Blood drenched the dusty ground around him. The rest of the platoon took cover. They fired their .303 rifles at the tribesmen, but were running short of ammunition.

'One of my mates told me he was standing behind a boulder and was picking up stones to throw at the tribesmen. I thought that wasn't good.' The best course of action was to call up reinforcements. They had radios but they did not work because of the high mountains around them. They had no choice but to strip off their equipment and three Highlanders ran three miles back to the camp in the intense heat. In the meantime, Blake was left lying on the ground out in the open with Smith next to him writhing in extreme pain.

I thought that was it. If the tribesmen come over now, we've had it. They'll cut our throats. I thought of my mum. I was only on National Service. I wasn't a regular.

But the Yemeni tribesmen didn't advance on the wounded platoon. They had seen the Highlanders go down, but the fire coming back from them was so intense they chose to avoid any more combat and disappeared into the landscape. The ferocity of the Camerons had saved their lives. In the meantime, the three Highlanders got back to their camp at Dhala. A relief column was quickly formed of Camerons and allied native tribesmen, known as Aden Protectorate levies. An Irish medical officer, Captain Brian O'Dowd, accompanied them on foot all the way. As they approached the ambush spot they were shot at, but none was hit.

By the time they got to the wounded men, it was dark. They could hardly be moved and had to spend a freezing night in a nearby mud house, where O'Dowd gave Smith painkilling drugs. Low-lying mountain cloud prevented an RAF Sycamore helicopter from landing in the morning, but it returned later and took the seriously wounded to Dhala and then on to Aden. A few days later, RAF Shackleton bombers and Venom jets dropped bombs on the villages of tribal leaders as punishment for their part in the ambush. No one was killed but the houses were destroyed.

Amazingly, Corporal Smith, despite his terrible stomach wound, eventually made a good recovery. 'I was sure he would die,' said Blake. 'We were out there for a long time.' Blake had his wounds tended and he spent the last few months of his National Service as a batman to a Cameron Major. 'You had to do all your time.' The fighting grew worse in Aden in the early 1960s when the Soviet Union supplied more weapons to Yemen and it became yet another Cold War battleground.

Forty-five years after the ambush in Dhala, Blake was lying in his bath at home in Bermondsey when he felt something sharp in his backside. The army medics had patched him up after the fight but they had left one bullet inside his buttock. Over the years it had slowly pushed its way to the surface. He went to hospital and had the bullet removed. As he stared at the piece of bent metal that had sat inside him for over four decades, he nodded his head – it was a .303.

I thought so. It was one of our own bullets. From a Bren gun. One of our guns had gone missing from our camp. It was the local tribesmen, they must have sold it on. They set us up for the ambush.

The sixty-five-year-old former Private Blake wanted to go back to the land he had served in and that had claimed the lives of two Camerons, but the British Foreign Office told him it was too dangerous. In 2002 the forgotten fight at Dhala was commemorated when the name of Private Henry McKenzie was added to the Portsoy war memorial in Aberdeenshire after an interval of forty-five years. His mother had just celebrated her ninetieth birthday.[15]

Chapter 19
Highlanders Betrayed

In October 2004 a battlegroup of Black Watch Highlanders were re-deployed from the British sector in southern Iraq several hundred miles north to the infamous 'Triangle of Death' near Baghdad. Alone among British troops, they had been selected to help the Americans stiffen their forces as they prepared for an assault on the *mujahideen* base of Fallujah. When the Highlanders arrived at US Camp Dogwood they set up their own little part of it and called it 'Ticonderoga' after one of their victories in North America nearly 250 years earlier. For those who understood the reference, it underlined the unstinting fighting history of the Black Watch.

As the troops prepared to face a significant increase in personal danger, they were plagued by a nagging question: was the Black Watch going to be around for much longer? War correspondents insisted that their regiment was high on a government list to be disbanded. Their commanding officer, Lieutenant-Colonel James Cowan, diplomatically avoided the explosive topic. 'I am sure,' he said, 'the Black Watch has a long, fine future ahead of it.'[1] But he was wrong. As a regiment, the Black Watch was doomed.

Less then two years later, in March 2006, veterans of the Black Watch, proudly wearing their campaign medals, gathered on a drizzly day outside Balhousie Castle, their regimental headquarters in Perth. Nearby were monuments remembering their fallen comrades from past wars and their most recent losses in Iraq. They raised their bonnets adorned with the famous red hackles and with three solemn cheers marked the end of 267 years of regimental history. A lone piper played *Lochaber No More*. Elsewhere in Scotland, similar ceremonies marked the disappearance of the regiments of the Argyll and Sutherland Highlanders and the Highlanders (incorporating the Seaforths, Gordons and Camerons). They were all to be reduced to battalion status within a new Royal Regiment of Scotland.

At Edinburgh Castle, the colours of the Royal Regiment of Scotland were paraded and there was much bright talk about a new chapter in Scottish military history, but back in Perth the old Highlanders were bitter. 'These buggers in Whitehall don't have a clue about what we are losing,' said seventy-nine-year-old Major Peter Watson. 'They haven't seen really gutsy service with the regiments, and they don't understand what Scots are about.'[2] There was a widespread sense of betrayal and bafflement. What on earth had possessed the British government to bring an end to the very Highland regiments that had served them so well for over two centuries?

*

The creation, amalgamation and extinction of Highland regiments have continued throughout the existence of the British Army since the eighteenth century. The raising of new regiments to fight wars has been countered by the need to cut costs as soon as the combat is over. But after the Second World War the pace of this reduction became more rapid, to the point where it concerned many key units in the army. It was matched by a headlong decline of the British Empire – the machine once powered by the Highlanders – as colonies across the globe were granted independence. As the Empire shrank so did the Highland Regiments.

Straight after the war, the cuts began. In 1948 the second battalions of all Highland regiments were absorbed into the first battalions. Ten years later a more profound plan was formulated. In 1957 a Defence White Paper announced the shocking news that Highland regiments with hundreds of years of separate history were to be amalgamated. The Seaforth Highlanders were to join with the Queen's Own Cameron Highlanders, while the Highland Light Infantry were to be removed from the Highland Brigade and transferred to the Lowlands to join the Royal Scots Fusiliers. The Highland Light Infantry had for a good part of their history been without a kilted uniform because of their designation as Light Infantry, but they still considered themselves Highlanders. 'They have persistently and continuously maintained their Highland ancestry and traditions,' declared one correspondent to *The Times*. 'It most certainly means that, if there is no going back, two famous Scottish regiments will die ...'[3]

At Cortachy Castle near Kirriemuir in the eastern Highlands, the Earl of Airlie – also Lord Lieutenant of Angus – made his feelings known to the Chief of the Imperial General Staff and the Secretary of State for War. In a letter of 22 August 1957, he wrote to Field Marshal Templer, saying: 'I must point out that I feel the authorities do not fully appreciate upon what dangerous ground they are treading in the interference of tradition, and I do not honestly feel that they fully realize what a serious step they are taking in view of the present low ebb at which recruiting stands.'[4]

Lord Airlie told the Field Marshal that he had been born into the Black Watch, just as his father had before him. When he joined the regiment before the Great War, 'it took the place of father, mother, sister and brother, sweetheart and everything all rolled into one'. After he left the regular army, he took command of the local Territorial battalion. He fully appreciated the need of the British Army to reduce its numbers, but said that if they started messing around with the identity of the Highland Regiments this would impact on the morale of 'troops that can be and have been the finest in the world'.

In the Defence White Paper, alongside the amalgamations, there was a proposal that regimental cap badges be replaced by a single Highland Brigade badge. There was even the suggestion that the red hackle, so beloved of the Black Watch, be taken away. Airlie recognized that the Highland Brigade had played a significant role in past wars, but it could not supplant the devotion that soldiers had to their centuries-old regiments. 'A new cap badge to extinguish the regimental badges will be a severe irritant,' warned the Lord, 'and will merely invite opposition from officers and soldiers who are doing their best to co-operate ... It won't help appealing to tradition in one paragraph and taking it away in another.'

Field Marshal Gerald Templer replied to Airlie while he was flying over the China Sea to Hong Kong. He took exception to the accusation that he did not fully appreciate the delicate situation provoked by the White Paper. 'I can only believe that you think all of us a lot of asses,' he blustered, 'who know nothing about the Army.' This was a weak comeback as Airlie would have known full well that the Field Marshal had an illustrious military career in both world wars and had won the DSO in Palestine. If regiments were not amalgamated, explained Templer, then they faced total disbandment. 'So we thought it best to go the whole hog and go for a brigade cap badge for everybody in the Infantry of the Line.'

'I am afraid it is useless asking me,' continued the Field Marshal in his remarkably candid letter, 'to use my influence to stop the rot. This sounds as if we senior soldiers who are responsible for it have had all this foisted on us by the politicians. We have not ...' It was simply the challenge of marrying available government money to affordable manpower. Templer argued that the rest of the British Army had accepted cutbacks with good grace, with the exception of the Highland Light Infantry, but he expected that to be resolved too. Then came the sting in the tail.

> If you really want to know what I think, I'd make a very large bet that the Highland Brigade (to take one example) would be absolutely prepared for the Brigade to be turned into the Highland Regiment now, with the 1st Battalion of the Highland Regiment having the title (Black Watch) and so on. But nothing would induce me on the present Army Council to try and force the pace on that issue.[5]

It was a stark warning. Lord Airlie's concerns about regimental cap badges could well be replaced by the destruction of the very regiments themselves. Clearly, half a century before their actual demise, the British Army was considering bringing an end to the history of the Highland regiments – and incorporating them as battalions into a super-regiment. It was a very black cloud to serve under, but some Highlanders would not go down without a fight.

*

In the post-war period, the decline of the British Empire was accompanied by moments of both heroism and ineptitude. A combination of cock-up and military swagger characterized the end of the British

Protectorate of Aden. In October 1967 a suspected leak from government indicated that British troops would be hastily withdrawn from Aden in just a couple of weeks.[6] In an earlier Foreign Office report there was exasperation at the failure to find a political solution to the future of the region. 'We see signs of the old South Arabian vice of inertia and unwillingness to take positive decisions or responsibility,' concluded an ambassador. 'If they go on fooling around, we shall have finally to fix the date which suits us best and make them accept the consequences.'[7] On the ground in Aden, it had been up to a unit of Highlanders to impose some discipline on the chaos and they had carried it out with a ruthless efficiency that embarrassed the government. The author of this moment of high imperial bravura was 'Mad Mitch'.

Lieutenant-Colonel Colin Mitchell was a London-born Highlander. His father, a West Highlander, had won a Military Cross in the Argyll and Sutherland Highlanders, and when he accompanied him to their Presbyterian church in West Croydon, Colin always wore a kilt. At the age of eighteen, Mitchell was commissioned into the army and joined the 8th Battalion of the Argylls in Italy for their final campaign of World War Two. After the war, he was posted to Palestine, where he narrowly missed being blown up in the King David Hotel in Jerusalem by Jewish terrorists. He then served in Korea, Cyprus and Kenya, but it was in Aden in 1967 at the age of forty-two that he savoured the moment he said, 'was worth all my quarter century of soldiering'.

In that year, Mitchell and the Argyll and Sutherland Highlanders were in Aden on peacekeeping duties. It was still the major base for British forces in the region but an insurgency against British rule had begun in 1963 and the Arab Gulf port was caught up in the Cold War politics of the Middle East, with the Russian-backed Communists of North Yemen continuing to threaten the area.

By 1967 the endgame was within sight, with the British government determined to establish an independent Federation of South Arabia; but fearful of their future, local army and police officers mutinied in the old port district of Crater. They attacked the British peacekeeping forces and killed twenty-two soldiers, including three Argylls. Mitchell was outraged and grew even angrier as the British government sat on its hands about what to do next – worried about provoking a blood bath. As commanding officer of the

Argylls, he wanted to go in straight away to punish the mutineers. Ordered to hold back, he ignored senior advice and went on to plan an operation – and on 3 July 1967 took decisive action.

At 7.00 p.m. it was beginning to get dark when Mitchell gave the order for his troops to move into the old Crater district. Many of them knew the men who had been killed by the Arabs and every armoured car of the Queen's Dragoon Guards accompanying them had the red and white feather hackles of dead Northumberland Fusiliers tied to their wireless aerials. They hoped for tough opposition from the 500-strong mutineers so they could wreak their vengeance. Rather than sneak into the Arab streets, Mitchell ordered his Pipe Major to sound the Regimental Charge – *Monymusk*.

> It is the most thrilling sound in the world to go into action with the pipes playing, it stirs the blood, reminds one of the great heritage of Scotland and the Regiment. Best of all, it frightens the enemy to death! In an Internal Security operation against a lot of third-rate, fly-blown terrorists and mutineers ... it seemed utterly appropriate.[8]

Machine gun fire erupted from an Arab palace and everyone ducked down, except for Pipe Major Kenneth Robson who kept on playing as he marched forward. The Highlanders returned fire and the enemy guns were silenced. The Argylls advanced into the warren of streets and shot one gunman as he tried to escape – and that was it. There was no blood bath as feared by the British government. Instead, Mitchell and his quietly determined Highlanders had taken back the streets of Crater under their strict authority. They took over the Treasury Building held by mutinous armed police by simply talking their way in. Early the next morning, Mitchell informed the local population that the Highlanders were in charge by having his pipers play on the roof of the Educational Institution as though they were standing on the battlements of their regimental home in Stirling Castle. They imposed a strict regime of nightly patrols and immediate punishment, which became known as 'Argyll Law'. Some locals protested at the robust law enforcement, but it worked, keeping a lid on any further trouble for the next five months.

There was general acclaim for Mitchell and his Highlanders in the British press. *The Times* called him 'irrepressible' and described the operation as a 'smooth takeover',[9] while the *Daily Telegraph* declared 'British troops have shown the combination of skill, tact and cool courage for which they are unequalled'.[10] But Mitchell was bitterly disappointed that the mutineers who had killed British soldiers were not handed over for punishment. His primary concern was the honour of his regiment, and the operation had been carried out, in part, to add another page of distinction to their history and to counter the weight of their loss. But there was worse to come.

Shortly after they returned home, the Argylls were threatened with disbandment. The Highlanders were dismayed at this stab in the back. Their success in Crater, plus earlier valour in Korea, had assured them of national praise and they were the most popular Highland unit for new recruits. For a year the regiment lived on in denial, until confirmation arrived on 11 July 1968 that they were to be axed. Captain DP Thomson was keeping the regiment's daily record of events. 'The Bn's reaction was', he wrote, 'disappointment, resentment and surprise. For several days now the Jocks have appeared on local and national TV and in the Press, and there had perhaps been built up a feeling that, in the last resort, this would never happen to us. Now it has.'[11]

Later that afternoon, Lieutenant-Colonel Mitchell spoke to his men. He told them that the disbandment would not take place before 1970 at the earliest and 1972 at the latest. 'While there's life there's hope,' he said, 'a lot can happen in four years – in particular a General Election, and with a new Party in power, a new Defence Policy.'[12] The Highlanders gave him a standing ovation. The press besieged the Argylls as they became a focal point for those who disagreed with the Labour government's defence policy.

A few days later, the fight got dirty when Tam Dalyell, the Labour MP for West Lothian, accused Mitchell of disobeying the orders of his senior officers when he retook the Crater district. He took exception to the tough discipline exerted by the Argylls on the Arabs and went as far as to say that he did not wish to be represented abroad by men such as Mitchell. One High Commission official called the Argylls a 'bunch of Glasgow thugs' – a statement for which he later apologized. Seeing that his actions in the Crater were getting in the way of the survival of his regiment, Mitchell promptly resigned.

Reaction to this in the armed forces was best expressed by Marshal of the Royal Air Force Sir John Slessor.

What I find profoundly disturbing about this Argylls affair is this. If potential recruits to the commissioned or other ranks of the Army come to believe that if in a dangerous emergency or actually in action they ever do anything unorthodox or even a bit undisciplined – with conspicuously successful results including the avoidance of unnecessary casualties – they will be subjected to this sort of witch-hunt and their careers abruptly terminated (perhaps even their regiments disbanded), then they will not join the Army.[13]

Clearly, there was perceived to be a link between Mitchell's action in the Crater and the disbandment of his regiment – the Argylls were being punished for their bold commander. 'Never in 53 years' service,' concluded Slessor, 'have I been so worried about the future of the British Army as I am today.'

Swept up into what was becoming a national *cause célèbre*, Mitchell joined a public campaign to 'Save the Argylls'. In his book, aimed squarely at critics in the Labour government, Mitchell wrote that the 'Argylls were a symbol of all that was best in the British race'.

It was my firm belief that if Britain was to survive as a democracy into the Twenty-first Century she must restore her national spirit by stopping this constant erosion of the sound and solid virtues without which any nation must surely perish.[14]

It was an eloquent statement that could describe the value of all Highland regiments within the British Army. Hundreds of thousands of people signed the petition to save the regiment, while the Scottish Conservative Party took full advantage of the controversy to pledge their support. As Mitchell predicted, a general election did intervene to change the fate of the Argylls, but as the secret minutes of a cabinet meeting reveal in July 1970, now that the Conservatives were in power, they found the whole Argylls affair to be a trifle awkward.

In a cabinet meeting at Downing Street, entitled 'Rundown of the British Army', the Minister of State for Defence proposed that regiments threatened with disbandment should be offered the option of surviving as units of squadron or company size, because 'on balance the political arguments for accepting it outweighed the financial arguments'. But it was also noted that 'any measure which appeared to single out the Argylls for special treatment would be at least as likely to provoke political criticism, from those who would argue that the government was yielding to a pressure group'.[15]

The result was that the Argyll and Sutherland Highlanders were reinstated in 1970 but only at company strength. The political compromise was profoundly disappointing for Mitchell, who by this time had become the Conservative MP for West Aberdeenshire. 'A strength of 150 is too low to form an independent company with its own support weapons and transport,' he said. 'The Socialists were going to hang the Argylls, while under the Tories they are going to be drawn and quartered.'[16]

Two years later, the 1st Battalion was restored to its full strength. Mitchell felt there was little more he could achieve in parliament and he resigned his seat in 1974.[17] The Argylls might have survived their disbandment, but they came under attack from a different angle in 1973. The Chairman of the Animals' Vigilantes Trust, whose President was the comedian Spike Milligan, wrote to the Queen protesting at the wearing of badger-head sporrans by the Highland regiment. The letter was passed on to the Army Dress Committee, which dealt with the matter by contacting the Colonel of the Argyll and Sutherland Highlanders.

Writing from their HQ in Stirling Castle, Colonel Tom Slessor explained that the majority of badger-head sporrans were second-hand and were passed down by officers and NCOs leaving the army. If properly looked after, they could last for over fifty years, meaning that only four new sporrans had been requested over the previous decade. 'It should be stressed that badgers are not specifically killed for the purpose of making sporrans,' insisted Slessor. 'Skins for making sporrans are obtained from animals either killed on the road, accidentally trapped or those dying of natural causes.'[18] This was confirmed by a veterinary surgeon working for the government, but in order to placate the critics, Slessor agreed to investigate the possibility of producing a synthetic badger sporran, 'although it is anticipated that it will not be an easy task and may take some time'.

A more recent assault on the Highland sporran has come from the European Commission, which moved closer to a complete ban on seal products in 2008. As 90 per cent of sporrans are made from sealskin, it would mean the end of the traditional Scottish sporran-making industry.[19] A licence is currently required in the UK to wear sporrans made from the fur of endangered animals, such as otters. Another attack on traditional Highland culture came from the European Union in 2008. Their health and safety laws imposed a limit of 85 decibels on pipe and drum bands, which meant they had to tone down their pipes or wear earplugs, which would cause a major problem when tuning their instruments. 'These limits are far too low,' said Ian Hughes, head of an RAF pipe band in Fife. 'If we have to go with these regulations, pipe bands won't exist. Every pipe band in the world will be above the maximum volume level.'[20]

*

Four Highland regiments survived in the British Army into the last decade of the twentieth century – the Black Watch, the Royal Highland Fusiliers, the Highlanders, and the Argyll and Sutherland Highlanders. The Royal Highland Fusiliers, formed in 1959, were descended from the Highland Light Infantry and the 71st and 74th Highlanders, as well as the Royal Scots Fusiliers. In their new incarnation they took part in the 1991 Gulf War – alongside the Queen's Own Highlanders – and helped liberate Kuwait. The Highlanders were the result of an amalgamation in 1994 of the Queen's Own Highlanders (Seaforth and Camerons) and the Gordon Highlanders. All three tartans of these venerable regiments were retained in their new dress uniform: soldiers wore a Gordon tartan kilt with a patch of Cameron tartan in their Balmoral bonnet, and Mackenzie of Seaforth tartan for their trews. But even this was not enough to stave off their inevitable end.

In 1997 Highlanders of the Black Watch stood on parade in Hong Kong as the last possession of the British Empire in the Far East was handed over to China. With the end of empire had the purpose of the Highland regiments come to an end too? In the same year, a Labour government came to power in London and pursued a determined policy of devolution for the United

Kingdom. Two years later, Scotland regained its own parliament and this development strengthened the hand of the Scottish National Party (SNP). In 2007 SNP leader Alex Salmond became First Minister of Scotland and with further election successes the SNP seem poised to put a strong case for independence for Scotland. With the end of empire just ten years earlier, the popular triumph of the SNP signalled that the end of Great Britain might also be fast approaching. Affection for the Union seemed to be waning both north and south of the border as arguments raged over the Barnett Formula – the government system used to calculate the distribution of public spending between the component parts of the UK – and the considerable spending gap between England and the three better-funded devolved territories. Highland regiments were once a proud part of a united kingdom, but now seemed increasingly dislocated from life south of the border. Events in Iraq in 2004 underlined this disaffection.

The Black Watch were part of the western coalition occupying Iraq when, in a most unusual move, they were ordered away from the British sector in the south of the country to the more dangerous region around Baghdad – the so-called Sunni triangle, full of insurgents using car bombs and roadside explosions against the occupiers. Operation Bracken was intended to bolster US forces so they could take on the *mujahideen* in Fallujah, but just as the Black Watch were taking on their most difficult task, the British government announced plans to merge them and other Highland regiments into one Scottish 'super' regiment. It would mean the end of over 250 years of regimental history and caused an immediate outcry. It did little to enhance the morale of the Highland troops in Camp Ticonderoga at the sharp end of the action. Then came tragedy.

At 1.00 p.m. on 4 November 2004, a car slowly approached a Black Watch checkpoint a short distance across the river Euphrates from Camp Dogwood. The unshaven driver smiled at the Highlanders and then detonated his suicide car bomb. The enormous explosion killed Sergeant Stuart Gray, Private Scott McArdle, Private Paul Lowe and their Iraqi interpreter. Eight soldiers were wounded. The terrorist bomb was synchronized with mortar shells that fell among the company, inflicting more casualties. Undeterred, the surviving Black Watch pressed forward under fire to help their fallen comrades. Privates Currie and McLaughlin distinguished themselves by administering first aid without any thought to their own safety and managed to prevent the condition of the casualties from deteriorating further. An American Black Hawk helicopter eventually arrived to remove the wounded. The dead were placed in a Warrior armoured vehicle by the Company Sergeant Major, who tried to shield the horrific injuries from the younger soldiers. It had been a terrible day for the Black Watch.

'For a close knit family such as the Black Watch, their deaths are indeed a painful blow,' said their commanding officer, Lieutenant Colonel James Cowan, shortly afterwards. 'But while we feel this blow most keenly, we are the Black Watch and will not be deterred from seeing our task through to a successful conclusion.'[21]

The events of that day were later dramatized in an internationally successful National Theatre of Scotland production called *Black Watch*, first performed in Edinburgh in 2006 and written by Gregory Burke. At the heart of the show was the belief that Highlanders did not fight primarily for Queen or Country but to embellish the military tradition of their regiment. In an especially effective sequence, a Black Watch soldier slips on and off the uniforms of past campaigns from the eighteenth to twentieth centuries, demonstrating a link between soldier and regiment that has carried on over generations of family members.

'The whole experience was a testing one and all ranks of the Black Watch drew together in adversity and came through the stronger for it,' concluded a regimental account of their mission to Iraq. 'The deployment had a certain surreal quality. As a regiment that had never sought the limelight, the Black Watch emerged blinking into the glare of public scrutiny. We now look forward to prolonged but less public service to Crown and Country.' But this could not be. For many, the sacrifice of a total of five Black Watch soldiers in five weeks, with seventeen wounded, for a mission that seemed more political than military, left a bad taste in the mouth – especially when the government, on the one hand, was happy to make a political gesture with these soldiers and yet, on the other, was disbanding the very regiment they expected so much from.

While official regimental comments might be muted, individual soldiers were less restrained. Captain Tam Henderson of the Black Watch was caught up in a controversial friendly fire incident in Iraq in 2003. On appeal he was exonerated, has now left the army and feels free to express his upset at the end of his regiment. 'I was born into the Black Watch as a seventeen-year-old boy,' he says. 'It taught me everything, gave me standards and values. When you dilute those within a completely different identity in a new regiment then you lose something valuable – you lose your identity. The family I joined is now gone. That loyalty is a powerful thing to throw away.'[22]

The *Scotsman* newspaper started a campaign to save the Highland regiments and it was anticipated that a crusade like that for the Argyll and Sutherland Highlanders, thirty years before, might well force the government into a U-turn. But the Chief of the General Staff, General Sir Michael Jackson, was implacable in his plans to turn all British Army regiments into battalions in regional super-regiments. Against those who argued that he was destroying the recruitment links between local areas and families, he claimed that traditional regiments had been failing to meet their recruitment targets for some time, with the Royal Scots having to depend on fresh troops from as far away as Fiji.[23]

To make matters worse, as the regiments were set to become battalions so they would lose much of their individual identity. In August 2005 a new cap badge was unveiled for the Royal Regiment of Scotland which would supersede the cap badges of all individual regiments. It featured a lion rampant superimposed on the Saltire topped by the crown of Scotland. 'A better and more appropriate badge might be a dagger in the back superimposed on a white flag,' said Lieutenant-Colonel Stuart Crawford, a former tank officer. 'Those who had the power to halt this unwanted mass amalgamation have failed to do so and have let down their own men and the whole of Scotland.'[24]

A further blow came with the announcement that all the Scottish battalions within the new regiment would wear kilts – the wearing of trews by Lowlanders would be abolished – since as far as the government was concerned they were all Highlanders now. From a Labour government so sensitive to the ethnic identities of new immigrants to the UK, it seemed a monumentally arrogant move. There was even a threat that Highland regimental museums – repositories of hundreds of years of military history – would be shut down as government funding was cut.

Despite passionate protests, petitions and marches throughout

Scotland by Highlander veterans, over 250 years of British Army Highlander history came to an end on 28 March 2006. Today, four of the five regular battalions of the Royal Regiment of Scotland bear the name of Highlander. They are the Royal Highland Fusiliers, 2nd Battalion, the Black Watch, 3rd Battalion, the Highlanders, 4th Battalion, the Argyll and Sutherland Highlanders, 5th Battalion. The 51st Highland, 7th Battalion, is one of two Territorial battalions.

There has been a clear attempt to retain some of the history of the Highlanders from the last three centuries, and the value of their military spirit remains, but recruitment north of the border has been badly affected. 'Regimental recruiters say volunteers have walked away,' reported the Glasgow *Herald*, 'after being told that they might not be able to enlist in the family units of their choice, in which their fathers, grandfathers and great-grandfathers served before them.'[25] A sacred link has been broken. That said, Highland units continue to see action in the most dangerous operations undertaken by the British Army – and will continue to do so – because Highlanders expect to be at the front of any action.

In 2008, Britain's most senior casualty in Afghanistan was a Highlander. Lieutenant-Colonel David Richmond, the forty-one-year-old commanding officer of the Argyll and Sutherland Highlanders, 5th Battalion Royal Regiment of Scotland, was leading an operation in Helmand Province when he was struck by a Taliban bullet. He survived, but in that same year – the bloodiest so far for British forces committed to Afghanistan in the twenty-first century – three Highland soldiers were killed: Sergeant Jonathan Mathews of Edinburgh, the Highlanders, 4th Battalion Royal Regiment of Scotland; Corporal Barry Dempsey of Ayrshire, the Royal Highland Fusiliers, 2nd Battalion Royal Regiment of Scotland; and Lance-Corporal James Johnson of Drumchapel, the Argyll and Sutherland Highlanders, 5th Battalion Royal Regiment of Scotland. Sergeant Mathews was on a joint foot patrol with the Afghan Army when he was warned that Taliban fighters lay ahead. He didn't hesitate to advance into danger and confront the terrorists when he was hit by a single shot. Highlanders have and always will be 'stormers' – it is their very nature.

Appendix
Highlander Victoria Cross Winners

Crimean War

Private T. Beach, 92nd Gordon Highlanders, 1854

Indian Mutiny

Ensign R. Wadeson, 75th Regiment, 1857
Private P. Green, 75th Regiment, 1857
C/Sgt C. Coughlan, 75th Regiment, 1857
Lt A.C. Bogle, 78th Highlanders, 1857
Lt J.P.H. Crowe, 78th Highlanders, 1857
Lt H.T. MacPherson, 78th Highlanders, 1857
Surgeon J. Jee, 78th Highlanders, 1857
Asst Surgeon V.M. McMaster, 78th Highlanders, 1857
C/Sgt S. MacPherson, 78th Highlanders, 1857
Pte H. Ward, 78th Highlanders, 1857
Pte J. Hollowell, 78th Highlanders, 1857
Capt. W.G.D. Stewart, 93rd Highlanders, 1857
C/Sgt J. Munro, 93rd Sutherland Highlanders, 1857
Sgt J. Paton, 93rd Sutherland Highlanders, 1857
L/Cpl J. Dunlay, 93rd Sutherland Highlanders, 1857
Private P. Grant, 93rd Sutherland Highlanders, 1857
Private D. MacKay, 93rd Sutherland Highlanders, 1857
Private G. Rodgers, 71st Highland (Light Infantry), 1858
Lt F.E.H. Farquharson, 42nd Highland Regiment, 1858

QMS J. Simpson, 42nd Highland Regiment, 1858
Private J. Davis, 42nd Highland Regiment, 1858
Private E. Spence, 42nd Highland Regiment, 1858
L/Cpl A. Thompson, 42nd Highland Regiment, 1858
C/Sgt W. Gardner, 42nd Highland Regiment, 1858
Lt A.S. Cameron, 72nd Duke of Albany's Own Highlanders, 1858
Lt W. McBean, 93rd Sutherland Highlanders, 1858
Private W. Cook, 42nd Highland Regiment, 1859
Private D. Millar, 42nd Highland Regiment, 1859

Ashanti Wars

L/Sgt S. McGraw, 42nd Highland Regiment, 1874
Sgt J. MacKenzie, Seaforth Highlanders, 1900

Afghanistan

L/Cpl G. Sellar, 72nd Duke of Albany's Own Highlanders, 1879
Major G. White, 92nd Gordon Highlanders, 1879
Lt W.H. Dick-Cunyngham, 92nd Gordon Highlanders, 1879

Egypt & Sudan

Lt W.M.M. Edwards, 2nd Bn Highland Light Infantry, 1882
Private T. Edwards, 1st Bn The Black Watch, 1884
Cpl A.G. Hore-Ruthven, 3rd Bn Highland Light Infantry, 1898

North-West Frontier

Private E. Lawson, 1st Bn Gordon Highlanders, 1897
Piper G.F. Findlater, 1st Bn Gordon Highlanders, 1897

Boer War

Capt. J. Shaul, 1st Bn Highland Light Infantry, 1899
Captain M.F. Meiklejohn, 2nd Bn Gordon Highlanders, 1899
Sgt Maj. W. Robertson, 2nd Bn Gordon Highlanders, 1899
Private C. Kennedy, 1st Bn Highland Light Infantry, 1900
Captain E. Towse, 1st Bn Gordon Highlanders, 1900
Captain W.E. Gordon, 1st Bn Gordon Highlanders, 1900
Cpl J.F. Mackay, 1st Bn Gordon Highlanders, 1900
Captain D.R. Younger, 1st Bn Gordon Highlanders, 1900
Sgt D.D. Farmer, 1st Bn The Queen's Own Cameron Highlanders, 1900

First World War

Private G. Wilson, 2nd Bn Highland Light Infantry , 1914

Lt W.L. Brodie, 2nd Bn Highland Light Infantry , 1914

Pte R. Tollerton, 1st Bn The Queen's Own Cameron Highlanders, 1914

Dmr W. Kenny, 2nd Bn Gordon Highlanders, 1914

Lt J.A. Brooke, 2nd Bn Gordon Highlanders, 1914

L/Cpl W. Angus, 8th Bn Highland Light Infantry , 1915

L/Cpl D. Finlay, 2nd Bn The Black Watch, 1915

Lt Col. A.F. Douglas-Hamilton, 6th Bn The Queen's Own Cameron
    Highlanders, 1915

Cpl J.D. Pollock, 6th Bn The Queen's Own Cameron Highlanders, 1915

Capt J.A. Liddell, 3rd Bn Argyll and Sutherland Highlanders & Royal
    Flying Corps, 1915

Sgt J.Y. Turnbull, 17th Bn Highland Light Infantry, 1916

Cpl S.W. Ware, 1st Bn Seaforth Highlanders, 1916

Dmr W. Ritchie, 2nd Bn Seaforth Highlanders, 1916

Capt N.G. Chavasse, 1 /10 (Scottish) Bn King's (Liverpool) Regiment,
    1916

L/Cpl J.B. Hamilton, 9th Bn Highland Light Infantry, 1917

Private C. Melvin, 2nd Bn The Black Watch, 1917

A/Lt Col. L.P. Evans, The Black Watch, 1917

Capt N.G. Chavasse, 1/10 (Scottish) Bn King's (Liverpool) Regiment,
    1917

L/Sgt T. Steel, 1st Bn Seaforth Highlanders, 1917

Lt D. MacKintosh, 2nd Bn Seaforth Highlanders, 1917

Sgt A. Edwards , 6th Bn Seaforth Highlanders, 1917

L/Cpl R. McBeath, 5th Bn Seaforth Highlanders, 1917

Private G.I. McIntosh, 1/6th Bn Gordon Highlanders, 1917

Lt J.R.N. Graham, 9th Bn Argyll and Sutherland Highlanders, 1917

Capt A. Henderson M.C., 4th Bn Argyll and Sutherland Highlanders,
    1917

Cpl J.Ripley, 1st Bn The Black Watch, 1917

Lt Col. W.H. Anderson, 12th Bn Highland Light Infantry, 1918

Cpl D.F. Hunter, 5th Bn Highland Light Infantry, 1919

Sgt J.M. Meikle M.M., 4th Bn Seaforth Highlanders, 1918

Lt A.E. Ker, 3rd Bn Gordon Highlanders, 1918

2nd Lt J.C. Buchan, 7th Bn Argyll and Sutherland Highlanders, 1918

Temp Lt D.L. MacIntyre, Argyll and Sutherland Highlanders, 1918

Lt W.D. Bissett, 8th Bn Argyll and Sutherland Highlanders, 1918

Second World War

Major E.G. Blaker, M.C., Highland Light Infantry, 1944

Lt-Col. L.M. Campbell D.S.O.J.D., 7th Bn Argyll and Sutherland
    Highlanders, 1943

Major I.T. McK.Anderson D.S.O., 8th Bn Argyll and Sutherland
  Highlanders, 1943

Korean War

Major K. Muir, 1st Bn Argyll and Sutherland Highlanders, 1950
Private William Speakman, Black Watch, with 1st Bn King's Own
  Scottish Borderers, 1951

Notes

Prologue

1 Letter from Revd George Innes in Forres to Robert Forbes; see Forbes, R, *The Lyon in Mourning*, Edinburgh: University Press, 1895, Vol I, pp276–7.

2 Extract from the Prince's battlefield orders published in the *Newcastle Courant*, 19–26 April 1746, p3.

3 Brown, IG, & Cheape, H (editors) *Witness to Rebellion: John Maclean's Journal of the Forty Five*, East Linton: Tuckworth Press, 1996, p21.

4 Tayler, H (editor), *A Jacobite Miscellany*, Oxford: Roxburghe Club, 1948, p155.

5 Johnstone, Chevalier de, *Memoirs of the Rebellion in 1745 and 1746*, London: Longman, Hurst *et al*, 1822, p187.

6 *Maclean's Journal*, p35.

7 Letter dated 17 April, published in *Newcastle Courant*, 19–26 April 1746, p3.

8 *Newcastle Courant*, 7–14 June 1746, p3.

9 Johnstone, p214, and further quotes pp190, 194–5 & 196.

10 Narrative given by Alexander Murray to Robert Forbes, July 1746; see Forbes, Vol I, p251.

11 *Newcastle Courant*, 26 April–3 May 1746, p2.

12 Johnstone, p449.

Chapter 1

1 James VI, *Basilicon Doron*, anglicized edition published in Edinburgh in 1599, Second Book, p42. Facsimile edition published by Menston: Scolar Press Ltd, 1969.

2   Major, J, *A History of Greater Britain as well England as Scotland*, 1521, translated by Archibald Constable, Edinburgh: Scottish History Society, 1892, p49.

3   McNeill, PGB, & MacQueen, H (editors) *Atlas of Scottish History to 1707*, Edinburgh: Scottish Medievalists and Department of Geography, University of Edinburgh, 1996, p13.

4   Major, p240.

5   Fairweather, B, *Old Highland Farming*, Fort William: Glencoe and North Lorn Folk Museum, 1978, pp11–12.

6   *Memoirs of the Life of Duncan Forbes of Culloden*, London, 1748, pp11 & 21.

7   Captain Edmund Burt, *Letters from a Gentleman in the North of Scotland to his friend in London*, London: S Birt, 1754. Reprinted Edinburgh: Birlinn, 1998, p267.

8   Cannan, F, 'Gaelic World at War', *Military Illustrated*, No 234, Totternhoe: ADH Publishing, November 2007, p28.

9   Major, p32 & pp48–9.

10 *Memoirs of William Veitch and George Brysson*, 1825, p518, quoted in Elder, JR, *The Highland Host of 1678*, Glasgow: University Press, 1914, p133. Second quote from Elder, p134.

11 Mackay, Maj Gen H, *Memoirs of the War carried on in Scotland and Ireland 1689–1691*, Edinburgh: Bannantyne Club, 1883, p51.

12 McBane, D, *The Expert Sword-Man's Companion*, reprinted in *Highland Swordsmanship*, Union City: Chivalry Bookshelf, 2001, p26. Quoted anonymously in Stewart, Col David, *Sketches of the Character, Manners and Present State of the Highlanders of Scotland; with details of the Military Service of the Highland Regiment*, Edinburgh: Archibald Constable & Co, 1822, Vol I, p66. For the suggestion that McBane may have worn Highland garb at Killiecrankie see Thomson, J, 'A Soldier of Fortune', *Dispatch – the Journal of the Scottish Military Historical Society*, No 139, pp4–6.

13 Drummond of Balhaldy, J, *Memoirs of Sir Ewen Cameron of Locheill, chief of the Clan Cameron*, Edinburgh: Abbotsford Club, 1842, pp270–1.

14 Letter to Lord Melvill [*sic*], written at Strathbogie, 17 August 1789. See Mackay p265.

15 Mackay, Lt Gen H, *Rules of War for the Infantry*, Edinburgh: Edm Bohun, 1693, XVII.

16 Goldstein, E, *The Socket Bayonet in the British Army 1687–1783*, Lincoln, Rhode Island: Andrew Mowbray, 2000, p9.

Chapter 2

1   Thomson, W, *Memoirs of the Life and Gallant Exploits of the Old Highlander Serjeant Donald Macleod*, 1791, reprinted London & Glasgow: Blackie & Son, 1933, p48.

2 *An Act for the more Effectual Securing the Peace of the Highlands in Scotland*, Edinburgh 1716, p4. Pamphlet collected in *Jacobite Tracts*, Vols 22–59, British Library c.115.i. 3 (54).

3 *A Remonstrance of the Gentlemen of the Highland Clans of Scotland to General Wade*, undated, but probably 1725, *Jacobite Tracts*, Vols 22–59.

4 Anonymous pamphlet published in Perth in 1716, *Jacobite Tracts* Vols 22–59.

5 Macleod *Memoirs*, p39.

6 Stewart, Col David, *Sketches of the Character, Manners and Present State of the Highlanders of Scotland; with details of the Military Service of the Highland Regiment*, Edinburgh: Archibald Constable & Co, 1822, Vol I, pp33–4.

7 *Memorial to George I concerning the State of the Highlands*, by Simon, Lord Lovat, 1724. Reprinted as an appendix in Jamieson, R (editor), *Letters from a Gentleman in the North of Scotland to his friend in London*, London: Rest Fenner, 1818, Volume II, p258.

8 *Marshal Wade's Proceedings in the Highlands of Scotland*, 1724. Reprinted as an appendix in Jamieson, Volume II, p273.

9 Wade, p271.

10 Captain Edmund Burt, *Letters from a Gentleman in the North of Scotland to his friend in London*, London: S Birt, 1754. Reprinted Edinburgh: Birlinn, 1998, p283.

11 For a detailed discussion of the early Black Watch uniform and tartans, see Haythornthwaite, PJ, 'The First Highland Regiment', *Military Illustrated*, No 10, London, December/January 1988, pp23–30, & Scarlett, JD, *The Origins and Development of Military Tartans – A Re-appraisal*, Leigh-on-Sea: Partizan Press, 2003.

12 Macleod *Memoirs*, pp48–54

13 Ibid., pp61–2. For a truer version of events, see Macwilliam, HD (editor), *The Official Records of the Mutiny in the Black Watch – a London incident of the year 1743*, London: Forster Groom, 1910, & Prebble, J, *Mutiny – Highland Regiments in Revolt 1743–1804*, London: Secker & Warburg, 1975.

Chapter 3

1 *An Authentic Account of the Late Action between the Army of the High Allies … in the neighbourhood of Tournay …* Translated from the Dutch, London: M Cooper, 1745, p4. *Tracts 64–82*, British Library: 1493.c.17.

2 *Two Genuine Private Letters from the Army of Flanders …* London: W Webb, 1745, p4. *Tracts 64–82*, British Library.

3 Doddridge, P, *Some Remarkable Passages in the Life of the Hon Colonel JAS Gardner*, Edinburgh: M'Cliesh & Campbell, 1808, pp232–3.

Quoted in Stewart, Col David, *Sketches of the Character, Manners and Present State of the Highlanders of Scotland; with details of the Military Service of the Highland Regiment*, Edinburgh: Archibald Constable & Co, 1822, Vol I, p272.

4   *Memoirs of the Life and Gallant Exploits of the Old Highlander Serjeant Donald Macleod*, 1791, reprinted London & Glasgow: Blackie & Son, 1933, p64.

5   Macpherson, L, *A New Form of Prayer as used (since the battle of Fontenoy) by the British Troops in the Allied Army of Flanders*, London: T Lion, 1745, p4 & p8. *Tracts 64–82*, British Library.

6   Letter from Lord Lovat to the Lord President, written at Beaufort, 11 October 1745, *Culloden Papers*, London, 1815, p230.

7   Letter from Lord Lovat to the Lord President, c. 20 October 1745, *Culloden Papers*, London, 1815, p234.

8   *The Life, Adventures, and many Great Vicissitudes of Fortune of Simon, Lord Lovat, the head of the family of Frasers*, London: J Stanton, 1746, p172. The authorship of this book is credited to an anonymous 'gentleman, who has been conversant with his Lordship, near forty years'. The entire letter was published in London: M Cooper, 1745, and is contained in *Tracts 64–82* in the British Library.

9   Letter from Sir Harry Munro to Lord Forbes, 22 January 1746, reprinted in Mackenzie, A, *History of the Munros of Fowlis*, Inverness: A & W Mackenzie, 1898, p134.

10 Letter of 22 June 1746, quoted in *The Life, Adventurers, and many Great Vicissitudes of Fortune of Simon, Lord Lovat, the head of the family of Frasers*, London: J Stanton, 1746, p186.

11 Letter from Ralph Bigland to Alexander Macmorland in Leith, 3 March 1748/9, contained in Forbes, R, *The Lyon in Mourning…*, Edinburgh: University Press, 1895, reprinted 1975, Vol I, pp254–5.

Chapter 4

1   Report written by James Wolfe at Camp Montmorency, River of St Lawrence, 2 September 1759: National Archives, Kew, file CO5/51.

2   Stewart, Col David, *Sketches of the Character, Manners and Present State of the Highlanders of Scotland; with details of the Military Service of the Highland Regiment*, Edinburgh: Archibald Constable & Co, 1822, Vol II, pp16–7.

3   Knox, Capt John (ed Doughty, AG), *An Historical Journal of the Campaigns in North America*, Toronto: Champlain Society, 1914, Vol II, p96.

4   'Even an out-of-condition 52-year-old can manage it in little more than 10 minutes!' Reid, S, 'Taking Quebec', *Military Illustrated*, No 227, London, April 2007, p35.

5   Fraser, Col Malcolm, *Extract from Manuscript Journal relating to the Siege of Quebec in 1759*, Quebec: Literary and Historical Society, 1867, p20.

6   Just a month later, the *Return of the State of His Majesty's Forces under command of Brig-Gen Robert Moncton left at Quebec*, 12 October 1759, lists the 78th as having 800 men fit for duty: National Archives, Kew, file CO5/51.

7   For doubts over whether Wolfe was involved at all in this incident, see Reid, S, *Wolfe*, Staplehurst: Spellmount, 2000, pp69–70.

8   Fraser, p20.

9   Knox, p101.

10 Fortescue, JW, *A History of the British Army*, London: MacMillan & Co, 1910, Vol II, p387.

11 Keegan, J, *Warpaths*, London: Hodder & Stoughton, 1995, pp135 & 138.

12 Fraser, p21.

13 Ibid., p23.

14 See Colley, L, *Britons: Forging the Nation 1707–1837*, London: Pimlico, 1994, p103.

15 Stewart, Col David, *Sketches of the Character, Manners and Present State of the Highlanders of Scotland; with details of the Military Service of the Highland Regiment*, Edinburgh: Archibald Constable & Co, 1822, Vol I, pp399–400.

16 Ibid., Vol II, pp75–6.

17 Klieforth, AC & Munro, RJ, *The Scottish Invention of America, Democracy and Human Rights*, Maryland: University Press of America, 2004, p263.

18 See Cage, RA (editor), *The Scots Abroad*, London: Croom Helm, 1985, pp226–30.

19 Frederick Davis, T, *MacGregor's Invasion of Florida, 1817*, Jacksonville: Florida Historical Society, 1928, p6.

20 Anonymous, *Narrative of the Expedition under General MacGregor against Porto Bello*, London: C&J Ollier, 1820, p52.

Chapter 5

1   Alexander Grant's fourteen-page account of the attack on Calcutta quoted in Busteed, HE, *Echoes from Old Calcutta*, Calcutta: Thacker Spink, 1882, pp6–12.

2   Ibid.

3   Grant, R, *A Sketch of the History of the East India Company*, London: Black Parry, 1813, p156. He says Calcutta 'was gallantly, although not very skilfully, defended …'.

4 Holwell, JZ, *A genuine narrative of the deplorable deaths of the English Gentlemen and others, who were suffocated in the Black Hole in Fort William*, London: A Millar, 1758.

5 Embree, AT, *Charles Grant and British Rule in India*, New York: Columbia University Press, 1962, p23. See also Morris, H, *Charles Grant*, London & Madras: Christian Literature Society, 1905.

6 Alexander Grant had an illegitimate son, William. William's second son, James Grant, moved to Mexico where he became involved in the Texan war of independence as an agent working for the British trying to keep Texas out of American hands. See Reid, S, *The Secret War for Texas*, College Station: Texas A&M University Press, 2007, pp13–14.

7 Embree pp209–10.

8 Tipu's mechanical tiger now resides in the Victoria & Albert Museum in London.

9 Hook, TE, *The Life of General Sir David Baird*, London: Richard Bentley, 1832, p48.

10 *Diary of Colonel Cromwell Massy*, Bangalore: Mysore Government Press, 1876, p13.

11 Ibid., letter from Henry George Jennings Clarke, p17.

12 Beatson, A, *A View of the Origin and Conduct of the War with Tippoo Sultan*, London: W Bulmer, 1800, ppciii–civ.

13 See Harrington, P, *British Artists and War*, London: Greenhill Books, 1993, pp61–4.

14 Hibbert, C, *Wellington*, London: HarperCollins, 1997, p43.

15 Weller, J, *Wellington in India*, London: Greenhill, 1993, p157.

16 Ibid., p194.

17 *General Orders of his excellency the most noble the Governor General in council*, Fort William, 30 October 1803, in Gurwood, Lt Col, *Dispatches of Field Marshal the Duke of Wellington*, London: John Murray, 1834, Vol 1, pp397–8.

Chapter 6

1 Transcript of Private Dixon Vallance's *Narrative of the Battle of Quatre Bras by a soldier of the 79th Highlanders* in the archive of the Highlanders' Regimental Museum, Fort George; quoted with thanks to them. Passages from this have only previously been published in *The 79th News* of 1892 and the *Hamilton Advertiser*, July 1922.

2 Ibid., p12.

3 Transcript of the diary of Captain Thomas Hobbs, 92nd Highlanders, p14, in the archive of the Gordon Highlanders Museum, Aberdeen; quoted with thanks to them.

4   Siborne, HT (editor), *Waterloo Letters*, London: Cassell & Co, 1891, p359.

5   Vallance, p14.

6   Oman, CWC, *A History of the Peninsular War*, Oxford: Clarendon Press, 1911, Vol IV, p334.

7   Bell, GC, *Rough Notes by an Old Soldier*, London: Day & Son, 1867, Vol I, p104.

8   *Historical Records of the Cameron Highlanders*, Edinburgh: Blackwoods, 1909–62, quoted in McCorry, H (editor), *The Thistle at War*, Edinburgh: National Museum of Scotland, 1997, pp18–19.

9   Haythornthwaite, P, *Waterloo Men*, Ramsbury: Crowood Press, 1999, p54.

10 *Gordons and Greys at Waterloo*, by Major Robert Winchester, transcript in the archive of the Gordon Highlanders Museum, Aberdeen; quoted with thanks to them. See shorter version of the letter, dated 24 November 1834, in Siborne, HT (editor), *Waterloo Letters*, London: Cassell & Co, 1891, pp382–4.

11 Siborne, HT (editor), *Waterloo Letters*, London: Cassell & Co, 1891, pp81–2.

12 Vallance p22.

13 For a moving description of the wounded after Waterloo see Crumpling, MKH, & Starling, P, *A Surgical Artist at War: The Paintings and Sketches of Sir Charles Bell 1809–1815*, Edinburgh: Royal College of Surgeons, 2005.

14 *A Soldier of the Seventy-first*, originally published in Edinburgh, 1819, reprinted Moreton-in-Marsh: Windrush Press, 1996, p111. The authorship of this has been ascribed to Thomas Howell, but this has been disputed, with no soldier of that name appearing on the muster rolls of the 71st. See Reid, S, 'Who was the soldier of the 71st?', *JSAHR*, No314, Summer 2000, pp138–9, and Reid, S, 'The Mysterious Highlander', *Military Illustrated*, October 2008, No245, pp16–23.

15 Transcript of Journal of James Gunn, written sixty-four years after he enlisted, in the Black Watch Museum, Perth, pp54–5; thanks for permission to quote from this from the Trustees of the Black Watch Museum.

Chapter 7

1   Robertson, JI, *The First Highlander – Major-General David Stewart of Garth*, East Linton: Tuckwell Press, 1998, pp58–9.

2   Stewart, Col David, *Sketches of the Character, Manners and Present State of the Highlanders of Scotland; with details of the Military Service of the Highland Regiment*, Edinburgh: Archibald Constable & Co, 1822, Vol I, pp417–18.

3   See Gibson, JG, *Traditional Gaelic Bagpiping*, Edinburgh: NMS Publishing, 1998.

4   *The Times*, London, 16 June 1787, p3.

5   Stewart, Vol 1, p214.

6   Campbell, A, *Two Hundred Years*, London: Highland Society of London, 1983, p26.

7   *Remarks on Colonel Stewart's Sketches of the Highlanders*, Edinburgh: Bell & Bradfute, 1823, p2, sixty-six-page booklet contained in British Library *Tracts* T:1099.

8   Faiers, J, *Tartan*, Oxford: Berg, 2008, p167.

9   Prebble, J, *The King's Jaunt*, London: Collins, 1988, pp74–5.

10 'The King's Visit to Scotland – Carle, now the King's come!', *The Times*, 14 August 1822, p3.

11 'His Majesty's Visit to Scotland', *The Times*, 15 August 1822, p3.

12 See Trevor-Roper, H, 'The Invention of Tradition: The Highland Tradition of Scotland', *The Invention of Tradition* (edited by E Hobsbawn), Cambridge: University Press, 1983, pp15–41, & Trevor-Roper, H, *The Invention of Scotland*, London: Yale, 2008.

13 'Pipe dream – glorious history of Scotland's iconic instrument is made up, says expert', *Guardian*, 19 April 2008. See Cheape, H, *Bagpipes: A National Collection of a National Instrument*, Edinburgh: National Museums Scotland, 2008.

14 'Death of Mackay, the celebrated piper', *The Times*, 16 April 1859, p7.

15 Abler, TS, *Hinterland Warriors and Military Dress*, Oxford: Berg, 1999, pp139–40.

Chapter 8

1   Currie, FG, *Letters from the Crimea*, Fareham: Henry Payne, 1899, letter 1; archive of the Highlanders' Regimental Museum, Fort George.

2   Transcript of journal by William Nairn in the Argyll and Sutherland Highlanders Museum, Stirling Castle, pp1–2.

3   Currie, letter 11.

4   Transcript of Crimean recollections by Sergeant Edward McSally of the 42nd, in the archives of the Black Watch Museum, Perth, p6; thanks for permission to quote from the Trustees of the Black Watch Museum.

5   McSally, p7.

6   Currie, letter 11.

7   Nairn, p2.

8   McSally, pp11–12.

9   'The life of Colin Campbell, Lord Clyde', *The Times*, 21 March 1881, p10.

10 See Lt Gen Shadwell, CB, *The Life of Colin Campbell, Lord Clyde*, Edinburgh & London: William Blackwood, 1881.

11 Currie, letter 12.

12 Fletcher, I, & Ishchenko, N, *The Crimean War*, Staplehurst: Spellmount, 2004, p169.

13 Nairn, p3.

14 Transcript of diary of George Greig in the Argyll and Sutherland Highlanders Museum, Stirling Castle, p7.

15 Russell, W, *The British Expedition to the Crimea*, 1858, extract reprinted in Hudson, R (editor), *William Russell Special Correspondent of The Times*, London: Folio Society, 1995, pp29–30.

16 Fletcher, p170.

17 'Art in Scotland', *The Times*, 2 April 1881, p10.

18 *The Times*, 29 June 1883, p6.

19 Currie, letter 13.

20 Letter of 7 November 1854 from Balaklava Heights by Capt Thomas Henry Montgomery, in the archives of the Black Watch Museum, Perth; thanks for permission to quote from the Trustees of the Black Watch Museum.

21 Transcript of Diary of Private William Duguid in the Argyll and Sutherland Highlanders Museum, Stirling Castle, p8.

22 Letter No 6, 7 August 1855, 'Crimean Letters of 3932 George Conn', *Aberdeen University Review*, Vol XXXVIII, 2, No 121, Autumn 1959, p134.

23 Currie, letter 32.

Chapter 9

1 Transcript of Diary of George Wells in the archive of the Highlanders' Regimental Museum, Fort George.

2 See Ward, A, *Our Bones are Scattered*, London: John Murray, 1996, pp417–30.

3 Munro, W, *Reminiscences of Military Service*, London: Hurst & Blackett, 1883, pp128–9.

4 Letter written by M de Banneroi, extract published in *The Times*, 14 December 1857, p3. Forbes-Mitchell backed up the truth of the story by saying he had spoken to a woman who was in the same room as Jessie in the Residency. See Forbes-Mitchell, W, *Reminiscences of the Great Mutiny*, London: Macmillan, 1893, pp114–19.

5 Forbes-Mitchell.

6 Ibid., p57.

7   Ibid., p72. Curiously, in a paraphrase of Forbes-Mitchell's account of the same scene, published in Kinsley, DA, *They Fight Like Devils*, London: Greenhill Books, p141, Campbell rounds on the soldier angrily saying 'Damn your medals! You fight for the honour, not honours, of your country.' Is this made up or a different version of the same event?

8   Forbes-Mitchell, p198.

9   Transcript of Diary of George Wells in the archive of the Highlanders' Regimental Museum, Fort George.

10 Ibid.

11 Munro, p221. See also Forbes-Mitchell, p213, and Creagh, Sir M, *The VC and DSO*, London: Standard Art Book Company, 1924, Vol 1, p51.

12 Wimberley, Capt D, *Some account of the part taken by the 79th Regiment of Cameron Highlanders in the Indian Mutiny Campaign of 1858*, Inverness, 1891, p40, in the archive of the Highlanders' Regimental Museum, Fort George.

Chapter 10

1   Herman, A, *How the Scots Invented the Modern World*, New York: Crown Publishers, 2001, p328.

2   Finley, JH, *The Coming of the Scot*, New York: Charles Scribner, 1940, p175.

3   See Bradley, ES, *Simon Cameron, Lincoln's Secretary of War – a political biography*, University of Pennsylvania Press, 1966.

4   For illustrations re-creating the 79th New York Highlanders' dress uniform, see Haythornthwaite, P, *Uniforms of the American Civil War*, Poole: Blandford Press, 1975, plate 20, & Troiani, D, *Regiments & Uniforms of the Civil War*, Mechanicsburg: Stackpole Books, 2002, p42.

5   *New York Times*, 18 May 1864, p4.

6   Todd, W, *The Seventy-Ninth Highlanders: New York Volunteers in the War of Rebellion*, Albany: Brandow, Barton & Co, 1886, p32.

7   Stevens, H, *The Life of Isaac Ingalls Stevens*, Boston & New York: Houghton, Mifflin & Co, 1900, Vol II, p324. This book was written by Stevens's son, Hazard.

8   Richards, KD, *Isaac I Stevens*, Pullman: Washington State University Press, 1993, p364.

9   Todd, pp160–1.

10 Another unit of Scottish descent fighting on the side of the South was the Memphis-raised Highland Guard, which dressed in 'the picturesque uniform of the Highlands of Scotland, plaid, kilt and trews'. See Field, R, *American Civil War Confederate Army*, London: Brassey's, 1996, p87.

11 Stevens, p485.
12 'Crowd Sees Scots Go to Church in Kilts', *New York Times*, 15 May 1911, p10.
13 'Highlanders at Sport', *New York Times*, 7 September 1883, p3.
14 Stout, G, *Yankees Century: 100 years of New York Yankees baseball*, Boston: Houghton Mifflin, 2002, p18, & Graham, F, *New York Yankees: an informal history*, Carbondale: Southern Illinois University Press, 2002, p8. Thanks to Steve Steinberg for these references.

Chapter 11

1   Letter written at Camp Suakin, 16 March 1884 by Captain Andrew Scott Stevenson; transcript in the Black Watch Museum, Perth; thanks for permission to quote from this from the Trustees of the Black Watch Museum.
2   Ibid., p1.
3   Ibid., p4.
4   Royle, T, *The Black Watch*, Edinburgh & London: Mainstream Publishing, 2006, p101–2; Linklater, E & A, *The Black Watch*, London: Barrie & Jenkins Ltd, 1977, p127.
5   Stevenson, p5.
6   Egerton, G, *With the 72nd Highlanders in the Sudan Campaign*, London: Eden Fisher, 1909, p11. Author-annotated copy in the archive of the Highlanders' Regimental Museum, Fort George; quoted with thanks to them.
7   Ibid., p15.
8   Witnessed by Lieutenant Samuel Cox of the Lincolnshire Regiment, quoted in Meredith, J, *Omdurman Diaries 1898*, Barnsley: Leo Cooper, 1998, p88.
9   Egerton, p18.
10 Diary of Lieutenant Angus McNeil quoted in Harrington, P, & Sharf, FA (editors), *Omdurman 1898*, London: Greenhill Books, 1998, p144.
11 Letters to the editor, *The Times*, 15 September 1880, p10.
12 Ibid., 18 November 1880, p6.

Chapter 12

1   Masters, J, *Bugles and a Tiger*, New York: Viking Press, 1956, p218.
2   Ibid., p47.
3   Wimberley, Capt D, *Some account of the part taken by the 79th Regiment of Cameron Highlanders in the Indian Mutiny Campaign of 1858*, Inverness, 1891, p34, in the archive of the Highlanders' Regimental Museum, Fort George.

4   Russell, W, *My Diary in India*, 1860, extract reprinted in Hudson, R (editor), *William Russell Special Correspondent of The Times*, London: Folio Society, 1995, p153.

5   Barthorp, M, *Afghan Wars and the North-West Frontier 1839–1947*, London: Cassell, 2002, p90.

6   Gardyne, Lt Col CG, *The Life of a Regiment – the History of the Gordon Highlanders*, London: Medici Society Ltd, 1929, Vol II, p288.

7   Ibid., p290.

8   Slessor, Capt AK, *The 2nd Battalion Derbyshire Regiment in Tirah*, London: Swan Sonnenschein & Co, 1900, p68.

9   Ibid., p74.

10 Lockhart in Gardyne, p291.

11 London Gazette citation in Creagh, Sir O'Moore, *The VC and DSO*, London: Standard Art Book Co, 1924, Vol I, p109.

12 Hutchinson, Col HD, *The Campaign in Tirah 1897–1898*, London: MacMillan & Co, 1898, p74.

13 Quoted in diary of Captain VR Ormsby of the 1/3 Gurkha Rifles, p32, transcript provided by Gavin Edgley-Harris of the Gurkha Museum, Winchester.

14 Barthorp, M, *The Frontier Ablaze*, London: Windrow & Greene, 1996, p104.

15 Fraser, GMcD, *The General Danced at Dawn*, London: Barrie Jenkins, 1970, p148.

16 Diary of Corporal James H Noble of the 1st Argyll and Sutherland Highlanders, in the archive of the Argyll and Sutherland Highlanders Museum, Stirling Castle.

17 Letter from Private James Williamson, A Company 2nd Black Watch, in the Black Watch Museum, Perth; thanks for permission to quote from this from the Trustees of the Black Watch Museum.

18 'Not Fighting, but Suicide', *Morning Leader*, London, 11 January 1900.

19 'Letter from a Private in the 1st A and S Highlanders who had been reported killed', *West Lothian Courier*, 30 December 1899.

20 'Roughing it', *Manchester Evening Chronicle*, 21 March 1900.

21 *Morning Leader*, London, 6 January 1900.

22 'Roughing it'.

Chapter 13

1   Barber, G, *My Diary in France*, Liverpool: Henry Young & Sons, 1917, p3. Privately published, this diary is in the archive of the National War Museum, Edinburgh Castle.

2   Ibid., p71.

3   Ibid., p3.

4 Campbell, A, *Two Hundred Years*, London: Highland Society of London, 1983, p47.
5 Parliamentary report, *The Times*, 12 April 1902, p9.
6 Bull, S, *World War One British Army, History of Uniforms*, London: Brassey's, 1998, pp19–24.
7 Sutherland, Captain D, *War Diary of the Fifth Seaforth Highlanders*, London: Bodley Head, 1920, p69.
8 Ibid., p83.
9 Ibid., p88.
10 Chappell, M, *Scottish Units in the World Wars*, London: Osprey, 1994, p5.
11 Lewis, JE (editor), *True World War I Stories*, London: Robinson Publishing, 1997, p205.
12 London Gazette citation in Creagh, Sir O'Moore, *The VC and DSO*, London: Standard Art Book Co, 1924, Vol I, p253.
13 Creagh, p252.
14 Snelling, S, *VCs of the First World War – Passchendaele 1917*, Stroud: Sutton Publishing, 1998, p35.
15 Ibid., p36.
16 Creagh, p253.
17 Farrell, FA, *The 51st (Highland) Division War Sketches*, Edinburgh: TC & EC Jack, 1920, p29.

Chapter 14

1 Orpen, N, *The Cape Town Highlanders*, Cape Town: Cape Town Highlanders History Committee, 1970, p4.
2 Ibid., p91.
3 *The Calcutta Scottish Regimental Chronicle*, December 1933, Vol I, No 3, p1.
4 Ibid., August 1933, Vol I, No 2, p3.
5 Ibid., April 1934, Vol II, No 5, p13.
6 Winsley, Captain TM, *A History of the Singapore Volunteer Corps 1854–1937*, Singapore: Government Printing Offices, 1938, p91.
7 For a list of their tartans, see Barnes, Maj MR, *The Scottish Regiments*, London: Seeley Service & Co, 1960, p343.
8 See Prentis, MD, *The Scots in Australia*, Sydney University Press, 1983.
9 See Barnes for details, pp321–4.
10 For a full list, see Barnes, pp305–20.
11 Cook, T, *No Place to Run: The Canadian Corps and Gas Warfare in the First World War*, Vancouver: UBC Press, 1999, pp20 & 28.

12 Hutchison, Col PP, *Canada's Black Watch – the First Hundred Years*, Montreal: Armoury Association, 1962, p76.

Chapter 15

1 'Memoirs of a Conscript', unpublished typescript by Private Andrew Meldrum in the Black Watch Museum, Perth, p3; thanks for permission to quote from this from the Trustees of the Black Watch Museum.

2 Unpublished typescript by Private John Clarke in the Black Watch Museum, Perth, p2; thanks for permission to quote from this from the Trustees of the Black Watch Museum.

3 Longden, S, *Dunkirk – the men they left behind*, London: Constable, 2008, p136.

4 Reoch, E, *The St Valery Story*, Inverness: privately published, 1965, p210.

5 Liddell Hart, BH (editor), *The Rommel Papers*, London: Collins, 1953, p65.

6 Churchill, W, *The Second World War*, abridged edition, London: Cassell, 1959, p286.

7 David, S, *Churchill's Sacrifice of the Highland Division*, London: Brassey's, 1994, pp238–41.

8 Clarke, p3

9 Borthwich, Capt J, *The 51st Highland Division in Africa & Sicily*, Glasgow: D MacKenzie & Co, 1945, p15.

10 Salmond, JB, *The History of the 51st Highland Division 1939–1945*, Edinburgh: William Blackwood & Sons, 1953, p39.

11 Transcript of interview with Alex Clark, July 2004, in the archive of the Gordon Highlanders Museum, Aberdeen; quoted with thanks to them.

12 Fuller, A, *Drawn in Battle: Sketches of the 51st Highland Division from El Alamein until the defeat of Rommel and the Afrika Korps*, Storrington: Historic Military Press, 2002, p21.

13 Laffin, J, *British VCs of World War 2*, Stroud: Sutton Publishing, 1997, p93.

14 Borthwich, p36.

15 London Gazette citation, quoted in Laffin, p96.

16 Finlay, A (editor), *The Armstrong Nose – Selected Letters of Hamish Henderson*, Edinburgh: Polygon, 1996, p4.

17 Clark, p31.

18 Quoted in Borthwich, p15.

19 Davies, DT (editor), *The Daily Telegraph Book of Military Obituaries*, London: Grub Street, 2003, p198.

Chapter 16

1 Transcript of interview with Bob Boyce in March 2005 in the archive of the Gordon Highlanders Museum, Aberdeen; quoted with thanks to them.
2 David, S, *Mutiny at Salerno*, London: Brassey's, 1995, p56.
3 Hansard, parliamentary debate, 22 March 2000.
4 Boyce, p2.
5 Ibid., p5.
6 This is a more genteel version of the traditional story, supposedly involving Black Watch soldiers enjoying carnal relations with a sheep, while jumpy Gordons are said to have shot up their own ration party.
7 Lindsay, M, *So few got through: Personal diary July 1944–May 1945*, London: Collins, 1946, p226.
8 'Memoirs of a Conscript', unpublished typescript by Private Andrew Meldrum in the Black Watch Museum, Perth, p8; thanks for permission to quote from this from the Trustees of the Black Watch Museum.

Chapter 17

1 Review by Mordaunt Hall, *New York Times*, 23 May 1929.
2 Robinson, G, 'Wee Willie Winkie – Hollywood's version of a Highland Regiment on the North West Frontier', *Soldiers of the Queen*, Victorian Military Society, issue 76, March 1994, p30. See also Newark, G, 'The Hollywood Regiment', *Military Illustrated*, London, No 121, June 1998, pp16–19.
3 Niven, D, *The Moon's a Balloon*, London: Hodder & Stoughton, 1971, pp63–4.
4 Ibid., p259.
5 Colman, JB, *A Very Private Person – Ronald Colman*, London: WH Allen, 1975, pv.
6 Lauder, Sir H, *Roamin' in the Gloamin'*, London: Hutchinson & Co, 1928, p191.
7 Package on display in the Museum of Packaging and Advertising, London.
8 Grigor, M&B, *Scotch Myths*, exhibition catalogue, Edinburgh International Festival, 1996.
9 McLaren, D, *The Rise and Progress of Whisky-Drinking in Scotland*, Glasgow: Scottish Temperance League, 1858, p19.
10 Thanks to Eileen Stuart and William Grant & Sons Distillers Ltd.
11 Thanks to expert toy soldier collector James Opie.

12 MacDonald Fraser, G, *The Hollywood History of the World*, London: Michael Joseph, 1988, p137.

13 Glancy, HM, *When Hollywood Loved Britain*, Manchester University Press, 1999, p191.

14 Pearson, J, *James Bond – a fictional biography*, London: Pan, 1973, p28.

15 Hunter, J, *Great Scot – the Life of Sean Connery*, London: Bloomsbury, 1993, p77.

16 Roberts, A, *A History of the English-Speaking Peoples Since 1900*, London: Weidenfeld & Nicolson, 2006, p579.

Chapter 18

1 Brown, AW, *A Memoir from Music to Wars*, Aberdeen: privately published, 2001, pp17–18.

2 Ibid., p108.

3 Mackay, D, *The Malayan Emergency 1948–60*, London: Brassey's, 1997, p58.

4 Author interview with Brown, 9 September 2008.

5 Statement by Independent Witness, signed by Major JB Ghillies, 12 October 1950, National Archive: WO 32/14012. See also Hickey, M, *The Korean War*, London: John Murray, 1999, pp79–80.

6 'He can't forget the freezing trenches of the Korean War', *Sunday Post*, 25 June 2000, p12.

7 Brown, p126.

8 Ibid., pp133–4.

9 'Pte Speakman gets his VC Ribbon', *The Times*, 31 December 1951, p3.

10 Halley, D, *The Iron Claw – A Conscript's Tale*, Finavon: privately published, 1998, pp69 & 75.

11 Author interview with Halley, 9 September 2008.

12 'The Hook Again, May 1953', *The Red Hackle*, May 2003, p20.

13 Author interview with Blake, 6 June 2008.

14 Special Order of the Day, 1st Battalion Queen's Own Cameron Highlanders, collection of Private Blake.

15 'Family touched by memorial tribute', *Banffshire Journal*, 13 November 2002, p3.

Chapter 19

1 *Daily Telegraph*, 25 October 2004.

2 'Death of a Regiment, birth of battalion', *Daily Telegraph*, 29 March 2006, p6.

3 'No going back', letters to the editor, *The Times*, 17 October 1957, p11.

4 Letter from Lord Airlie to Field Marshal Templer, 22 August 1957, National Archives: WO 32/17178.

5 Letter from Field Marshal Templer to Lord Airlie, 6 September 1957, National Archives: WO 32/17178.

6 Press Association report of 27 October 1967, followed by government investigation into leak, National Archives: CAB 164/129.

7 Report to Foreign Office from Aden, 23 September 1967, National Archives: CAB 164/139.

8 Mitchell, Lt Col C, *Having been a Soldier*, London: Hamish Hamilton, 1969, p179.

9 'Crater fully under British control', *The Times*, 6 July 1967, p4.

10 Mitchell, p187.

11 Historical Record of Argyll & Sutherland Highlanders, 1st Battalion, Period 1 April '68–31 March '69, written by Captain DP Thomson, p18, National Archives: WO 305/3487.

12 Ibid.

13 Letters to the editor, *The Times*, 22 July 1968, p7.

14 Mitchell, p242.

15 Minutes of Cabinet Meeting, 30 July 1970, National Archives: CAB 130/472.

16 'Half a Reprieve for the Argylls' by Tom Pocock, *London Evening Standard*, 6 August 1970.

17 Lt-Col Colin Mitchell's last public campaign was to set up a charity to clear mines from war zones. He died in 1996.

18 Letter from Colonel Slessor to the Ministry of Defence, 16 November 1973, National Archives: WO 32/19828.

19 'Scotsman's sporran doomed by European ban on sealskins', *Independent*, 25 July 2008, p26.

20 'Pipe down! Brussels slaps a noise order on heart of Scotland', *Sunday Times*, 20 April 2008, p7.

21 *The Red Hackle*, May 2005, p36.

22 Author interview with Tam Henderson, 7 November 2008. See also Capt Henderson, T, & Hunt, J, *Warrior*, Edinburgh: Mainstream Publishing, 2008.

23 'No reprieve for Scots Regiments', *Scotsman*, 17 July 2004, p12.

24 'Badge of pride or shameful betrayal?', *Herald*, Glasgow, 17 August 2005, p3.

25 Ibid.

Bibliography

For all unpublished sources, magazine and newspaper articles, see footnotes.

Abler, TS, *Hinterland Warriors and Military Dress*, Oxford: Berg, 1999.

Anonymous, *The Life, Adventurers, and many Great Vicissitudes of Fortune of Simon, Lord Lovat, the head of the family of Frasers*, London: J Stanton, 1746.

Anonymous, *Memoirs of the Life of Duncan Forbes of Culloden*, London, 1748.

Anonymous, *Narrative of the Expedition under General MacGregor against Porto Bello*, London: C&J Ollier, 1820.

Anonymous, *A Soldier of the Seventy-first*, Edinburgh, 1819; reprinted Moreton-in-Marsh: Windrush Press, 1996.

Barber, G, *My Diary in France*, Liverpool: Henry Young & Sons, 1917.

Barnes, Maj MR, *The Scottish Regiments*, London: Seeley Service & Co, 1960.

Barthorp, M, *The Frontier Ablaze*, London: Windrow & Greene, 1996.

Barthorp, M, *Afghan Wars and the North-West Frontier 1839–1947*, London: Cassell, 2002.

Beatson, A, *A View of the Origin and Conduct of the War with Tippoo Sultan*, London: W Bulmer, 1800.

Bell, GC, *Rough Notes by an Old Soldier*, London: Day & Son, 1867.

Borthwich, Cap J, *The 51st Highland Division in Africa & Sicily*, Glasgow: D MacKenzie & Co, 1945.

Bradley, ES, *Simon Cameron, Lincoln's Secretary of War – a political biography*, 1966.

Brown, AW, *A Memoir from Music to Wars*, Aberdeen, 2001.

Brown, IG, & Cheape, H (editors), *Witness to rebellion: John Maclean's Journal of the Forty Five*, East Linton: Tuckworth Press, 1996.

Burt, Captain E, *Letters from a Gentleman in the North of Scotland to his friend in London*, London: S Birt, 1754. Reprinted Edinburgh: Birlinn, 1998.

Busteed, HE, *Echoes from Old Calcutta*, Calcutta: Thacker Spink, 1882.

Cage, RA (editor), *The Scots Abroad*, London: Croom Helm, 1985.

Campbell, A, *Two Hundred Years*, London: Highland Society of London, 1983.

Chappell, M, *Scottish Units in the World Wars*, London: Osprey, 1994.

Cheape, H, *Bagpipes: a National Collection of a National Instrument*, Edinburgh: National Museums Scotland, 2008.

Colley, L, *Britons: Forging the Nation 1707–1837*, London: Pimlico, 1994.

Colman, JB, *A Very Private Person – Ronald Colman*, London: WH Allen, 1975.

Cook, T, *No Place to Run: The Canadian Corps and Gas Warfare in the First World War*, Vancouver: UBC Press, 1999.

Creagh, Sir M, *The VC and DSO*, London: Standard Art Book Company, 1924.

Currie, FG, *Letters from the Crimea*, Fareham: Henry Payne, 1899.

David, S, *Churchill's Sacrifice of the Highland Division*, London: Brassey's, 1994.

David, S, *Mutiny at Salerno*, London: Brassey's, 1995.

Davis, TF, *MacGregor's Invasion of Florida, 1817*, Jacksonville: Florida Historical Society, 1928.

Devine, TM, *Scotland's Empire 1600–1815*, London: Penguin, 2004.

Diary of Colonel Cromwell Massy, Bangalore: Mysore Government Press, 1876.

Doddridge, P, *Some Remarkable Passages in the Life of the Hon Colonel JAS Gardner*, Edinburgh: M'Cliesh & Campbell, 1808.

Douglas, H, *Jacobite Spy Wars*, Stroud: Sutton, 1999.

Drummond of Balhaldy, J, *Memoirs of Sir Ewen Cameron of Locheill, chief of the Clan Cameron*, Edinburgh: Abbotsford Club, 1842.

Duffy, C, *The '45*, London: Cassell, 2003.

Egerton, G, *With the 72nd Highlanders in the Sudan Campaign*, London: Eden Fisher, 1909.

Elder, JR, *The Highland Host of 1678*, Glasgow: University Press, 1914.

Embree, AT, *Charles Grant and British Rule in India*, New York: Columbia University Press, 1962.

Faiers, J, *Tartan*, Oxford: Berg, 2008.

Fairweather, B, *Old Highland Farming*, Fort William: Glencoe and North Lorn Folk Museum, 1978.

Farrell, FA, *The 51st (Highland) Division War Sketches*, Edinburgh: TC & EC Jack, 1920.

Finlay, A (editor), *The Armstrong Nose – Selected Letters of Hamish Henderson*, Edinburgh: Polygon, 1996.

Finley, JH, *The Coming of the Scot*, New York: Charles Scribner, 1940.

Fletcher, I, & Ishchenko, N, *The Crimean War*, Staplehurst: Spellmount, 2004.

Forbes, R, *The Lyon in Mourning*, reprinted Edinburgh: Scottish Academic Press, 1975.

Forbes-Mitchell, W, *Reminiscences of the Great Mutiny*, London: MacMillan, 1893.

Fortescue, JW, *A History of the British Army*, London: MacMillan & Co, 1910.

Fraser, GMcD, *The General Danced at Dawn*, London: Barrie Jenkins, 1970.

Fraser, GMcD, *The Hollywood History of the World*, London: Michael Joseph, 1988.

Fraser, Col Malcolm, *Extract from Manuscript Journal relating to the Siege of Quebec in 1759*, Quebec: Literary and Historical Society, 1867.

Fry, M, *The Scottish Empire*, Edinburgh: Tuckwell Press, 2001.

Fry, M, *Wild Scots: Four Hundred Years of Highland History*, London: John Murray, 2005.

Fuller, A, *Drawn in Battle: Sketches of the 51st Highland Division from El Alamein until the defeat of Rommel and the Afrika Korps*, Storrington: Historic Military Press, 2002.

Gardyne, Lt Col CG, *The Life of a Regiment – the History of the Gordon Highlanders*, London: Medici Society Ltd, 1929.

Gibson, JG, *Traditional Gaelic Bagpiping*, Edinburgh: National Museums Scotland, 1998.

Glancy, HM, *When Hollywood loved Britain*, Manchester University Press, 1999.

Goldstein, E, *The Socket Bayonet in the British Army 1687–1783*, Lincoln, Rhode Island: Andrew Mowbray, 2000.

Grant, R, *A Sketch of the History of the East India Company*, London: Black Parry, 1813.

Grigor, M&B, *Scotch Myths*, Edinburgh International Festival, 1996.

Gurwood, Lt Col, *Dispatches of Field Marshal the Duke of Wellington*, London: John Murray, 1834.

Halley, D, *The Iron Claw – A Conscript's Tale*, Finavon: privately published, 1998.

Harrington, P, *British Artists and War*, London: Greenhill Books, 1993.

Harrington, P, & Sharf, FA (editors), *Omdurman 1898*, London: Greenhill Books, 1998.

Haythornthwaite, P, *Waterloo Men*, Ramsbury: Crowood Press, 1999.

Henderson, DM, *The Scottish Regiments*, London: HarperCollins, 1996.

Henderson, Capt T, & Hunt, J, *Warrior*, Edinburgh: Mainstream Publishing, 2008.

Herman, A, *How the Scots Invented the Modern World*, New York: Crown Publishers, 2001.

Hibbert, C, *Wellington*, London: HarperCollins, 1997.

Hickey, M, *The Korean War*, London: John Murray, 1999.

Holwell, JZ, *A genuine narrative of the deplorable deaths of the English Gentlemen and others, who were suffocated in the Black Hole in Fort William*, London: A Millar, 1758.

Hook, TE, *The Life of General Sir David Baird*, London: Richard Bentley, 1832.

Hudson, R (editor), *William Russell Special Correspondent of The Times*, London: Folio Society, 1995.

Hunter, J, *Great Scot – the Life of Sean Connery*, London: Bloomsbury, 1993.

Hutchinson, Col HD, *The Campaign in Tirah 1897–1898*, London: MacMillan & Co, 1898.

Hutchison, Col PP, *Canada's Black Watch – the First Hundred Years*, Montreal: Armoury Association, 1962.

James VI, *Basilicon Doron*, Edinburgh, 1599. Facsimile edition, Menston: Scolar Press Ltd, 1969.

Jamieson, R (editor), *Letters from a Gentleman in the North of Scotland to his friend in London*, London: Rest Fenner, 1818.

Johnstone, Chevalier de, *Memoirs of the Rebellion in 1745 and 1746*, London: Longman, Hurst *et al*, 1822.

Keegan, J, *Warpaths*, London: Hodder & Stoughton, 1995.

Kinsley, DA, *They Fight Like Devils*, London: Greenhill Books, 2001.

Klieforth, AC, & Munro, RJ, *The Scottish Invention of America, Democracy and Human Rights*, Maryland: University Press of America, 2004.

Knox, Capt John (ed Doughty, AG), *An Historical Journal of the Campaigns in North America*, Toronto: Champlain Society, 1914.

Lauder, Sir H, *Roamin' in the Gloamin'*, London: Hutchinson & Co, 1928.

Lenman, B, *Jacobite Clans of the Great Glen 1650–1784*, London: Methuen, 1984.

Lindsay, M, *So few got through: Personal diary July 1944–May 1945*, London: Collins, 1946.

Linklater, E & A, *The Black Watch*, London: Barrie & Jenkins Ltd, 1977.

Longden, S, *Dunkirk – The Men They Left Behind*, London: Constable, 2008.

McCorry, H, *The Thistle at War*, Edinburgh: National Museums of Scotland, 1997.

Mackay, D, *The Malayan Emergency 1948–60*, London: Brassey's, 1997.

Mackay, Lt Gen H, *Rules of War for the Infantry*, Edinburgh: Edm Bohun, 1693.

Mackay, Maj Gen H, *Memoirs of the War carried on in Scotland and Ireland 1689–1691*, Edinburgh: Bannantyne Club, 1883.

Mackenzie, A, *History of the Munros of Fowlis*, Inverness: A & W Mackenzie, 1898.

McLaren, D, *The Rise and Progress of Whisky-Drinking in Scotland*, Glasgow, Scottish Temperance League, 1858.

Maclean, F, *Highlanders*, London: Viking Books, 1995.

Maclean-Bristol, N, *Clan to Regiment, 600 Years in the Hebrides*, Barnsley: Pen & Sword, 2007.

McNeill, PGB, & MacQueen, H (editors), *Atlas of Scottish History to 1707*, Edinburgh: Scottish Medievalists and Department of Geography, University of Edinburgh, 1996.

MacQuoid, GS (editor), *Jacobite Songs and Ballads*, London: Walter Scott, c.1917.

Macwilliam, HD (editor) *The Official Records of the Mutiny in the Black Watch a London incident of the year 1743*, London: Forster Groom, 1910.

Major, J, *A History of Greater Britain as well England as Scotland*, translated by Archibald Constable, Edinburgh: Scottish History Society, 1892.

Masters, J, *Bugles and a Tiger*, New York: Viking Press, 1956.

Memoirs of the Life and Gallant Exploits of the Old Highlander Serjeant Donald Macleod, 1791, reprinted London & Glasgow: Blackie & Son, 1933.

Meredith, J, *Omdurman Diaries 1898*, Barnsley: Leo Cooper, 1998.

Mileham, P, *The Scottish Regiments 1633–1996*, Staplehurst: Spellmount, 1996.

Mitchell, Lt Col C, *Having been a Soldier*, London: Hamish Hamilton, 1969.

Morris, H, *Charles Grant*, London & Madras: Christian Literature Society, 1905.

Munro, W, *Reminiscences of Military Service*, London: Hurst & Blackett, 1883.

Neillands, R, *The Dervish Wars*, London: John Murray, 1996.

Newark, T, *Celtic Warriors*, Poole: Blandford Press, 1986.

Niven, D, *The Moon's a Balloon*, London: Hodder & Stoughton, 1971.

Oman, CWC, *A History of the Peninsular War*, Oxford: Clarendon Press, 1911.

Orpen, N, *The Cape Town Highlanders*, Cape Town: Cape Town Highlanders History Committee, 1970.

Parker, J, *Black Watch*, London: Headline Publishing, 2005.

Paterson, RC, *A Land Afflicted*, Edinburgh: John Donald, 1998.

Pearson, J, *James Bond – a fictional biography*, London: Pan, 1973.

Pittock, MGH, *A New History of Scotland*, Stroud: Sutton Publishing, 2003.

Pittock, MGH, *The Myth of the Jacobite Clans*, Edinburgh: Edinburgh University Press, 1995; new edition, 2009.

Prebble, J, *Culloden*, London: Secker & Warburg, 1961.

Prebble, J, *Mutiny – Highland Regiments in Revolt 1743–1804*, London: Secker & Warburg, 1975.

Prebble, J, *The King's Jaunt*, London: Collins, 1988.

Prentis, MD, *The Scots in Australia*, Sydney University Press, 1983.

Preston, D, *The Road to Culloden Moor*, London: Constable, 1995.

Ramsay, AAW, *Challenge to the Highlander*, London: John Murray, 1933.

Reid, S, *Like Hungry Wolves*, London: Windrow & Greene, 1994.

Reid, S, *1745 – A Military History*, Staplehurst: Spellmount, 1996.

Reid, S, *Highlander*, London: Publishing News, 2000.

Reid, S, *Wolfe*, Staplehurst: Spellmount, 2000.

Reid, S, *Cumberland's Army*, Leigh-on-Sea: Partizan Press, 2006.

Reid, S, *The Secret War for Texas*, College Station: Texas A&M University Press, 2007.

Reoch, E, *The St Valery Story*, Inverness, 1965.

Richards, KD, *Isaac I Stevens*, Pullman: Washington State University Press, 1993.

Roberts, A, *A History of the English-Speaking Peoples Since 1900*, London: Weidenfeld & Nicolson, 2006.

Robertson, JI, *The First Highlander – Major-General David Stewart of Garth*, East Linton: Tuckwell Press, 1998.

Robson, B, *Fuzzy Wuzzy: The campaigns in the Eastern Sudan 1884–85*, Tunbridge Wells: Spellmount, 1993.

Royle, T, *The Black Watch*, Edinburgh & London: Mainstream Publishing, 2006.

Salmond, J, *Wade in Scotland*, Edinburgh: Moray Press, 1936.

Salmond, JB, *The History of the 51st Highland Division 1939–1945*, Edinburgh: William Blackwood & Sons, 1953.

Scarlett, JD, *The Origins and Development of Military Tartans – A Re-appraisal*, Leigh-on-Sea: Partizan Press, 2003.

Shadwell, Lt Gen CB, *The Life of Colin Campbell, Lord Clyde*, Edinburgh & London: William Blackwood, 1881.

Siborne, HT (editor), *Waterloo Letters*, London: Cassell & Co, 1891.

Sked, P, *Culloden*, Edinburgh: National Trust of Scotland, 1997.

Slessor, Capt AK, *The 2nd Battalion Derbyshire Regiment in Tirah*, London: Swan Sonnenschein & Co, 1900.

Stevens, H, *The Life of Isaac Ingalls Stevens*, Boston & New York: Houghton, Mifflin & Co, 1900.

Stewart, Col David, *Sketches of the Character, Manners and Present State of the Highlanders of Scotland; with details of the Military Service of the Highland Regiment*, Edinburgh: Archibald Constable & Co, 1822.

Sutherland, Captain D, *War Diary of the Fifth Seaforth Highlanders*, London: Bodley Head, 1920.

Tayler, H (editor), *A Jacobite Miscellany*, Oxford: Roxburghe Club, 1948.

Taylor, W, *The Military Roads in Scotland*, Newton Abbot: David & Charles, 1976.

Thomson, W, *Memoirs of the Life and Gallant Exploits of the Old Highlander Serjeant Donald Macleod*, 1791; reprinted London & Glasgow: Blackie & Son, 1933.

Todd, W, *The Seventy-Ninth Highlanders: New York Volunteers in the War of Rebellion*, Albany: Brandow, Barton & Co, 1886.

Trevor-Roper, H, 'The Invention of Tradition: The Highland Tradition of Scotland', *The Invention of Tradition* (edited by E Hobsbawn), Cambridge: University Press, 1983.

Trevor-Roper, H, *The Invention of Scotland*, London: Yale, 2008.

Vetch, Col RH, *Life, Letters and Dairies of Lieut-General Sir Gerald Graham VC GCB RE*, Edinburgh: William Blackwood, 1901.

Ward, A, *Our Bones are Scattered*, London: John Murray, 1996.

Weller, J, *Wellington in India*, London: Greenhill, 1993.

Wimberley, Capt D, *Some account of the part taken by the 79th Regiment of Cameron Highlanders in the Indian Mutiny Campaign of 1858*, Inverness, 1891.

Winsley, Captain TM, *A History of the Singapore Volunteer Corps 1854–1937*, Singapore: Government Printing Offices, 1938

Woosnam-Savage, RC (editor), *1745 – Charles Edward Stuart and the Jacobites*, Edinburgh: HMSO, 1995.

Index

Abbreviations used: VC = Victoria Cross